the
Idea-a-Day
Guide
to Super Selling
and
Customer Service

**250 Ways to Increase Your
Top *and* Bottom Lines**

the Idea-a-Day Guide

to Super Selling and Customer Service

250 Ways to Increase Your Top *and* Bottom Lines

Tony Alessandra, Ph.D.
Gary Couture
Gregg Baron

DARTNELL

4660 N. Ravenswood Ave.
Chicago, IL 60640
1-800-621-5463

Chicago / Boston / London / Sydney

Dartnell is a publisher serving the world of business with books, manuals, newsletters, bulletins, and training materials for executives, managers, supervisors, salespeople, financial officials, human resources professionals, and office employees. In addition, Dartnell produces management and sales training films and audiocassettes, publishes many useful business forms, and offers many of its materials in languages other than English. Established in 1917, Dartnell serves the world's complete business community. For catalogs and product information write: THE DARTNELL CORPORATION, 4660 Ravenswood Avenue, Chicago, Illinois 60640-4595 USA. Phone 800-621-5463. In Illinois: (312) 561-4000.

This publication is designed to provide accurate and authoritative information in regard to the subject matter covered. It is sold with the understanding that the publisher is not engaged in rendering legal, accounting, or other professional service. If legal advice or other expert assistance is required, the services of a competent professional person should be sought.

From a Declaration of Principles jointly adopted by a Committee of the American Bar Association and a Committee of Publishers.

Published by The Dartnell Corporation
4660 Ravenswood Avenue
Chicago, Illinois 60640
Chicago/Boston/London/Sydney

© 1992 Dartnell Corporation
ISBN 0-85013-185-5
Library of Congress Catalog Card Number: 91-076594
Printed in the USA by The Dartnell Press
1 0 9 8 7 6 5 4 3

DEDICATION

To my maternal grandmother, Grace Imbriani.

Tony

To my parents, for their love and ever-present support.

Gary

To Nancy, my wife and my joy.

Gregg

ABOUT THE AUTHORS

Dr. Tony Alessandra

Tony Alessandra, Ph.D., is one of America's most dynamic, entertaining and thought-provoking keynote speakers. Since 1975 he has given over 1000 speeches throughout the world on Relationship Strategies, Customer-Driven Selling, and Customer-Driven Service.

Tony received his B.B.A. from the University of Notre Dame, his M.S.B. from the University of Connecticut, and his Ph.D. from Georgia State University. He has written eight books including *Non-Manipulative Selling* and *People Smart,* recorded numerous audio programs such as *Super Selling Skills* and *Relationship Strategies,* and has been featured in films and videos including *The Power of Listening* and the comprehensive video training program, *Customer-Driven Selling.*

Gregg Baron

Gregg Baron is an international customer service and team development trainer and consultant. He is president of Success Sciences, Inc., which develops behavior change training programs, and strategies for customer service and team development, sales and leadership. Success Sciences' clients include IBM Rolm, McCaw Cellular Communications (Cellular One), Tupperware International, Continental Airlines, Novell, and Chase.

Gregg holds degrees in accounting and management from the University of South Florida, and is a Certified Associate Trainer in Neurolinguistic Programming.

Dr. Gary Couture

Gary Couture, Ph.D., has motivated business audiences throughout the world to greater personal achievement for more than twenty years. His Success by Design programs take the individual through a practical, step-by-step process that provides bottom-line results in management, selling, marketing, customer service, and personal development.

Gary received his Ph.D. from Pepperdine University. In 1983 he and Tom Peters received the Oscar for speaker of the year from the Sales and Marketing Executives Club of San Francisco.

CONTENTS

ACKNOWLEDGMENTS

The authors would like to thank Garry Schaeffer for his substantial writing assistance. Robert Coates for sharing his expertise in service and development. Rick Barrera, co-author of *Non-Manipulative Selling*, for his invaluable feedback, insights, and creative ideas. Jim Cathcart, co-author of *Relationship Strategies,* for sharing and developing many concepts found in this work. Dr. John Monoky, co-author of *Be Your Own Sales Manager,* for his contributions to many of the planning and targeting worksheets. Ed Reese and Dan Bagley, authors of *Beyond Selling—How to Maximize Your Personal Influence,* for their expert contributions on NLP. Lastly, we'd like to express our appreciation to Rich Hagle, for working so closely with us, motivating us, and refining the final product.

INTRODUCTION

This is your book—not just because you purchased it but because of the way it was made. The *Idea-a-Day Guide to Super Selling and Customer Service* was conceived, designed, and developed with the needs of you—the working sales rep or sales manager—in mind. And it could be the most important book you'll ever use. Not just read—**use.** Because the *Idea-a-Day Guide to Super Selling* is organized to meet your day-to-day success needs with 250 practical, ready-to-use sales ideas. It will help you build and increase your short- and long-term success the way the real pros do it: day after day, one day at a time, all year long.

This book has three key components to unlocking the door to success.

First is a self-diagnostic test located in the Appendix at the back of the book. Make two copies of the test. Fill out one yourself. Give a copy to your supervisor, manager, or a colleague to fill out. Give the remaining copy to a customer to fill out. You'll not only have a thorough self-assessment and the beginnings of an action plan for your future growth. You'll also get important feedback—to "see yourself as others see you"—that you will be able to incorporate into your self-assessment. The result will be a comprehensive, objective picture of your current professional development.

The second and third components—FYIs and Worksheets—work together as the main components of the book. FYIs are key facts, important insights, and sure-fire ideas that will help you improve your productivity and effectiveness. The Worksheets help you organize your thoughts, test your ideas, and put them into action today, tomorrow, and all year long. Altogether, you get 250 fresh, new, money-making ideas, one for each working day of the year.

YOUR CHOICE

What makes *Idea-a-Day Guide to Super Selling and Customer Service* so important, so useful to your sales career, is that you can use it **any way you want.** The FYIs and Worksheets are all self-contained on a single page (the few exceptions, which give you more space for writing your own notes, are two pages). So you can:

1. Flip through the book, read a single page, get an idea, close the book, and go out and take one more step down the road to success; Or

2. Look over the exhaustive table of contents, pick out a particular section devoted to a particular set of skills, and read that entire section and get a whole grouping of ideas that meet your immediate needs in a particular skills area; Or

3. Read the entire book straight through, from page one to the end, and benefit that way.

The point is, you can use this book any way you want and still get its benefits. It is the most flexible and most usable sales book you will ever own.

FIVE MINUTES A DAY IS ALL IT TAKES

There is more than one way you can use this book. Whether you've been in sales for 20 days or 20 years, you'll have an easy-to-use daily reference for getting a new idea or double-checking ones you haven't used for awhile. Since the main components—the Self-Test, the FYIs, and the Worksheets—cover key points in selling success, you'll turn to *Idea-a-Day* for new insights and a mini-"refresher" course in sales success. And you'll be able to use it every day of the year because it's organized on a page-by-page basis that takes only five minutes a day to use.

GET STARTED NOW

There's one easy thing about success. There's only one time and place to start: here and now. So, right now, while the book is in your hands, turn to the table of contents and pick an area—all areas are represented, from territory and time management to prospecting, responding to customer concerns, and ways to confirm the sale, as well as some newer ones, such as neurolinguistic programming. Spend the minutes we mentioned above. We're sure you'll be impressed. More important, we're sure you'll be on your way to greater success in your sales career.

1 Setting goals for success

WHAT'S IN IT FOR YOU

- Get where you want to go faster—by knowing exactly how you'll get there.
- Examine what is important to you in life
- Determine your strengths and weaknesses
- Set goals for improving your personal and professional skills
- Continually enhance your skills by evaluating your performance
- Appreciate the value of measuring your sales activities and performance as a way to help you increase sales

Someone once said, "Speed isn't everything. If you don't know where you're going, the faster you go, the more lost you'll get." It is impossible to overstate the importance of having a set of well-defined goals. They provide incentive, motivation, and a sense of accomplishment because they provide the ability to measure your progress in concrete terms. They also help you redefine and redirect your activities because you can more clearly identify what you want to change to since you know where you are coming from. This section shows you ways to increase your success by developing clear personal and professional goals.

WORKSHEET

WHAT'S IN IT FOR YOU

- Gain a greater understanding of your values
- Clarify what you think is important in life

EVALUATING YOUR PERSONAL GOALS

1.1 Clarify Your Life Definitions

The first step in setting goals is to inventory your values. Define what the following terms mean and how important they are to you. Write in sentences, phrases or single words—it doesn't matter.

1. Freedom is ... _____

2. Success is ... _____

3. Happiness is ... _____

4. Prosperity is ... _____

5. Challenge is ... _____

6. Competence is ... _____

7. Being in control is ... _____

What values would you add to this list? Take a moment and prioritize your top five values.

WORKSHEET

EVALUATING YOUR PERSONAL GOALS

1.2 Define Your Organizational Goals

Address the following questions to better understand your company's expectations of you. Use a blank sheet of paper if you need more room.

1. What is the current mission of the sales force in my firm (e.g., to increase market share, increase profitability)?

   _____

2. What components of the product mix am I being asked to sell and what is the relative importance of each?

   _____

3. What market segments are we going after and what are their relative priorities?

   _____

4. How frequently and on what criteria will my performance be measured?

   _____

5. What constitutes good selling behavior in terms of these tasks and activities?

   _____

6. Are these organizational goals and priorities consistent with my personal goals?

   _____

WORKSHEET

EVALUATING YOUR PERSONAL GOALS

1.3 Areas to Improve

Rate yourself on a scale of one to ten on the following:

Setting Priorities ...

1.   2.   3.   4.   5.   6.   7.   8.   9.   10.

Concentration and Focus ...

1.   2.   3.   4.   5.   6.   7.   8.   9.   10.

Intensity and Commitment ...

1.   2.   3.   4.   5.   6.   7.   8.   9.   10.

Goal Setting ...

1.   2.   3.   4.   5.   6.   7.   8.   9.   10.

Devising Strategies ...

1.   2.   3.   4.   5.   6.   7.   8.   9.   10.

Setting and Meeting Deadlines ...

1.   2.   3.   4.   5.   6.   7.   8.   9.   10.

Measuring Results ...

1.   2.   3.   4.   5.   6.   7.   8.   9.   10.

Managing Time on a Day-to-Day Basis

1.   2.   3.   4.   5.   6.   7.   8.   9.   10.

Now, write out ways to improve each of these areas.

WORKSHEET

EVALUATING YOUR PERSONAL GOALS

1.4 Goal-Setting Dream List

Do a little soul searching. Without being concerned about priority, quickly list the first ten images that come to your mind regarding things you would like to have or achieve in your lifetime.

1. _____

2. _____

3. _____

4. _____

5. _____

6. _____

7. _____

8. _____

9. _____

10. _____

WORKSHEET

EVALUATING YOUR PERSONAL GOALS

1.5 Personal Strengths and Weaknesses

For each area of your life that you targeted in your dream list (and for organizational goals), fill out the following "personal inventory." It will give you a snapshot of where you are now and what you need to do to move toward your goals.

For each area of your life that you targeted in your dream list (and for organizational goals), fill out the following "personal inventory." It will give you a snap shot of where you are now and what you need to do to move toward your goals.

Goal/Area to Improve	Past Accomplishments	Current Strengths	Current Weaknesses	How You Will Improve

WORKSHEET

EVALUATING YOUR PERSONAL GOALS

1.6 Wrapping Up Loose Ends

Imagine yourself on your deathbed. You are looking back, taking stock of your life. What would you be happy about—what would give you a sense of accomplishment? What would you regret not having done? Your regrets should be included in your goal setting.

    1.
    2.
    3.
    4.
    5.
    6.
    7.

Now list all the major loose ends in your life at present. Include incomplete projects, unattained goals, unresolved relationship issues and other frustrations.

    1.
    2.
    3.
    4.
    5.
    6.
    7.
    8.
    9.
    10.

Look at the list and cross out the unimportant loose ends.

List the loose ends that you can live with even if they are unresolved.

    1.
    2.
    3.
    4.

List the loose ends that are most important to complete.

    1.
    2.
    3.
    4.
    5.

Now, with this insight, list the five highest priority goals and projects to start working on today.

    1.
    2.
    3.
    4.
    5.

✏ ● WORKSHEET

EVALUATING YOUR PERSONAL GOALS

1.7 Key Goal Action Plans

- Commit to your goals by writing them out, assigning completion dates and determining how you will achieve and measure them.

Copy this sheet and use it to answer the following questions regarding as many aspects of your life as you want. Some areas to explore are your career, family life, intellectual development, social situation, spiritual needs, physical fitness and financial goals.

Answer the following questions regarding as many aspects of your life as you want. Some areas to explore are your career, family life, intellectual development, social situation, spiritual needs, physical fitness and financial goals.

What is the goal I would like to achieve?
What are the potential obstacles that stand in my way?
What is driving my desire to achieve this goal?
What is my action plan? How will I specifically reach the goal? Who can help? What other resources do I have?
What is my target date/deadline for implementing the goal?
How and when will I measure my success?

? F Y I

EVALUATING YOUR PERSONAL GOALS

1.8 Numbers Can't Lie

The flip side of setting goals is measuring performance. Measurement helps you determine what you are doing right and wrong. If you don't keep records, you won't have a clue as to how to improve your performance and reach your goals.

There are many ways to measure and evaluate performance. Only you can determine which methods make the most sense for you, given your industry and the nature of your sales process. The methods you choose should complement—if not be identical to—the ones used by your sales manager. The five areas to measure are Sales Calls, Sales Expenses, Nonselling Activities, Market Opportunities and Results.

To interpret your records, look for two things: changes from last year, and current ratios that are poor. Current ratios are excellent indicators of areas that need work. For example, a life insurance salesperson whose appointments-per-call ratio is low may need to work on her phone script. A low sales-per-appointment ratio may indicate a need to improve presentation skills. If the number of calls she makes per day is low, she is simply not picking up the phone.

Sales is a numbers game. Keeping records will show how those numbers apply to you. For example, knowing that you have to contact 25 prospects to average ten appointments to make five presentations to make one sale is valuable information.

The model in FYI 1.9 shows you how evaluating performance fits into the overall scheme of things.

EVALUATING YOUR PERSONAL GOALS

1.9 Salesperson's Management Model

- Understand the logic behind setting goals, measuring performance, and making behavioral corrections.

This diagram shows you how measuring performance aids you in meeting goals and correcting problems.

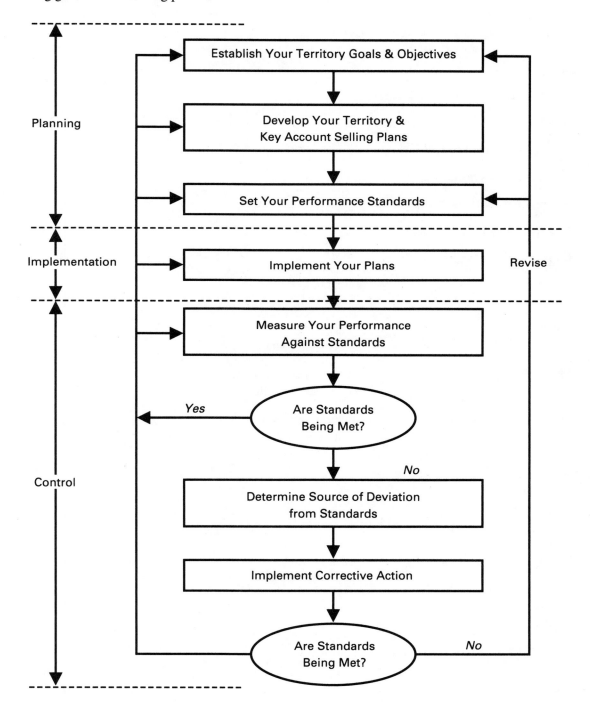

WORKSHEET

EVALUATING YOUR PERSONAL GOALS

1.10 Measuring Sales Calls

- Understand the many ways to measure sales calls and determine which are appropriate for your business

Measuring the number of sales calls and the number of customer prospect contacts is a key method of measuring performance. Most salespeople don't like to spend their time on measuring. They'd rather be selling. But top performers consistently measure what they do, so they can leverage what's working and develop what isn't working.

Sales Calls:

- Number made on current customers

- Number made on potential new accounts

- Average time spent per call

- Number of sales presentations

- Selling time versus nonselling time

- Call frequency ratio per customer type

- Calls per day

- Calls-per-day ratio $=$ $\dfrac{\text{Number of calls}}{\text{Number of days worked}}$

- Calls-per-account ratio $=$ $\dfrac{\text{Number of calls}}{\text{Number of accounts}}$

- Planned call ratio $=$ $\dfrac{\text{Number of planned calls}}{\text{Total number of calls}}$

- Orders-per-call (hit ratio) $=$ $\dfrac{\text{Number of orders}}{\text{Total number of calls}}$

EVALUATING YOUR PERSONAL GOALS

1.11 Measuring Sales Expenses

- Understand the many ways to measure sales expenses and determine which are appropriate for you

Cost control is a watchword in business today. Here is a simple approach.

Sales Expenses:

- Average per sales call

- Expenses as a percentage of sales quota

- By customer type

- By product category

- Direct selling expense ratios

- Indirect selling expense ratios

- Sales expense ratio $= \dfrac{\text{Expenses}}{\text{Sales}}$

- Cost-per-call ratio $= \dfrac{\text{Total Costs}}{\text{Number of calls}}$

❓FYI

EVALUATING YOUR PERSONAL GOALS

1.12 Measuring Nonselling Activities

- Understand the many ways to measure nonselling activities and determine which are appropriate for you

Direct customer contact is only one important part of sales. It's equally important—maybe more important—to keep track of essential nonselling activities.

Nonselling Activities:

- Letters written to prospects

- Telephone calls made to prospects

- Number of formal proposals developed

- Advertising display set-ups

- Number of meetings held with distributors/dealers

- Number of training sessions for distributor/dealer personnel

- Number of calls on distributor/dealer customers

- Number of service calls made

- Number of customer complaints received

- Number of overdue accounts collected

EVALUATING YOUR PERSONAL GOALS

1.13 Measuring Opportunities

The following information, available from your company or from your own analysis, will help you plan and work your territory and evaluate your performance.

- Territory Potentials

- Market Segment Potentials

- Account Potentials

- Number of Accounts

- Size of Territory

? F Y I

EVALUATING YOUR PERSONAL GOALS

1.14 Measuring Results

Results come in many shapes and sizes. Consider these measures for determining your results.

- Total dollar contribution

- Average contribution margin

- Contribution in margin dollars per call

- Current versus past sales

- Current sales per call

- Account penetration ratio = $\dfrac{\text{Accounts sold}}{\text{Total accounts available}}$

- New account conversion ratio = $\dfrac{\text{Number of new accounts sold}}{\text{Total number of potential new accounts}}$

- Lost account ratio = $\dfrac{\text{Prior accounts not sold}}{\text{Total number of accounts}}$

- Sales-per-account ratio = $\dfrac{\text{Sales dollar volume}}{\text{Total number of accounts}}$

- Average order size ratio = $\dfrac{\text{Sales dollar volume}}{\text{Total number of orders}}$

- Order cancellation ratio = $\dfrac{\text{Number of cancelled orders}}{\text{Total number of orders}}$

Profitable territory management

WHAT'S IN IT FOR YOU

Boost your reputation as a knowledgeable sales consultant

- Know your company, products, and services
- Determine your company's strengths and weaknesses
- Analyze your competitors' strengths and weaknesses
- Discover your customers' most important buying criteria

Avoid sales slumps and benefit from sales peaks

- Anticipate the effects of economic, political, and regulatory trends on your industry

Focus on profit

- Determine your best source of sales
- Categorize and prioritize your accounts

In territory management, the name of the game is control. Like a young basketball player, you have to master dribbling and ball-handling before you can turn your attention to the hoop and the possibility of becoming a high scorer. Control in sales is gained by gathering information that helps you see how the relevant details of your territory fit into the "big picture" of a constantly changing market—so you can strategically cover and exploit the potential in your territory.

More often than not, a well-informed salesperson is a successful salesperson. That's why the first three exercises in this section increase your knowledge of your company, customers and industry, and the economic and business cycles that affect them.

? F Y I

MIND YOUR OWN BUSINESS—
AND THE FACTORS THAT AFFECT IT

- Fully understand how the steps of the sales process make your job easier in the long run by optimizing your time

2.1 The Sales Planning Process

Two-Stage Sales Planning Process

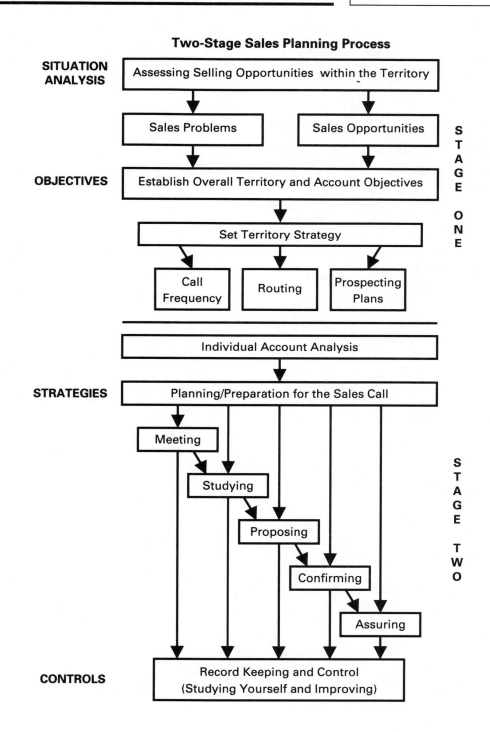

SITUATION ANALYSIS — Assessing Selling Opportunities within the Territory

Sales Problems | Sales Opportunities

OBJECTIVES — Establish Overall Territory and Account Objectives

Set Territory Strategy

Call Frequency | Routing | Prospecting Plans

STAGE ONE

Individual Account Analysis

STRATEGIES — Planning/Preparation for the Sales Call

Meeting

Studying

Proposing

Confirming

Assuring

STAGE TWO

CONTROLS — Record Keeping and Control (Studying Yourself and Improving)

MIND YOUR OWN BUSINESS— AND THE FACTORS THAT AFFECT IT

2.2 Where to Find the Market

Because managing your territory often requires market or competitor research, you have to know where to find information you need. In the following sources you will find answers to virtually any question on the marketplace, your competition, your company and your prospects.

Standard & Poor's Industry Surveys
Moody's Industrial Manual
Forbes Annual Report on Business
S & P's Corporate Record
Dunn & Bradstreet Reference Book of Corporate Management
Encyclopedia of Business Information Sources
Financial periodicals
Funk & Scott Index of Corporations and Industries

Government publications from:
    U.S. Department of Commerce
    Bureau of Economic Analysis
    Local Chambers of Commerce
    Internal Revenue Service
    U.S. Treasury Department
    Department of Labor
    Bureau of Census

Newspapers, especially:
    The Wall Street Journal
    New York Times
    Barron's
    Washington Post

Business magazines
Professional and trade journals
Consulting firms
Annual reports, stock prospectuses, stock performance guides
Company sources, including marketing department, ad agencies
Personal contacts
Trade associations
Trade shows
University libraries and research centers

✎ WORKSHEET

MIND YOUR OWN BUSINESS—
AND THE FACTORS THAT AFFECT IT

- Increase your knowledge of your company
- Give better, more credible presentations
- Boost your ability to market your product/service

2.3 Know Your Company

Answer these critical questions about your company. If you don't know an answer offhand, interview or research until you find the information you need.

1. List the key personnel of your company and their unique contributions to the firm.

_____

2. What unique capabilities or technical advantages does the company have?

_____

3. What is the company's image and reputation among:

   a. Present customers?

   b. Prospects?

   c. The competition?

_____

4. What are its relative strengths and weaknesses compared to the competition? How do these affect business?

_____

5. What is the marketing philosophy of your company?

_____

6. What are the present and future markets of your company?

_____

7. What has the company's sales history been during the last 3-5 years?

_____

8. What is your company's standard policy regarding:

   a. Pricing?_____

   b. Discounts? _____

   c. Guarantees? _____

   d. Service? _____

   e. Negotiating? _____

WORKSHEET

WHAT'S IN IT FOR YOU

- Increase your knowledge of your products/services
- Understand how your product//services compare to competitors'

MIND YOUR OWN BUSINESS— AND THE FACTORS THAT AFFECT IT

2.4 Know Your Products/Services

A solid grasp of your products/services—and how they compare to competitors'—will increase your credibility and help you sell the right product to the right customer.

1. What specific benefits do present and prospective customers seek in your product/service?

2. How does your product/service compare to the competition's in providing those benefits?

3. Are there any features that make your product/service better than the competition's? If so, why?

4. How does your product/service compare to the others in your territory in the following aspects:

   a. Quality

   b. Price

   c. Delivery

   d. Value-added

   e. Reliability

   f. Service

5. What factor(s) might prevent a customer from purchasing your product/service?

   What can you do about it?

6. Is your company a leader (developer) or follower (imitator) in its field? Why?

? FYI

MIND YOUR OWN BUSINESS— AND THE FACTORS THAT AFFECT IT

2.5 The Economic Climate

Understanding the economic factors that influence your business can help you forecast variations in your sales activity and plan strategies to accommodate or even prevent them. Consider the direct influence of the following factors on your industry, and then use the worksheet to determine the impact of local, regional, and national economic trends—directly and indirectly—on your customers and your business.

Economic Factors	*Impact*
1. Interest Rates	Corporate spending, housing construction, consumer durables
2. Unemployment	Consumer spending— durable goods, nonnecessities
3. Industrial Production	Corporate spending, changes in unemployment
4. Corporate Profits	Corporate spending, employment levels; indirect impact on
5. Inflation	Consumer spending All areas of spending on corporate and consumer levels
6. Consumer Income	Consumer spending, especially nonnecessities

Sources of information on economic trends include Chambers of Commerce, newspapers, trade journals, business publications, and trade associations.

WORKSHEET

MIND YOUR OWN BUSINESS—
AND THE FACTORS THAT AFFECT IT

- Identify the economic factors that may positively or negatively affect your industry, company, and territory

2.6 The Economy and Your Business

To summarize the economic influences on your territory, evaluate in general terms the economic trends and their probable direct and indirect impact on your business. For example, say a local plant closing has made unemployment soar in your area. What does that mean for your business? Your customers? Use the extra space to add any categories that may be unique to your industry.

KEY: + Increasing   - Decreasing   0 Holding steady

Factor		Trend	Implication for Our Business	Impact on Key Market Groups	Threat/ Opportunity
1. General Economy	Local				
	Reg.				
	Natl.				
2. Unemployment	Local				
	Reg.				
	Natl.				
3. Corporate Profits	Local				
	Reg.				
	Natl.				
4. Inflation	Local				
	Reg.				
	Natl.				
5. Consumer Spending	Local				
	Reg.				
	Natl.				
6. Interest Rates	Local				
	Reg.				
	Natl.				
7. Other	Local				
	Reg.				
	Natl.				

WORKSHEET

MIND YOUR OWN BUSINESS— AND THE FACTORS THAT AFFECT IT

2.7 Political and Regulatory Trends

- Gain an awareness of the political and regulatory trends that affect your business and your customers
- Quickly profit from opportunities created by favorable trends
- Avoid losses by preparing ahead of time for changes that negatively affect you

Political and regulatory changes can happen swiftly—and their repercussions can be dramatic. CEOs and executive managers must keep on their toes to adapt to (or head off) the changes; salespeople must understand how they will be affected as well.

To keep abreast of potential changes in your field, make the time to read trade publications, local business newspapers, national business magazines and, especially, *The Wall Street Journal*.

Use the worksheet on the following page to analyze the impact that political and regulatory changes may have on your business.

Political and Regulatory Trends

Level	Proposed Legislation	Effect	Implication for Your Business	Implications For Customers	Threat/ Opportunity
1. Federal					
2. State					
3. Local					

WORKSHEET

WHAT'S IN IT FOR YOU

MIND YOUR OWN BUSINESS—
AND THE FACTORS THAT AFFECT IT

2.8 Industry Trends

In the following table, write down the changes that are likely to take place in your industry over the next year, and describe their potential impact.

- Maintain an awareness of industry trends that may affect various market segments
- Anticipate industry changes that can influence how you attack your territory
- Capitalize on industry changes to increase sales in strong market segments, and avoid sales slumps in weak market segments

Description of Trend or Condition	Likelihood of Occurrence	Market Segment(s) Affected	Impact Sales
1.			
2.			
3.			
4.			
5.			
6.			
7.			
8.			
9.			
10.			

WORKSHEET

WHAT'S IN IT FOR YOU

ANALYZING YOUR ACCOUNTS

2.9 Breakdown of Current Year's Sales

For each product line and market segment, fill in the dollar amounts and percentages of current year's sales.

- Develop a clear picture of where your company's current sales come from
- Gain insight into your company's promotional effectiveness, market saturation, and customer loyalty

Market Segment _____

Product Line	Existing Customers	New Customers	Total
1.	_____ $ _____ %	_____ $ _____ %	_____ $ 100 %
2.	_____ $ _____ %	_____ $ _____ %	_____ $ 100 %
3.	_____ $ _____ %	_____ $ _____ %	_____ $ 100 %
Total	_____ $ _____ %	_____ $ _____ %	_____ $ 100 %

WORKSHEET

ANALYZING YOUR ACCOUNTS

- Understand your company's plans for growth

2.10 Projection of the Coming Year's Sales

Through research and/or discussions with your sales manager, find out where next year's sales are expected to come from in various market segments.

Market Segment_____

Product Line	Existing Customers	New Customers	Total
1.	_____ $ _____ %	_____ $ _____ %	_____ $ ___100___ %
2.	_____ $ _____ %	_____ $ _____ %	___100___ $ _____ %
3.	_____ $ _____ %	_____ $ _____ %	_____ $ ___100___ %
Total	_____ $ _____ %	_____ $ _____ %	_____ $ ___100___ %

WORKSHEET

ANALYZING YOUR ACCOUNTS

2.11 Market Segment Categories

List the various market segments in your territory by the combination of profitability and your company's strength of position.

Territory: _____

Very High — 2		1
4		3 — **Very Low**

PROFITABILITY

Very Low — STRENGTH OF POSITION — Very High

WORKSHEET

ANALYZING YOUR ACCOUNTS

2.12 Analysis of Key Market Segments

- Identify factors that are important to customers and prospects when they compare your company to the competition
- Know what to emphasize when selling the strong points of your company

Because no two market segments are the same, they cannot be approached identically. To help you customize your approach, use this worksheet to identify what is important to your market segments when they evaluate competing companies. Twelve examples of selection criteria are given. Add or delete as you see fit. Use your judgment, consult with your sales manager, and talk to customers to determine the importance of these criteria.

Market Segment: _____

	IMPORTANCE		
Selection Criteria	**1** **Not** **Important**	**2** **Important**	**3** **Very** **Important**
1. General reputation			
2. Quality of products carried			
3. Range of products carried			
4. Prices of product carried			
5. Quality of outside sales personnel			
6. Quality of inside sales personnel			
7. Availability of products			
8. Delivery reliability			
9. Ability to follow up on complaints			
10. Quality of service			
11. Financial strength			
12. Size of firm			
13.			
14.			
15.			

ANALYZING YOUR ACCOUNTS

2.13 Buying Influences

The notion that selling is a one-on-one interaction between a corporate buyer and a salesperson is a bit too simple. The bigger the company, the more influences come to bear on a buying decision. Understanding these influences is important. Take them into account when planning your sales approach.

The Environment

The environment is everything outside the company that has an impact on market conditions or the company itself, such as economic, political, legal, technological, and competitive factors.

The Organization

You might call this the internal environment. Every company has a unique culture that affects the structure and functioning of the buying process. The bigger the purchase, the more the "personality" of the organization influences the buying process.

The Group

The personalities and positions of the decision makers play a big role in shaping the buying process. Other influences include their decision criteria, the risks involved in the purchase, and the unwritten rules of behavior within the group.

The Individual

Your contact's agenda and behavioral style are major influences. If you are involved in selling to a prospect's team, the individual dynamics become even more complex and deserving of attention.

ANALYZING YOUR ACCOUNTS

2.14 How Decision Makers Obtain Information

People in different target markets gather information differently. By knowing the various media that are effective in reaching decision makers, you will be able to better promote your product/services and yourself.

Use the following worksheet to comment on the effectiveness of each promotional strategy as a way to reach decision makers in each market segment. Fill in as you see fit, and make additional copies if necessary.

Information Source	Target Market Segment		
	1.	2.	3.
1. Catalogs			
Comments:			
2. Price Lists			
Comments:			
3. Newspaper Ads			
Comments:			
4. Radio Advertising			
Comments:			
5. Direct Mail Promo			
Comments:			
6. Inside Salespeople			
Comments:			
7. Outside Salespeople			
Comments:			
8. Published Reports or Stories Comments:			
9.			
Comments:			
10.			
Comments:			

WORKSHEET

ANALYZING YOUR ACCOUNTS

- Identify current customers and prospects in each market segment you want to penetrate

2.15 Account and Prospect Identification

Break down each of your target markets into present and future customers. Complete the worksheet for each product/service you sell and market segment you are trying to penetrate. The order of your accounts is unimportant.

Account Identification

Market Segment _____ **Product Line** _____

Existing Customers/Clients	*Prospects*
_____	_____
_____	_____
_____	_____
_____	_____
_____	_____
_____	_____
_____	_____
_____	_____
_____	_____
_____	_____
_____	_____
_____	_____
_____	_____
_____	_____
_____	_____
_____	_____
_____	_____
_____	_____
_____	_____

WORKSHEET

ANALYZING YOUR ACCOUNTS

2.16 Volume and Profit Matrix

- Gain a clear picture of the desirability of your accounts
- Prioritize your sales calls
- Develop an effective strategy for working your accounts

List your accounts in the boxes that best correspond to the combinations of sales volume and profits. You goal should be to work your accounts so they move up in profitability and sales volume.

SALES VOLUME

	Low	Medium	High
High			
Medium			
Low			

PROFITABILITY

WORKSHEET

ANALYZING YOUR ACCOUNTS

- Classify your accounts in terms of profitability
- Prioritize your accounts
- Determine how and when to call on them

2.17 Key Account Categories

Using data from your most recent sales year, rank your accounts by their profitability. Complete a separate sheet for each product/service you sell.

Product/Service: _____

Date: _____ through _____

	Company	Contact	Phone
"A" ACCOUNTS Top 20% Very Profitable			
"B" ACCOUNTS Middle 30% Profitable			
"C" ACCOUNTS Bottom 50% Less Profitable			
PROSPECTS			

WORKSHEET

ANALYZING YOUR ACCOUNTS

2.18 Coverage of Key Accounts

To develop your personal Territory Coverage Planning Guide, determine the following:

1. Total number of present and prospective A, B and C accounts.

2. Average number of selling days during the sales planning cycle (quarterly, semiannual or annual).

3. The average time for a sales call for A, B and C accounts.

Fill in the following table and your allocation of time will become clear.

Account Classification	Number of Accounts	Call Frequency	Call Total	Time per Call (min.)	Total Time (min.)	Hours/ Cycle

Example: Based on six month cycle = 936 hours—hrs/day = 117 days

Account Classification	Number of Accounts	Call Frequency	Call Total	Time per Call (min.)	Total Time (min.)	Hours/ Cycle
A	10	12	120 x	40 min.	4800 min.	80
B	30	6	180 x	30 min.	5400 min.	90
C	500	2	1000 x	20 min.	20K min.	333
Travel Time			1300 x	20 min.	26K min.	433
					TOTAL # OF HOURS = 936	

 **FYI**

WHAT'S IN IT FOR YOU

SELLING AGAINST THE COMPETITION

2.19 Sources of Competitive Information

- Learn what your competitors say about themselves and what others say about them
- Keeping up on the competition can enhance your reputation as a knowledgeable sales rep, and help you compete more effectively in a crowded marketplace. Make the time to study your competitors, clipping and saving the most pertinent items you discover

Where to Find What Competitors Say About Themselves

Publications	Trade/ Professional	Government Sources	Investors/ Financial Services
Advertising	Manuals	SEC Reports	Annual reports
Promotional materials	Technical papers	Court cases	Prospectuses
Press releases	Licenses/applications	Regulatory agencies	Annual meetings
Speeches	Patents	One-time studies	
Books	Courses/seminars	Government publications	
Articles	Suppliers	Chambers of Commerce	
Personnel changes	Consultants		
Want Ads			
In-house publications			
Catalogs/brochures			
Products/services			

Where to Find What Others Say About Your Competitors

Newspapers	Former employees	Court cases	Security analysts
Consumer Groups	Customers	Federal/local Agencies	Dun & Bradstreet
Unions	Competitors	Government programs	Standard & Poor's
Market research	Suppliers	Environmental filings & other permits	Credit bureaus
Recruiting firms	Trade Publications		Commercial banks
Specialized university libraries	Industry studies		
Industrial research centers			

WORKSHEET

SELLING AGAINST THE COMPETITION

2.20 Identifying Competitors

Use this worksheet to list your major competitors for each product or service that you represent.

		MAJOR COMPETITORS				
		Target Market A	Target Market B	Target Market C	Target Market D	Target Market E
P R O D U C T	A					
	B					
	C					
	D					

WORKSHEET

SELLING AGAINST THE COMPETITION

2.21 Competitor Profile

Create a file on each of your competitors in every market segment that you sell. Keep an up-to-date copy of this form at the beginning of each file, adding to it other pertinent information you collect on each competitor.

Company _____

Location _____

Markets Served _____

_____

Key Personnel _____

Name _____   TItle _____

Name _____   Title _____

Name _____   Title _____

Number of Employees _____   Estimated Sales _____

Inside Sales Personnel _____   Outside Sales Personnel _____

Size of Facility _____ sq. ft.

Product Lines _____   _____

_____   _____

_____   _____

_____   _____

Marketing Approach

_____

_____

_____

_____

WORKSHEET

SELLING AGAINST THE COMPETITION

2.22 Competitors' Market Strengths

To find out how you compare to key competitors in your primary market segments, rate the relative market penetration and strength of your company versus your competitors in various market segments. Complete a separate sheet for each product or service you sell.

+ = Stronger market strength than your company
0 = The same market strength as your company
− = Less market strength than your company

Product/Service: _____

	Target Market A	Target Market B	Target Market C	Target Market D	Target Market E
Your Company					
Competitor A					
Competitor B					
Competitor C					
Competitor D					
Competitor E					
Competitor F					
Competitor G					

WORKSHEET

SELLING AGAINST THE COMPETITION

2.23 Competitors' External Strengths

How well are you serving your customers? How well are your competitors serving their customers? Ask your customers to rank your company and your competitors on a scale of one to three. Let them know that you appreciate their frank, candid point of view on each of the criteria listed in the left column. Ask them to mention any additional criteria that are important to them, and note how important each criterion is to your customers. Write your rating (and your competitors') in the spaces provided in the table on the following page.

- Find out what matters to your customers
- Determine how well your company is serving your customers
- Find out how well your competitors are serving their customers
- Learn about your company's strengths and weaknesses from your customers
- Assess the strengths and weaknesses of the competitors you are selling against

Target Market Segment _____

Selection Criteria or Attribute	Importance 3 = Very Important 2 = Important 1 = Not Important	Your Firm	Competitors 1. ___ 2. ___ 3. ___ 4. ___			
1. General reputation						
2. Quality of products carried						
3. Range of products carried						
4. Prices of product carried ,						
5. Quality of outside sales personnel						
6. Quality of inside sales personnel						
7. Availability of products						
8. Delivery reliability						
9. Ability to follow up on complaints						
10. Quality of service						
11. Financial strength						
12. Size of firm						
13.						
14.						
15.						

RATINGS   3 = Strong Performer
2 = Average Performer   1 = Poor Performer

WORKSHEET

SELLING AGAINST THE COMPETITION

2.24 Competitors' Internal Strengths

- Know, in detail, your competitors' strengths and weaknesses from customers' perspective

Using a separate sheet for each competitor in the primary market segments that you serve, describe your competitors' strengths and weaknesses as customers would see them. Add to the categories as you see fit.

Market Segment: _____

Competitor's Name: _____

Category	Strengths	Weaknesses
Personnel		
Marketing Approach		
Pricing Policies		
Promotional Efforts		
Customer Image		
Customer Service		
Financial Strength		
Products		

SELLING AGAINST THE COMPETITION

2.25 How to Win Competitors' Customers

"Stealing" customers from competitors is a fact of life for salespeople. Customers become dissatisfied and switch. Your market share will increase if they come to you. Here's how you entice prospects to switch.

1. **Think long term.** Don't give up when you hear, "I'm satisfied." Satisfaction may be temporary. Your prospect's needs may change, or you may provide a good reason for switching.

2. **Develop a relationship.** Once you've mastered the relationship strategies to be presented in Section 6, you will be able to determine quickly whether you can develop a rapport with a prospect, sale or no sale. By developing a friendship, you will be able to ...

3. **Study needs.** Take your time, do research and ask a lot of nonthreatening questions so you can find out your prospect's needs and how well they are being satisfied. The key is to find a need gap and offer a solution.

4. **Sell yourself.** Personal chemistry is important, but so is the knowledge that you are an enthusiastic, earnest, professional, ethical, caring expert who would be nothing but an asset to know and do business with. Come up with new ideas for your prospects. Show them that you are on their team, sale or no sale.

5. **Add value.** So many products and services are commodities that differentiation may be difficult. That is why you sell yourself. That is also why you have to differentiate your product with added value such as service and performance guarantees, superior service, better delivery schedules—whatever it takes to be better.

6. **Ask for a no-risk trial order.** Many customers are loyal to their suppliers, but will grant you a trial order if you ask for it. Make it a no-risk proposition. Ensure your prospect's satisfaction with some kind of guarantee, and bend over backward to make sure the trial order makes a very positive impression.

7. **Ask for a portion of their business.** "Stealing" a competitor's customer may not be an all-or-nothing deal. You may have to do it bit by bit, proving yourself slowly as you go along. Ask for a small percentage of the prospect's business and you may find that percentage will grow.

8. **Be persistent.** Nothing succeeds more than persistence. All things being equal, the persistent salesperson will win the account every time. Keep in touch with prospects, think long-term, be a consultant and ally and you will plant drought-resistant seeds.

SELLING AGAINST THE COMPETITION

2.26 Doing the Basics Right

It is amazing how many times success can be assured by attending to the basics of the job. For example, a study of 257 Fortune 500 companies found that only:

- 17 percent do not determine an approximate duration for each sales call.

- 23 percent do not use a computer to assist in time and territory management.

- 28 percent do not set profit objectives for their accounts.

- 37 percent do not use prescribed routing patterns in covering their territories.

- 46 percent do not look at their use of time in an organized way.

- 49 percent do not determine the *economical* number of calls for each account.

- 49 percent do not use prepared sales presentations.

- 70 percent do not use call schedules.

- 75 percent do not have a system for classifying customers according to sales potential.

- 76 percent do not set sales objectives for their accounts.

- 81 percent do not use a call report system.

3 Time management

WHAT'S IN IT FOR YOU

- Become aware of how you spend (and waste) your time
- Identify productive activities that deserve more time
- Identify and eliminate time wasters
- Learn time management skills that make you more efficient
- Delegate routine tasks

Time is life's most precious resource. *What* you do with your time *is* your business. Your career will flourish or flounder depending on how well you manage this valuable asset. Success in sales comes to those who are effective *and* efficient. Mastering selling and people skills makes you more effective. Time management skills make you more efficient.

Before you can manage your time, you must know what you are doing with it. The first step, therefore, is awareness. Time management experts believe that the more records you keep, the more you will be able to control your time.

Once you become aware of how you spend your time, you can control, change, modify, delegate and discard activities as you see fit. These incremental steps will set you on the road to developing efficient time management habits that will make every day more productive.

WORKSHEET

CONTROL YOUR TIME/ BOOST YOUR PRODUCTIVITY

3.1 The Time Log

Directions: Make ten copies of this log and fill out one a day for the next ten days. Once each hour, try to stop what you are doing and record your activities. It's really not difficult or time-consuming.

Time Log

Time Log For _____

Date _____ Day _____ Analysis

Hour	Time Frame	Actual Time	Description of Activities	Comments For Better Time Use
7	0-30			
	30-60			
8	0-30			
	30-60			
9	0-30			
	30-60			
10	0-30			
	30-60			
11	0-30			
	30-60			
12	0-30			
	30-60			
1	0-30			
	30-60			
2	0-30			
	30-60			
3	0-30			
	30-60			
4	0-30			
	30-60			
5	0-30			
	30-60			
6	0-30			
	30-60			
7	0-30			
	30-60			

WORKSHEET

CONTROL YOUR TIME/ BOOST YOUR PRODUCTIVITY

3.2 Daily Time Analysis Questions

Directions: Make ten copies of this worksheet. For the next ten days, answer these questions at the end of each workday. Be as detailed as possible. Try to state specifically how you will make the next day better.

1. What went right today? Why?

2. What went wrong today? Why?

3. What time did I start on my top priority task? Why? Could I have started earlier?

4. What patterns do I see in my time logs?

5. What part of the day was most productive? Least productive?

6. What were my three biggest time wasters today?

7. Which activities need more time? Which need less time?

8. Beginning tomorrow, what will I do to make better use of my time?

WORKSHEET

CONTROL YOUR TIME/ BOOST YOUR PRODUCTIVITY

3.3 Identify Good and Bad Habits

It's impossible to develop good time management habits unless you understand which activities deserve more time and which should be downplayed or pruned out altogether.

At the end of the ten days, look back over your daily time logs and questions. Determine the six most productive and least productive activities you engaged in during that period. Compute the total amount of time spent on these activities

My Six Most Productive Activities Between (Dates) _____

1. Total Time: _____

2. Total Time: _____

3. Total Time: _____

4. Total Time: _____

5. Total Time: _____

6. Total Time: _____

My Six Least Productive Activities Between (Dates) _____

1. Total Time: _____

2. Total Time: _____

3. Total Time: _____

4. Total Time: _____

5. Total Time: _____

6. Total Time: _____

WORKSHEET

CONTROL YOUR TIME/ BOOST YOUR PRODUCTIVITY

3.4 Identify Time Wasters

Some unproductive activities are all too common. In addition to the time wasters you identified in the last two exercises, see which of the following apply to you.

	Never	Sometimes	Always
1. Over-preparing for calls.	_____	_____	_____
2. Scheduling less important work before more important work.	_____	_____	_____
3. Starting a job before thinking it through.	_____	_____	_____
4. Leaving jobs before they are completed.	_____	_____	_____
5. Doing things that can be delegated to another person (across or down; not upward).	_____	_____	_____
6. Doing things that can be delegated to modern equipment (providing such exists in your work).	_____	_____	_____
7. Doing things that aren't actually part of your real job.	_____	_____	_____
8. Keeping too many, too complicated, or overlapping records.	_____	_____	_____
9. Pursuing prospects you probably can't sell.	_____	_____	_____
10. Paying too much attention to low-yield prospects.	_____	_____	_____
11. Handling too wide a variety of duties.	_____	_____	_____
12. Failing to build barriers against interruptions.	_____	_____	_____
13. Allowing conferences and discussions to wander.	_____	_____	_____
14. Conducting unnecessary meetings, visits, and/or phone calls.	_____	_____	_____
15. Chasing trivial data after the main facts are in.	_____	_____	_____
16. Socializing at great length between tasks.	_____	_____	_____

WORKSHEET

CONTROL YOUR TIME / BOOST YOUR PRODUCTIVITY

3.5 Steps to Eliminate Time Wasters

By looking at your most productive and least productive activities on worksheets 1.3 and 1.4, you can get a good idea of the activities you need to change. If you have worked through the exercises in Section 1, you know how to set goals. Use your goal-setting skills to establish three objectives and action plans for eliminating time wasters. (If you haven't worked on goal-setting yet, complete the exercises on pages 1 through 16 before finishing the rest of the exercises in this section.)

1. Time Waster: _____

Strategies for eliminating:

2. Time Waster: _____

Strategies for eliminating:

3. Time Waster: _____

Strategies for eliminating:

WORKSHEET

CONTROL YOUR TIME /
BOOST YOUR PRODUCTIVITY

- Understand which activities provide the greatest pay-off for you

3.6 Setting Priorities

There are two famous laws that govern the use of time (or so it seems):

Parkinson's Law: "Work expands to fill the time allotted for its completion."

Pareto's Principle: "Twenty percent of your time generates 80 percent of your results."

The secret to using time effectively lies in setting priorities. That means knowing which activities generate the most results. List the five highest pay-off activities in your job from the points of view of your manager, your prospects and customers, and yourself. Use these three lists to determine the activities that will benefit you most overall.

In the eyes of my sales manager:

1.

2.

3.

4.

5.

In the eyes of my customers and prospects:

1.

2.

3.

4.

5.

In my own eyes:

1.

2.

3.

4.

5.

My overall high-priority activities:

1.

2.

3.

4.

5.

WORKSHEET

CONTROL YOUR TIME/ BOOST YOUR PRODUCTIVITY

3.7 The Weekly Planning Guide

Effective time management is a discipline that must be practiced every day. You must learn to organize your days *and* weeks around activities that pay off for you.

If you spend Sunday evening planning the week ahead of you, you'll hit the ground running Monday morning. This worksheet will help.

Use your high priority worksheet to determine five objectives you can realistically achieve in one week. Write them in the large space below. Then jot down the activities required to achieve those objectives. Make a new plan every week.

OBJECTIVES (what I hope to have accomplished by the end of the week)

ACTIVITIES REQUIRED TO ACCOMPLISH OBJECTIVES	Priority	Time Needed	Which Day

●WORKSHEET

CONTROL YOUR TIME/
BOOST YOUR PRODUCTIVITY

3.8 The To-Do List

Your organization and productivity will increase if you organize your days around your high-priority activities. One of the best ways to do that is to use your organizer or calendar, whether it's paper or electronic.

If not, get organized by photocopying the "To-Do" list on the following page and filling it out every evening for the next day's work. List activities by priority, starting with the most important. Define specific amounts of time to be spent on each activity, as well as the desired outcomes.

Use this list as a "road map" for your day. Consult it regularly to make sure you are working to meet your daily objectives. At the end of the day, file your "To-Do" list for future reference.

Things To Do Today

Item	Priority	Time Needed	Done
			☐
			☐
			☐
			☐
			☐
			☐
			☐
			☐
			☐
			☐
			☐
			☐
			☐
			☐
			☐
			☐
			☐
			☐
			☐
			☐

Notes

Date

Scheduled Events

8:00	
8:15	
8:30	
8:45	
9:00	
9:15	
9:30	
9:45	
10:00	
10:15	
10:30	
10:45	
11:00	
11:15	
11:30	
11:45	
12:00	
12:15	
12:30	
12:45	
1:00	
1:15	
1:30	
1:45	
2:00	
2:15	
2:30	
2:45	
3:00	
3:15	
3:30	
3:45	
4:00	
4:15	
4:30	
4:45	
5:00	
5:15	
5:30	
5:45	
6:00	
Evening	

CONTROL YOUR TIME/ BOOST YOUR PRODUCTIVITY

3.9 The Paperwork Shuffle

Many people, in and out of sales, have desks that look like paper mountains. These strategies for handling mail and paperwork more efficiently will free you to attend to more important tasks.

1. Delegate as much as possible. What cannot be delegated must be streamlined.

2. If possible, have a secretary or assistant open your mail. Mail should be prioritized. Junk mail goes on the bottom, bills and information in the middle, and letters requiring immediate action on top.

3. If you open your own mail, set a time to do it and keep that time the same every day.

4. Answer correspondence immediately. Write on the backs of letters, or dictate your responses and have a secretary type them up.

5. Peruse magazines and clip articles of interest to read during downtime, travel, lunch, etc.

6. Paperwork other than mail ideally should be handled only once. Pick it up, act on it, and be done with it—or at least move it along to the next step toward completion.

? **FYI**

CONTROL YOUR TIME/ BOOST YOUR PRODUCTIVITY

3.10 Handling Interruptions

Do you ever get the feeling that, if it weren't for all the interruptions, you could get your work done? Interruptions, like time, need to be controlled. Here are some ways to prevent or skillfully handle them.

1. If you answer your own phone, you need to develop a tactful, but direct way of dodging calls. Try, "I'm extremely busy now, let me call you back," or "I'm in the middle of a meeting, let me call you back." Anything will do as long as you use it.

2. The best system is one in which a secretary or receptionist screens your calls. An answering machine is second-best.

3. If a secretary is screening your calls, devise a system to help her determine the urgency of a call. Create categories such as, "Direct to someone else"; "Take number, will call back"; "Interrupt me briefly"; and "Urgent, interrupt immediately."

4. When you return calls, be sure to call at the best time for your prospect or customer. These are covered in Section 5.

5. Prepare for your calls in advance. Pull files or call up a customer's data on the computer before you dial the number.

6. Keep your calls short by getting to the point. Be careful who you ask, "How are you?" You may get a long answer. Better: Say, "Hi, Janet, just returning your call. What can I do for you?"

7. When calling customers (as opposed to returning their calls), have your objectives clearly in mind. Write out key questions so you won't lose your train of thought. Respect your customers' time as you would have them respect yours.

8. Group your calls by type so you won't have to change your mindset. For example, sales calls, especially if you are cold calling, should be made together. Other types of calls include collection, appointment verification, and problem resolution.

9. Handle visitors as if you were a doctor. Appointments need to be made. If possible, don't interrupt meetings with phone calls. Set a finite amount of time for the visitor, unless it is a customer or prospect. Diplomatically end your meetings by standing up and hinting that the meeting is over.

CONTROL YOUR TIME/ BOOST YOUR PRODUCTIVITY

3.11 The Art of Delegation

The ability to delegate sets the leader apart from the followers. That's because many people find it difficult to give up control. But delegating duties and responsibility is essential in today's downsized organizations. Sales people have so much work that they must delegate some activities if they hope to significantly increase their sales volume.

These key points will help you master the art of delegation.

Find the right person for the project. Don't assign a project to any warm body, or just the closest one. That's fine if *any* outcome is acceptable. If you want the job done right, however, you must find the right person for the job. If none exists, find the most capable person and train him or her well.

Delegate authority and accountability. The worst thing you can do is delegate a task and then tie a person's hands. If you have picked the right person or trained someone well, you must then give them decision-making authority so that the job can be done without your supervision. In addition, you should make the person accountable for the quality of the work performed.

Make the task perfectly clear. Carefully explain the nature of the project to the person to whom you are giving responsibility. This may be done verbally or in writing, depending on the complexity of the task. The newer and more complex the task, the more questions your assistant will have. Remain open to these, and answer all questions promptly and thoroughly.

Agree on a deadline. When your assistant fully understands your expectations, both of you are in a position to determine a mutually acceptable deadline.

Review and coach. There is a learning curve associated with any new activity. During this time, you should periodically review your assistant's progress and offer additional coaching if needed.

Lay the groundwork for more delegation. Once you get your feet wet, you will find more things that can be done by others to free up your time. Begin training people to assist you in more operations and you will find yourself with more time to do what you do best: selling.

WORKSHEET

CONTROL YOUR TIME/ BOOST YOUR PRODUCTIVITY

3.12 Delegation Plan

To delegate effectively, you must let go emotionally of some of your routine tasks. This worksheet will help you categorize your activities and shed light on what can be delegated.

1. Activities I've already delegated:

   _____

   _____

2. Activities I haven't yet, but could delegate:

   _____

   _____

3. Activities I'm unsure about delegating:

   _____

   _____

4. Activities I must do myself:

   _____

   _____

5. Ways to change #3 and #4 above to #2's:

   _____

   _____

WORKSHEET

CONTROL YOUR TIME/ BOOST YOUR PRODUCTIVITY

3.13 Time Management Action Plan

Choose three areas in which to improve your control of time Prioritize them and choose the most important to work on first. Fill out the action plan that follows and experience some success with one change before implementing the other two. Photocopy this action plan and use it for other goals as well.

What is a major time management practice I would like to implement?

What are the potential obstacles to doing so?

What are the benefits to implementing this practice?

How, specifically, will I implement this practice?

What is my target date for implementing this?

How and when will I measure my success?

What will I have to give up to make this behavioral change/

How will I reward myself and when?

ELECTRONIC SALES SUPPORT

3.14 The Portable Electronic Office (Part I)

Just because you're on the road doesn't mean you have to live without the conveniences or necessities of your office.

Cellular Phones

These expensive luxuries are becoming more affordable as digital technology comes on-line in a greater number of cities. There are three types of cellular phones on the market, but more are on the way.

Portable or **hand-held phones** are used by construction supervisors and other people who are away from a power source. These phones can be as small as a cordless phone and may be plugged into a car's cigarette lighter for recharging.

Mobile phones are permanently installed in a vehicle. They have a higher power rating and use all 832 cellular channels.

Transportable phones are not unlike portables, but they are larger and have more transmitting power and features. Instead of weighing a pound or less, transportables weigh ten to fifteen pounds.

Fax Machines and Copiers

The technology involved in both of these office machines is so similar that they are frequently combined in smaller, more convenient packages. Some models can be used in cars, phone booths, hotel rooms, or out on the golf course. The smallest fax machines are paperless, seven-ounce portables that cost $750 and up.

Copy machines have also been miniaturized. Some are about the size of a college textbook and can be used on AC or batteries. Of course, fax machines also double as copiers.

Pagers and Beepers

You're never far from a phone message with one of these clipped to your belt. In fact, some people use them in lieu of car phones—at a tremendous savings. Paging companies vary, so shop around for the best service and price. There are several different types of pagers. The simplest ones beep when you have a message, requiring you to call the office for details.

More expensive pagers actually give you information on the spot. They have LCD displays that show a phone number and/or message, depending on the model. Some features to compare are: 1) length of message; 2) how long messages are displayed; 3) the pager's ability to store message; 4) optional flash to replace tone; and 5) its ability to be read at night.

Laptop Computers

If you spend a lot of time on airplanes, you will love a laptop computer, especially if you do not dictate your letters. Laptops have become lighter (four to seven pounds) and more powerful. With increased memory and bigger hard drives, some models are more powerful than desktop systems. Check the screen under different lighting conditions. Some can be difficult to read. Backlit screens are generally more legible.

ELECTRONIC SALES SUPPORT

3.15 The Portable Electronic Office (Part II)

Dictating Machines and Tape Recorders

If you write a lot of letters, take extensive notes after meetings or aspire to write a book, a dictating machine is worth its weight in platinum. The tapes now come in three sizes, standard, micro, and pico. One pico is only $4^1/_4$" x $1^1/_4$" x $^3/_4$" and weighs three ounces. That's small enough to swallow if you're dictating on a bumpy road.

To choose among the many microcassette machines on the market, look for features such as voice-activated recording and tape-end warning. Reputation and warranty are important as well. These machines are very fragile, so buy a well-known brand that can be serviced. Standard cassette recorders are the most durable, but their size may create limitations for some people. They are getting smaller. In fact, one weighs a mere eight ounces, and measures $4^1/_2$" x $3^1/_4$" x $1^1/_4$".

There are many creative uses for tape recorders. One is to use it for prospecting. Drive through a new town or new industrial park and record the names of the stores that look like prospects. Another use is for recording orders. You may have a busy, impatient customer who doesn't want to wait for you to fill out paperwork. Streamline the order-writing process with a tape recorder and transcribe it later. Worried about not having the customer's signature? Let's be real—customers accept orders because they *want* them, not because they've signed their names on a dotted line.

Audio/Video Systems

Audio/video aids to presentations are big these days. They run the gamut from flash cards and flip charts to multi-media computerized slide shows and films. The most portable are what interest us here.

Self-contained video players/monitors combine a video tape player and TV. Starting at around five pounds and $600, these battery-operated, two-person viewing units enable you to show a video virtually anywhere.

Video playback units are similar to VCRs, but are designed for travel. Some of them fit under a plane seat and have such handy features as remote, freeze-frame, and automatic repeat. The latter is ideal for trade show booths. These units need to be hooked up to a TV monitor.

Computer data projection panels are portable LCD screens that project a computer's screen onto an overhead projector. They vary in size, the smallest about one foot square. Used in conjunction with expandable computer graphics programs such as Hypercard, these panels can lend a very high-tech look to your presentation.

Pocket Organizers and Translators

These calculator-like devices offer dozens of functions, ranging from calendars and calculators to multi-year appointment planning, address and phone storage (with auto dialing), notepads, language translation, and dictionaries. Some even interface with a personal computer. The Sharp Wizard is a good example of one of these $10^1/_2$ ounce miracles.

Language translators are a must if you're doing business with the ECC and don't know French, German or a half-dozen other languages. One ten-inch, four ounce model translates 1,400 phrases into ten different European languages. At $150, it is far cheaper than taking a translator along.

Multi-function Briefcases

This is the item for the salesperson who has it all and needs it all. For a mere $7,500, you can own (if you prefer a lease, it's $195/mo.) the Teleport C.E.O. (Complete Electronic Office). This self-contained fax, cellular phone, high-speed modem, and laptop computer is enclosed in a sleek black case that measures only 18" x 13" x 4" and weighs just 19 pounds (with batteries).

Prospecting for results

WHAT'S IN IT FOR YOU

- Discover the many sources for finding prospects
- Identify the types of prospects that hold the most potential
- Identify the most effective ways to contact prospects
- Learn the fine points of direct mail promotion
- Create your own effective direct mail letter
- Promote yourself as a salesperson
- Boost your sales and exposure through trade shows
- Discover six ways to increase your profile among colleagues and in the community

Your sales success depends on your customers. This group will change over time, which is why you need to spend some of your time looking—prospecting—for new customers.

Prospecting for customers is very much like prospecting for gold. Just as an old-time prospector might pan a mountain's worth of rock, mud and gravel to find a few valuable gold nuggets, today's salesperson must "mine" a potential area in the hopes of finding individuals or companies that are truly worthy digging for. These "nuggets" can be extremely valuable and can appreciate over time through repeat and referral business. This section shows you how to identify them.

IDENTIFYING LUCRATIVE PROSPECTS

4.1 The Sales Pipeline

Understanding all the elements will help you identify the best prospects for you to work with.

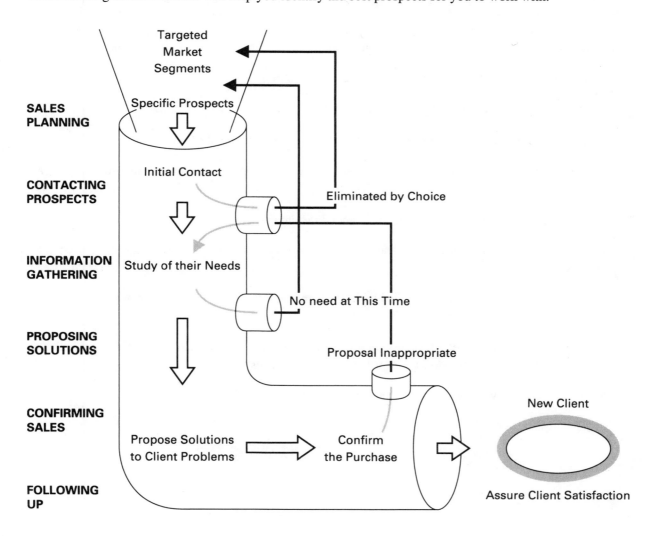

? F Y I

IDENTIFYING LUCRATIVE PROSPECTS

4.2 Qualifying Questions

Not every lead turns into a prospect, unless you don't mind wasting your time and money. There are a myriad of leads in your target market, so you must pare them down to a manageable number that hold the greatest promise. Of course, not every prospect can be an "A" account. To determine if a lead is worth upgrading to prospect status, ask yourself the following questions:

1. Does this company need the products/services I am selling?

2. Does this company perceive a need that I may fill?

3. Does this company have a sincere desire to solve this problem or fill this need?

4. Can this company's desire to solve its problem be converted into the belief that my product/service is the answer?

5. Does this company have the necessary financial resources?

6. Will this prospect's order be significant enough to be profitable, given the amount of time needed to make the sale?

7. Is the competition so well entrenched with this firm that it will take an inordinate amount of time to get an order, thus making it unprofitable at this time?

8. If the answer to 7 was yes, does this company have the potential to be a significant account in the future and, therefore, should I invest time now to plant seeds?

9. Are this company and its decision makers accessible to me?

IDENTIFYING LUCRATIVE PROSPECTS

4.3 Prospect Sources

Industrial	*Final Consumer*
existing customers	existing customers
other prospects	other prospects
company leads	company leads
direct mail	direct mail
directories	directories
trade associations	friends and social contacts
conventions and trade shows	professional groups
newsletters	centers of influence
chamber of commerce	canvassing
government publications	tip clubs or networking clubs
• federal	study groups
• state	
• local	seminars and classes
public speaking	personal observation
"orphan" accounts	public speaking

WORKSHEET

IDENTIFYING LUCRATIVE PROSPECTS

- Organize all information on your prospects on a standard sheet

4.4 Prospect Data Sheet

Use this form to make sure you gather pertinent data on every one of your prospects.

Prospect Data Sheet

Name of prospect _____

Address of prospect _____

_____

Products purchased:

Product A _____   Product B _____   Product C _____

Product volume:

Product A $ _____   Product B $ _____   Product C $ _____

Type of business

SIC Code

Has prospect been qualified?   Yes   No

Actions required to:

1. Qualify the prospect:

   •

   •

   •

2. Follow-up:

   •

   •

   •

WORKSHEET

IDENTIFYING LUCRATIVE PROSPECTS

- Keep track of prospecting methods for future analysis

4.5 Methods of Prospecting

Periodically you need to look back on your prospecting activities and evaluate which methods were most fruitful. This worksheet and the one that follows will help you. Start by keeping a record of the prospecting methods you have used with specific companies.

PROSPECTS (Company Name)	METHODS OF PROSPECTING					
	Company Leads	Direct Mail	Industrial Directories	Trade Shows	Trade Assns.	Other

Prospecting Performance Evaluation Form

WORKSHEET

IDENTIFYING LUCRATIVE PROSPECTS

4.6 Prospecting Performance Evaluation

Evaluate the effectiveness of prospecting methods by comparing your expected performance for each client with your actual performance.

Prospecting Performance Evaluation Form				
Prospecting Method	Objectives– Planned Performance	Actual Performance	Excess (shortage)	Explanation

✎ WORKSHEET

IDENTIFYING LUCRATIVE PROSPECTS

4.7 Identifying Ideal Customers

This worksheet will help you identify your ideal customers. Once you have done so, you will be able to look for prospects or market segments that have similar profiles.

1. List five of your best customers.

    1.

    2.

    3.

    4.

    5.

2. List the characteristics of your best customers.

3. List five of your worst customers.

    1.

    2.

    3.

    4.

    5.

4. List the characteristics of your worst customers.

5. What prospecting methods can you employ to find more "best" customers?

WORKSHEET

IDENTIFYING LUCRATIVE PROSPECTS

- Identify your most productive sources of prospects
- Brainstorm more sources of prospects

4.8 Creative Prospect Source List

One of the most important aspects of prospecting is creatively generating a list of potential clients or sources for clients.

List the top ten most fruitful sources of prospects you have used so far. Then brainstorm five less obvious sources.

Ten most-used sources of prospects

1.

2.

3.

4.

5.

6.

7.

8.

9.

10.

Five less-used, more creative sources of prospects

1.

2.

3.

4.

5.

WORKSHEET

IDENTIFYING LUCRATIVE PROSPECTS

4.9 Prospecting Action Plan

Write the five best prospect sources from the previous worksheet in the blank spaces below. Under each, brainstorm four ways to increase your exposure and generate more prospects.

1. _____

   a.

   b.

   c.

   d.

2. _____

   a.

   b.

   c.

   d.

3. _____

   a.

   b.

   c.

   d.

4. _____

   a.

   b.

   c.

   d.

5. _____

   a.

   b.

   c.

   d.

WORKSHEET

**WHAT'S IN IT FOR YOU**

IDENTIFYING LUCRATIVE PROSPECTS

- Brainstorm all the possible personal connections that may benefit you

4.10 The Friendship Tree

Growing a friendship tree is simple. List all the people you know who know your capabilities and professionalism. Evaluate age, occupation, length of time known, how well known, how often seen, ability to provide referrals, and how easy they are to approach. When you make your first contact, ask for two more names. Do the same for each person you contact. You'll find the list of prospects growing and spreading like the branches of a tree.

Friendship Tree

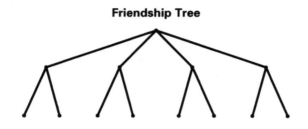

Type of Friend   *List Two Names*

School friends:

Friends of family:

Neighbors:

Known through spouse:

Known through children:

Known through hobbies:

Known through church:

Known through social clubs:

Known through community activities:

Known through past employment:

People you do business with:

Other:

FYI

AVOID SALES SLUMPS WITH DIRECT MAIL

4.11 The Direct Mail Solution[1]

Virtually every salesperson has experienced sales slumps, but few have mastered prospecting techniques that avoid them. The following direct mail system will eliminate or greatly reduce a sales slump by creating a steady stream of prospects. It also turns cold calling into warm calling, because it puts your name in front of your target market.

This unique system has several important elements.

1. You must work it for 90 days before modifying it to fit your personality, company, or industry.

2. It may take three to six months to smooth out your sales, depending on the normal sales cycle of your product or service.

3. It is more important for prospects to see your letter than it is to *read* it.

4. You are not trying to trigger a prospect's need, you are trying to establish name and company recognition. There is a big difference.

The Four-Letters-a-Day System

Your goal is to send one letter a week for four weeks to each prospect, then call for an appointment three to five days after sending the last letter. This is done by sending out four letters a day to your target market. Do not, however, send out more than four letters a day. After a couple of weeks, you will be sending out 12 to 16 letters a day. (First letters, second letters, third letters, etc.) If you become overly enthusiastic and contact more than four new prospects a day, you will be overwhelmed when it comes time to follow up.

If you have a computer, the system is quite easy. If you do not have a computer, farm out the work. Start by writing and entering the four letters (samples follow). Then enter the first month's 80 prospects, (four a day for 20 days). Next, print out all 320 letters, but stagger the dates printed on the letters. This will take some calculating, so use a calendar and think in terms of groups of four every day, starting with letter one in the first week.

After you have printed and signed all 320 letters, put them in envelopes. Before you seal them, write the date on which each letter should be mailed in the upper right corner. On the appropriate day, you will cover that spot with a stamp. Finally, print out a list of your prospects and the date they should have received the fourth letter so you will know when to call them.

[1]Adapted from *Direct Mail for Sales People* by Rick Barrera. Rick Barrera & Associates, P.O. Box 8164, La Jolla, CA 92038.

?FYI

AVOID SALES SLUMPS WITH DIRECT MAIL

4.12 Letters that Make Impressions

Although your letter may not be read from beginning to end, it must at least make an impression. To make an impression, it must be opened and read at least briefly. A letter that looks personal has the best chance of being opened.

How do you make a letter look personal?

- Address the envelope by hand or typewriter, not with a mailing label or personal computer. Also, write out the return address without your company name. A return address printed on the back of the envelope looks personal.

- Put a stamp on the envelope. Do not use a postage meter.

- To ensure that the letter gets opened first, make it lumpy. Why lumpy? When lumpy mail arrives, the recipient thinks, "What could this be? It must be a gift!" The letter gets opened. Try enclosing a cassette, a novelty, a piece of candy . . . anything related to the message you are conveying.

Five Keys to Effective Letters

1. Use a headline and a p.s. They should work together to convey your message succinctly, just in case the body of the letter is not read . . . and it usually isn't.

2. Write an upbeat, fun letter that focuses on problem-solving. Write several letters and get feedback from people. Edit, rewrite and perfect them before you mail them. Remember, you need to have four well-written letters.

3. Include a postage-paid reply card. This makes it easy for your prospect to respond.

4. Include a phone number, preferably a toll-free 800 number. This will encourage even more response than a reply card.

5. Follow the guidelines in worksheet 4.14, "Key Elements of Your Letters."

AVOID SALES SLUMPS WITH DIRECT MAIL

4.13 Two Sample Letters

These two sample letters illustrate catchy headlines, brief, easy-to-read text, and the effective use of a p.s.

Are You Tired of Feeling Like Goldilocks?

Dear _____ :

First you look at one hotel and the meeting space is *too big* . . . then you look at another hotel and it is *too small* . . . but at the Hotel Barrera you will find the meeting space is *just right!!*

Because of our flexible design system, we can customize our space to fit your needs exactly. Try us. We are the sensible alternative.

Sincerely,

Rick Barrera

p.s. Because we are at the world's largest airport you will also find flight schedules that fit just right.

SENT BY: Hotel Sales Person
TARGET MARKET: Corporate and Association Meeting Planners

Prescription Without Diagnosis Is Malpractice

Dear _____ :

In business as in medicine we believe this is a truism. That is why I'd like to meet with you soon to learn more about our business and to help you find some creative ways to meet your goals.

I'll be calling you in a couple of days to set up an appointment for us to get together.

Sincerely,

Rick Barrera

p.s. I've enclosed a copy of our latest issue. The article on Page 10 might be of particular interest to you.

SENT BY: Newspaper Advertising Sales Person
TARGET MARKET: Advertisers

WORKSHEET

AVOID SALES SLUMPS WITH DIRECT MAIL

- Create an effective sales letter, step-by-step

4.14 Key Elements of Your Letters

Other time-tested elements also increase the chances of a letter's success. Not every letter will incorporate every element below. Pick and choose as you need them.

1. **Make it personal.** For immediate identification, your letterhead should appear at the top. And you should *always* use the prospect's name in the salutation. Form letters almost always end up in the garbage.

2. **Cover only one idea.** Sell one thing at a time. You can sell a product, service, your company or yourself, but make it just one thing. Keep the letter focused and simple.

   The purpose of your letter is _____

3. **Sell benefits, not features.** Remember, you are a problem-solver, not an educator. Don't try to overwhelm people. Just write about two or three of the most impressive benefits. The three benefits you will mention in your letter will be:

   a. _____

   b. _____

   c. _____

4. **Write for readability.** Letters that are one page (maximum) in length and broken up into four or five paragraphs are easy to read. Consult an artist or direct mail specialist for ideas on how to make your letter attractive and inviting.

5. **Write with a logical flow.** Take the time to write out your answers to the questions that will naturally flow into your readers' minds:

   What is it? (Simple description) _____

   What does it do? _____

   How would I use it? _____

   Why do I need it? _____

   How can I be sure this is a legitimate offer and a good value?

   _____

   What risks are involved for me? _____

   Is it guaranteed? _____

   How much does it cost? _____

   How do I get one? _____

6. **Make a claim.** Tell your reader what is different and better about your product, service, company or you. This claim goes beyond the simple description. Your claim is:

_____

7. **Give examples.** Examples speak louder than descriptions and claims. Tell a brief success story. Use statistics and dollar amounts if you can. An example you can use is:

_____

_____

8. **Use testimonials.** Most prospects will read a direct mail letter with skepticism. Testimonials add credibility to your claims and examples, especially if they are from high-profile experts. List three people who would give you an impressive testimonial:

a. _____

b. _____

c. _____

9. **Guarantee your claim.** Money-back guarantees are powerful motivators. They take the risk out of buying. If you can, offer a guarantee and watch your response rate soar! Your guarantee will be:

_____

10. **Include a call for action.** At the end of your letter, give your readers a nudge to get them to call or write. Your call for action will be:

_____

11. **Make it easy to respond.** The easier, the better. Toll-free numbers make responding effortless. Self-addressed stamped envelopes are second best. If you promise to make a follow-up call (also desirable), be sure you call within two weeks. Your prospects will respond by:

_____

(We highly recommend the book *Words That Sell* by Richard Bayan.)

WORKSHEET

AVOID SALES SLUMPS WITH DIRECT MAIL

4.15 Mailing List Checklist

- Determine the specifications of your mailing list
- Determine the break-even return of your direct mail campaign
- Increase your understanding of some of the requirements of a direct mail campaign

Before you compile or buy a mailing list, you must know the "specifications" of your list. Fill in as many of the details as you can, and research what you don't know.

1. What are the characteristics of individuals and companies in your target market?

   Geographic location(s):_____

   Specific zip codes: _____

   Age range:_____

   Yearly income: _____

   Educational background: _____

   Occupations/industries:_____

   Interests: _____

   Targeted needs; _____

2. In what form will you need the mailing list?

   _____ Computer Disk (best for multiple use)

   _____ Address Labels (best for one-time use)

3. Will the list broker guarantee the list is current? What percentage can be guaranteed as "deliverable" or "clean"?

4. What is the total number of pieces to be mailed? _____

5. Will you need a disk so you can personalize letters through your computer's mail-merge function?

6. Will you enclose a brochure or other material that will need folding and stuffing? Who will do that work?

   _____

7. If you are sending over 500 pieces, you can use a bulk mail permit. Have you contacted the post office for details on doing so?_____

8. How many sales do you need to make this direct mail campaign break even? _____ To make a profit?_____ How much of a profit would you like in order to consider this mailing worth the effort? _____

9. Based on your answers to the question above, what response rate do you need in order to reach your goals (based on your sales/call average)?_____

10. Follow-up calls dramatically increase your response rate and overall success. Will phone numbers be supplied with the list and are calls possible within this target market? _____

11. Who will make the follow-up phone calls? _____

WORKSHEET

AVOID SALES SLUMPS WITH DIRECT MAIL

4.16 Direct Mail Campaign Budget

You need to know the cost of a direct mail campaign to make it successful. Use this worksheet to estimate costs, and you'll be able to pinpoint the response you need to break even.

Name of_____

Mail Piece: _____

Objective: _____

Date:_____

Prepared By: _____

_____

A. DIRECT EXPENSES

1. Planning/Administrative/Operating
   Salaries (Man Hours x Hourly Rate) $_____

2. Creative Costs/Preparations
   a. Copy $_____
   b. Layout $_____
   c. Artwork $_____
   d. Photography/Retouching $_____
   e. Printing Preparation $_____ $_____

3. Other enclosure $_____

4. Envelopes $_____

5. Mailing list rental/purchase $_____

6. Mailing list maintenance $_____

7. Mailing piece preparation $_____
   (folding, collating, inserting, labeling,
   addressing, metering, sorting, typing, etc.) $_____

8. Postage
   a. Outgoing $_____
   b. Return $_____ $_____

9. If Selling Merchandise
   a. Cost of merchandise $_____
   b. Handling $_____
   c. Postage/shipping $_____
   d. Royalties $_____
   e. Refunds/cancellations $_____
   f. Refurbish returns $_____
   g. Bad debts $_____
   h. Storage $_____ $_____

10. Other $_____

TOTAL DIRECT EXPENSES $_____

? F Y I

AVOID SALES SLUMPS WITH DIRECT MAIL

4.17 Sources of Direct Mail Lists

There are innumerable sources for prospects and information on companies in every industry. For ideas, pick the brain of a reference librarian at a large public or university library. The following categories of sources should not only get you started, but take you a long way:

Professional and trade associations

Clubs (golf, tennis and other hobby and sport clubs)

Civic groups (Kiwanis, Lions, Optimists)

Community business groups (Chambers of Commerce, convention and tourism groups)

Magazines (Lists of subscribers)

Women's organizations (NOW, League of Women Voters)

Special interest groups (Greenpeace, Cousteau Society, NAACP)

Business directories (Moody's, Poor's, Thomas Register)

The Yellow Pages

Religious groups (churches, businesses catering to religion)

List brokers (Dun & Bradstreet, TRW, local companies).

TRADE SHOWS

4.18 Why Work a Trade Show?

A trade show offers a microcosm of customers and competitors. You can learn a great deal and make many contacts in a very short time. If your company is picking up the tab for the booth, ask if you can help represent the company. If your company does not participate in trade shows, consider doing it yourself. The number of customers attending makes it a very wise use of your time.

1. Customers galore! You can't ask for a faster introduction to a large number of customers. Customers are there to do business. They want to see the latest. They want to be sold, by the right person, of course, but many intend to place orders. For the salesperson who can socialize and sell, there is a lot of money to be made.

2. Easy spying! Many of your competitors will be there. Of course, the secrets they reveal are the ones they want the public to see, but you will learn a lot. By talking to them—either openly or by posing as a customer—you will find out about their features, benefits, delivery capabilities, services, guarantees, pricing, and so on.

3. Polish your presentations! Put an end to doubts about your product knowledge or presentation skills. Spending all day giving presentations to prospects will make you the consummate pro.

4. Sell from either side. You don't have to rent a booth to take advantage of a trade show. You can attend and sell to customers who have booths. There is no rule saying that sales must be conducted from a booth. Selling flows both ways. It is less expensive to sell to people at *their* booths.

5. For more information on trade shows, see *How To Participate Profitably in Trade Shows* by Robert B. Konikow, Dartnell Press, 4660 Ravenswood Ave., Chicago, IL 60640.

?FYI

- Streamline your research into trade shows for your industry

TRADE SHOWS

4.19 Sources of Trade Show Information

How do you find out about trade shows? There are too many trade associations to mention here, but these resources can start your research.

1. Successful Meetings, Inc. publishes an annual *Directory of Conventions*. It is available from them at 1518 Walnut St., Philadelphia, PA. 19102, (215) 546-3295.

2. The National Trade and Professional Associations of the U.S. publishes meeting and convention dates and locations for each member association. Write: NTPA, Columbia Books, 777 14th St. NW #236, Washington, D.C. 20005, (202) 737-3777.

3. The *Tradeshow Week Data Book* is an annual publication of the Tradeshow Bureau. This features data on over 3,000 trade shows in over 100 categories. Contact them at 12233 W. Olympic Blvd. #236, Los Angeles, CA. 90064, (213) 826-5696.

4. Many trade and professional association publications have regular columns or annual special features on trade shows. For more information, contact your industry's trade publication.

5. If your city has a convention and visitor's bureau, ask them for a list of conventions scheduled for the next year.

- Introduce yourself to prospects
- Stimulate off-season sales
- Develop long-term relationships with customers
- Expand your customer base

PROMOTING YOURSELF

4.20 Blow Your Own Horn

Every company devises a marketing plan to promote its products or services. You, too, should promote yourself. Your company takes a global market view of promotions; you have to focus on your small piece of the earth—your territory.

Why bother? Most people think the company's advertising will bring in enough business to keep them busy. More often than not, this is not the case.

A well-executed promotional program will accomplish many things for you:

- Introduce you, your company, and product/service to prospects and smooth the way for follow-up calls

- Encourage more purchases by current customers

- Stimulate off-season business

- Keep abreast or ahead of your competition's promotional efforts

- Enlarge your customer base by spreading your sales activity to larger areas

- Keep in touch with customers; keep your name in the back of their minds; let them know you are just a phone call away

- Re-establish contact with former customers.

There are four means of promoting a company or an individual: advertising, sales promotions, publicity, and public relations. The first two are designed to influence sales directly; the latter two increase sales by boosting a person's or company's image.

Advertising
Yellow Pages ad
Direct mail
Ads in trade and professional publications
Television, radio, billboards
Brochures and flyers

Sales Promotions
Special discounts and package deals, coupons, cross-promotions
Novelties such as pens, calenders, letter openers
Trade show exhibits
In-store demonstrations and samples
Special events, open houses

Public Relations and/or Publicity
Sending Christmas, birthday, and special-occasion cards
Membership and involvement in professional and trade groups
Donations of time and/or money
Speaking engagements, seminars, consulting, teaching classes
Press releases, feature articles, interviews

?FYI

PROMOTING YOURSELF

4.21 Advertising

Many salespeople advertise on their own—especially in real estate, insurance, professional services, and multi-level marketing. Answer the following questions to determine if advertising is suitable for you.

1. What message(s) do you want to convey? Should more emphasis be put on you or your product/service?

2. Who is your target market?

3. What is the most effective way to reach your target market?

4. How much can you afford to spend on advertising this year? Can you afford *not* to advertise? Will your company supplement your advertising budget, or contribute in any other way?

5. When is the best time to schedule your advertising? Is your product/service seasonal? Is your product/service tied in with an activity such as the purchase of a new car or home?

After you have answered these questions, you will have a better idea of your advertising capabilities. The most important issue is money. Repeated advertising is not cheap; one-time advertising is usually ineffective. You'll be better off concentrating a modest budget on direct mail than blowing it all on one TV commercial.

Consider the following media carefully.

Brochures. Large or small, brochures should always be professionally designed, written, and printed on high-quality paper. Brochures increase credibility significantly.

Direct Mail. Letters and brochures are effective for name recognition and exposure in general. Direct mail's primary advantage is its ability to target your market with precision.

Novelties. Pens, calendars, and other novelties cheerfully remind customers of you. They are not inexpensive and, if possible, should be done with the financial help of your company.

Print Ads. Magazine and newspaper ads are effective, yet expensive. In industries such as real estate, there is no substitute for a picture and description of a listing.

Billboards. Billboards come in all shapes and sizes. For the budgets of individual salespeople, the bus stop seat billboard is the most realistic.

Radio. One of the most effective media if used repeatedly, radio reaches the demographic group you desire, but at a price. Air time and production are expensive.

Television. The king of mass media, this high-priced advertising vehicle reaches the most people at the highest price. It would be absurd for a salesperson to advertise on national TV, but local cable channels offer less expensive opportunities for exposure.

WORKSHEET

PROMOTING YOURSELF

4.22 Sales Promotions

Advertising is an on-going promotional activity. Sales promotions are one-time activities designed to stimulate sales for a special occasion. As a salesperson, you should think of ways to boost sales, especially if your company does not do this. Use your calendar to figure out when a product needs to be sold most heavily. Plan to begin your sales promotion well in advance, so that you gain the proper exposure. The time to run a Christmas special is not December 24.

What Can You Do? Brainstorm ways to use as many of the following sales promotions as possible.

1. Demonstrations of new products (either live or on video)

   _____

2. Trade show exhibit booths—volunteer to work trade shows that your company is attending, or put together your own booth. (See FYIs 4.18 and 4.19.)

3. **Promotional packages**—seasonal sales, year-end specials and discount coupons. What are some specials you could suggest to your company?

   _____

4. **Specialty advertising items**—Ideas for novelties, knickknacks and other things to be remembered by (be creative):

   _____

5. **Attractions**—celebrity sports, raffles, etc. What would be appropriate for your business?

In addition to devising promotions you launch yourself or present to your company, take advantage of promotions your company sponsors. Volunteer for trade shows, distribute novelties or calendars (with stamp your name, title and telephone number stamped on them), and get involved to increase your exposure.

WORKSHEET

PROMOTING YOURSELF

- Find creative ways to benefit from free ink in newspapers and trade journals

4.23 Publicity

The best advertising is free advertising. Publicity, which can be positive or negative, is a form of free advertising. Let's just concern ourselves with positive publicity.

Exposure in the news media is a promotional tactic that must be orchestrated. Publicity requires a newsworthy event such as a promotion, grand opening, new business, scientific breakthrough, award, or large contract. The event should be described in a press release—a one- to two-page article that the news medium can print as is, or follow up on for more details.

If the news is of greater significance—a scientific breakthrough, for example—a full-length, feature article may be in order. Articles and press releases must be written so that they do not sound like ads. That means no hype, no unsubstantiated claims, and no calls to action.

Sometimes a newspaper will accept an interesting or amusing photograph and caption. A photograph's first priority is journalistic merit; its second is publicizing you, your company, or your product/service.

Letters to the editor also serve as publicity. If you keep abreast of local issues, especially those in business, offer your opinion or insight in a letter. You'd be surprised how many people read the Op-Ed pages.

Publicity as a means to gain exposure and increase sales often succeeds where advertising fails due to three advantages:

- *Credibility* People are much more likely to believe the facts in an article than in an advertisement. Most of us are skeptical of ads, but suspend that disbelief when we read an article, which is why the tabloids sell so well.

- *Subtlety.* Readers of press releases and feature articles do not resist the news as they resist other forms of contact.

- *Dramatization.* Advertising tends to make products, services, and companies seem larger than life. Publicity can do the same thing, but in a different way. Publicity can convey the message, "We are your neighbors, with the same concerns that you have. Let's all work together to make this a better community."

Think of three ways to capitalize on each of these forms of publicity.

Press Releases:

1. _____

2. _____

3. _____

Feature Articles:

1. _____

2. _____

3.

Photographs:

1. _____

2. _____

3. _____

Letters to the Editor:

1. _____

2. _____

3. _____

Publicity, unlike advertising, is an occasional promotional strategy. The results are long term, and may not even be measurable. With advertising, you can pick the location of an ad in a publication. With publicity, you are completely at the mercy of the editor, which is why public relations firms are necessary. Their strategic knowledge and working relationships with editors will give you and your company a better shot at getting exposure.

? F Y I

PROMOTING YOURSELF

4.24 Public Relations

WHAT'S IN IT FOR YOU

- Determine ways to get involved in the community and gain favorable publicity
- Understand who your "publics" are

Public relations and publicity are often confused. Public relations is simply the company's image—or your image—in relation to the community. Positive P.R. comes from the goodwill, altruism, and charity generated by acts as small as sponsoring a Little League team or as large as donating a building to a local university.

As an individual salesperson, you can gain excellent exposure for yourself by getting involved in your local community. Join the Chamber of Commerce, volunteer at the Lung Association, answer phones at the Cancer Society, register people to vote, or spend time at a children's hospital. Do whatever altruistic deeds interest you, but do something!

You want to convey that—

- You care about your community and have a long-term interest in it

- You are an expert in your field

- You are open and accessible to help customers and noncustomers alike.

Who Are Your "Publics"?

"Publics" are groups of people who perceive you as a business person. Some publics act on their perceptions to increase your sales; others just like you as a person. It is important to identify your publics and choose promotional strategies that will increase your profile with the most important ones. For example, if you sell real estate, your publics are bankers, loan officers, people in title and escrow companies, other brokers, attorneys, property managers, and real estate buyers and sellers in your community.

How Do You Reach Your Publics?

In addition to community volunteer work, there are other ways to get involved.

- Contribute time or money to a worthy cause.

- Sponsor a team—bowling, Little League, volleyball.

- Give speeches or seminars free of charge. For example, an accountant might give a free lecture around tax time. A salesperson with an athletic shoe company might give a speech to high school students about getting into shape before the summer. The possibilities are unlimited.

- Provide public service spots on local television or radio stations. National Public Radio's local affiliates are often looking for local people to provide two- to three-minute spots about topics of interest.

- Organize an event. You can help put together a celebration or an event to commemorate a city anniversary, honor a local hero, or start an annual charity golf tournament.

- Get involved in trade or professional associations. Show that you care about the industry by volunteering for committees.

Rub shoulders with the right people and doors begin to open.

WORKSHEET

PROMOTING YOURSELF

- Brainstorm ways to promote yourself using all the strategies discussed

4.25 Promotional Strategies Worksheet

List all the creative ways you can think of to promote yourself and your company, using each of the following methods.

Advertising:

Publicity:

Clubs/organizations:

Brochures:

Newsletters:

Yellow Pages:

Seminars/speaking:

Publishing:

Directories:

Congratulation/welcome letters:

Other:

? F Y I

PROMOTING YOURSELF

4.26 Promote Yourself in Print

Publishing articles in local newspapers, magazines, trade journals, or company organs can help you gain clients, credibility, and recognition.

The best type of article for the beginning writer to tackle is the list article. It is easy to write, useful, and highly salable. In a list article, you discuss several points under a single theme, but its format gives you the freedom to jump from one topic to another. You do not have to worry about creating smooth transitions from one paragraph or section to the next.

The beauty of the list article is that it is the perfect vehicle for you to show your expertise. You can address a specific problem or issue in a how-to style. There are several types of list articles.

The Problem-Solving List Article

This is the most common form of list article. It answers the primary question posed in the article's introduction by devoting one item in the list to each solution. For example, a financial planner could write an article on how to avoid estate taxes. The article could list five ways and discuss each, one at a time.

The Step-By-Step List Article

This type of article uses a cookbook approach to giving information. For example, a salesperson in your industry might write an article on negotiating. The order of the steps would be important, as they would be in a recipe.

The General Information List

Some articles list information about people, places, companies, or products/services of interest. In this type of article, it is important to give the criteria on which your selection was made. For example, if you write an article on the five best ways to get leads in your business, tell your readers why these ways are *the best*.

The key to writing anything is organization and editing. Start out by organizing your article into an introduction, a list, and a conclusion. Outline as much as possible before sitting down to write. After you've written the article, let it sit for a few days. Then come back to it and read it again. Edit or rewrite spots that need work, and then give it to someone else for an objective opinion. Keep your ego out of the process, and remember that writing well takes patience and practice.

PROMOTING YOURSELF

4.27 Promote Yourself on the Podium

Whether you are selling yourself or your company, giving speeches will go a long way toward increasing your exposure, your credibility, and your sales.

Public speaking is many people's number one fear. Like everything else, however, it gets easier with practice. Keep these tips in mind as you prepare to mount the podium.

Give Yourself a Mental Edge. Realize that your audience will be *with* you, not against you. Think of the experience as a dialogue rather than a monologue.

Know Your Audience. What are their backgrounds, expectations, and business positions?

Define the Purpose of Your Speech. Is it to motivate, educate, persuade, or sell?

Use Visual Aids. Some speeches—especially brief ones—are fine without visual aids; others desperately need them.

Create a Catchy Title. A clever title not only describes your speech, it piques your audience's curiosity.

Do Your Homework. Company records, the library, magazines, and telephone interviews of industry experts are all sources of interesting information for your speech.

To put your speech together well, follow these steps.

Start With an Outline. Think in terms of a beginning, middle, and end of the speech. Edit your outline to include only relevant topics.

Concentrate on the Introduction and Conclusion. First, make a connection with your audience and answer the question, "Why should they listen to me?" Do it with impact. For your conclusion, do not simply restate your main points. Conclude by summarizing, but do it in a way that puts everything in a broader, more significant perspective. Your conclusion has to send people away changed (even slightly) for the better.

Use Statistics Wisely. Statistics can impress people, or put them to sleep. Consider the nature of your audience. If you are speaking to a group of engineers, use statistics. If you are talking to Socializers and Relaters, forget the statistics and use graphics instead. (See Section 6 for explanations of these types.)

Plan a Q & A Period. It's a good idea to rehearse the answers to probable questions. Put the Q & A session before your conclusion. This will allow you to tactfully cut off the questions and end your speech in control, with *your* ideas.

Use Index Cards. Know your material well enough to speak extemporaneously, with notes on index cards to jog your memory.

A speech is not unlike a sales presentation. The audience may be larger and the speech longer, but the following principles apply to both.

Rehearse Regularly. Practice your speech aloud in front of a mirror as often as necessary until it is smooth. Time your speech. Learn to pause. Record yourself and be ready for a surprise, but learn from it.

Make Sure All Systems Are Go. If you can, check out the room before your presentation. Make sure the P.A. system works, the slide projector is loaded and has a spare bulb, and the room temperature and lighting are comfortable.

Control Your Stage Fright. Everyone, yes, *everyone,* gets butterflies before going on stage. Expect stage fright but minimize it. Take some deep breaths. Tell yourself, "I am the expert; these people are going to like me; I don't have to be perfect (no one is) and I'm going to do a great job."

Vary Your Eye Contact During Your Speech. You'll relax more if you realize you are talking to nice people. Look at a lot of different people. Keep your eyes moving around the room and make a connection with your audience. They'll appreciate it as well.

Move Around During Your Speech. Few great speakers stand behind a podium as if they were perfectly relaxed robots. They wander around, become animated, go out into the audience and get people involved.

Persist. Comedians know this well. You cannot quit after you have died on stage. It happens to everyone. Come back for more. Practice. Improve yourself. The pay-off could be tremendous.

5 Contacting prospects

WHAT'S IN IT FOR YOU

- Learn the relative value of the three ways to contact prospects
- Learn to write an effective telephone script
- Learn to maximize your effectiveness and efficiency by organizing your calls
- Determine the best time to call various prospects
- Learn to write personal letters and form letters
- Realize the value of an initial benefits statement
- Learn to change your contacting style to conform to different peoples' behavioral styles

First impressions count—maybe more than they should. But they do leave a lasting impression on a prospect. Every customer wants to feel like an individual. By tailoring your approaches to prospects to their individual needs and personality, you will significantly increase your chances for success. Show that you recognize your prospect's individual needs and you will have taken a giant step toward making that prospect a long-term customer. This section gives you the tools for doing that.

WORKSHEET

MAXIMIZING PROSPECT CONTACTS

5.1 Sales Planning Guide

Before you call on an account, you have to have a purpose for the call. It can be as simple as calling to confirm that a delivery arrived on time, or as complex as meeting face to face for an information-gathering session. No matter what the reason, the more organized you are, the greater your chances are of accomplishing your objective for the call. Answer the most relevant questions below before each call.

- Organize yourself before each call
- Save time by having concrete purposes for each sales call
- Have complete prospect information in front of you during each call

Company _____ Type of Business _____

Location _____ Phone _____ Date _____

Key Contact _____ Title _____

Who is the decision maker? _____

Current Situation?

Goals and Objectives?

Potential Problem(s)/Need(s)?

What objectives should I seek to accomplish with this account?

Next Call:

Overall:

If the key contact is not the decision maker, how can he/she influence the objective(s) I am trying to achieve?

What questions can I ask to uncover, clarify, or amplify prospect problems, needs, and/or goals?

What decision-making criteria are important to this prospect?

Possible Benefits Prospect Is Seeking	Service/Company Features That Provide Those Benefits	Proof Material (Letters, Brochures, Testimonials, To Be Used if Necessary

How can I be of more benefit to this prospect than anyone else who has called on him/her?

Possible Prospect Objections	Potential Answers

Based on my objective(s), what specific commitment will I ask this prospect to make?

Why should the prospect want to make this commitment?

By what criteria will the prospect judge whether or not my product/service/company was a satisfactory solution to his problem/need?

What methods, procedures, or forms can I use to measure whether or not the actual results did in fact meet the above criteria?

WORKSHEET

MAXIMIZING PROSPECT CONTACTS

5.2 Prospect Knowledge Checklist

Learn all you can about the decision maker at a prospective company. You should be able to answer most of the following questions, noting the particulars in the prospect's file.

1. What are the prospect's personal style, idiosyncrasies and temperament?

2. What are his/her hobbies, sports and other interests?

3. What are his/her family's interests?

4. Does he/she buy on opinion, fact, friendship or reciprocity?

5. What is his/her present product usage?

6. Who is your current or potential competition for this account?

7. What are his/her specific needs for your product/service?

8. Why should he/she purchase from you rather than from a competitor?

9. What is his/her present volume of business and potential for expansion?

10. What type and quality of merchandise does he/she carry?

11. How is the merchandise marketed?

12. What is the company's credit rating?

13. Are there any industry trends that will affect the company's future purchasing pattern?

MAXIMIZING PROSPECT CONTACTS

5.3 Only Three Ways to Make Contact

Let's face it, there are only three ways to contact a prospect: in person, by letter, or over the phone. Each has its advantages and disadvantages. Most salespeople use a combination of all three. Whatever your methods of contact are, they must be accomplished in ways that are

- conducive to business

- cost-effective

- image-effective

- tension-reducing

- trust-building

If you were to grade the three ways to contact people, they would receive report cards that look like this:

Type of Contact	Quantity Possible	Quality Possible
In-Person	C	A
Telephone	B	B
Letter	A	C

Obviously, some combination of the three is the best tactic. Many salespeople start by sending a letter to a large number of people. The leads that come from those letters are then called on the phone for appointments. Finally, at the face-to-face (high-quality) meeting, the salesperson can really begin to build trust and establish the relationship. This is one of many possible combinations. Only you can determine the best strategy for your business.

To maximize your selling time, remember Pareto's 80-20 rule: 20 percent of your accounts will represent 80 percent of your sales volume. After you have categorized your accounts into A, B, C accounts, you will know which companies (the As) deserve the highest quality contact; that is, frequent personal visits. Your B accounts will receive fewer personal visits and more phone calls. The C accounts will be contacted primarily by letter, phone and occasionally in person.

? F Y I

MAXIMIZING PROSPECT CONTACTS

5.4 The Customer Perception Matrix

The way you contact a customer will determine the way or ways that he or she can perceive you. These perceptions could be limited or unlimited depending upon the method you choose. Being aware of the limitations will help you choose the most appropriate way to contact prospects and customers.

	Modes of Perceptions		
Ways to Contact	**Verbal**	**Vocal**	**Visual**
Letter	Words	Bold Face Italics Quotes Underline All Caps	Quality Type Style Illustrations Brochures
Phone	Words	Enthusiasm Accent Volume Pacing	Mental Pictures
In Person	Words	Enthusiasm Accent Volume Pacing	Image/Looks Facial Expressions Body Language

✏ **WORKSHEET**

MAXIMIZING PROSPECT CONTACTS

5.5 Common Brush-Offs

Occasionally you run into a prospect who tries to give you the brush-off before you've even had a chance to identify yourself. We've all heard the excuses: "I'm too busy," "I have everything I need," "I'm not interested," or "Not today."

In Section 10, we will discuss specific ways to handle these brush-offs. For now, it would be a valuable exercise to become aware of your five most common "early" prospect excuses.

1. Common Excuse: _____

   Your Response: _____

2. Common Excuse: _____

   Your Response: _____

3. Common Excuse: _____

   Your Response: _____

4. Common Excuse: _____

   Your Response: _____

5. Common Excuse: _____

   Your Response: _____

CONTACTING BY PHONE

5.6 How to Write a Telephone Script (Part 1)

WHAT'S IN IT FOR YOU

- Understand the seven steps covered in an effective phone script

Many prospects dislike receiving cold calls. For this reason, you must write your phone script so that it sounds natural, puts your prospect at ease, and accomplishes one or two specific goals: Introduces you, offers information, requests an appointment, requests a sale, or handles a problem. The guidelines in the next seven FYIs in this subsection will help you write a smooth, effective telephone script.

 **F Y I**

CONTACTING BY PHONE

5.7 Introducing Yourself and Your Company

WHAT'S IN IT FOR YOU

- Develop clear, concise openings for cold calls on the phone
- Put cold-call prospects at ease
- Get your cold-call phone presentations off to a good start

Most people don't like receiving cold calls. So remember, first impressions are important. Above all, be clear and concise when identifying yourself. Avoid lengthy explanations such as, "Hello, Mrs. Jones, this is Artimus Hercules Seidenspinner the Third with Goldstar Audio and Video Recording, which is a wholly-owned subsidiary of the United Electronics Consortium based in London." Forget it—your prospect will get lost in the maze of words. Just say, "Hello, Mrs. Jones, this is Art with Goldstar Recording, and this is what we do. . . . "

Take some time to think about how you introduce yourself to a customer. Are you too talkative? Do you make it easy for the consumer?

? F Y I

- Put a phone prospect at ease
- Increase your chances of making the sale

CONTACTING BY PHONE

5.8 Taking the Pressure Off the Call

Many prospects, especially consumers at home, immediately think to themselves, "Oh, brother, another sales call. What is this guy going to try to sell me now?" If you are calling a prospect at work, your call is an interruption. Make a statement that takes the rudeness out of the interruption, such as, "If you have a minute, I'd like to briefly introduce myself and tell you what we do. Would that be OK?" Or, "I'd like to take a moment to tell you who we are and what we do. Is this a good time for you?" If it's not a good time, ask when would be a better time. This way, you don't waste your customer's (or your) time.

Think about making cold calls. Do you try to take the pressure off your prospect? Can you think of ways to sound more natural and put the consumer at ease?

CONTACTING BY PHONE

5.9 Explaining the Purpose of the Call

- Establish rapport with your prospect by clarifying the reason for your call
- Increase your chances for moving the prospect toward confirmation

After you take the pressure off your consumer, you should follow with a brief, hard-hitting statement that explains why you have called. Do not, however, describe any of the benefits that you will present later. Some possible purposes for your call are:

- To follow up to see if a direct mail piece was received . . .

  "Mr. Smith, this is Gene Kelly with Toes-A-Tappin'. I just wanted to see if you received the brochure I sent you last week on our dancing services?" If Mr. Smith says no, you can say, "May I take a minute or so now to tell you what it's all about?"

- To mention a person who referred you to this prospect . . .

  Mrs. Maples, a good friend of yours, Donald Trump, suggested I call you. He thought you would be interested in knowing about our personalized security service."

- To tell your prospect about a product/service that your company has designed that is of particular interest to people like the prospect.

  "Dr. Lee, if you have a minute or so, I'd like to quickly tell you about our health insurance billing software that we designed specifically for chiropractors."

- To follow up on the prospect's response to your company's advertising.

  "Mrs. Regan, I'm calling in response to your inquiry about our psychic financial planning. Is this a good time for me to answer any questions you may have?"

Why are you calling your prospect? Think of other clear, concise ways to explain your purpose to your customer.

?FYI

CONTACTING BY PHONE

5.10 Capturing Interest with a Powerful Statement

WHAT'S IN IT FOR YOU

- Draw the prospect into the conversation to identify benefits to the prospect
- Increase the likelihood of a sale

To answer two of the prospect's questions—"What's this all about?" and "What's in it for me?"—make a claim that includes a benefit, financial reward, or service. An example: "Mr. Schmidt, our software was designed to increase your staff's productivity by 25 percent while also decreasing overhead by 15 percent. And I'm aware of several companies in your industry that have achieved even better results. Are those numbers that you would like to achieve?"

Asking a question after your captivating statement will help keep your prospect's attention focused on you and your claim. What kind of captivating statement do you make about your products? Can you think of a strong follow-up question to that captivating claim?

? FYI

- Increase prospect involvement
- Increase potential for a sale

CONTACTING BY PHONE

5.11 Making a Request from your Prospect

If you don't ask, you don't get. So ask for an appointment, for an address where you can send more information, or for a sale—whatever is appropriate to your situation. If you are asking for an appointment, it's a good idea to tell your prospect how much time you are requesting. "I can show you everything in about 20 minutes. When might be a good time for us to get together?"

Avoid giving part of your presentation on the phone. That puts you at a significant disadvantage. Because selling is very much a people business, the opportunity to meet face-to-face can help create a rapport—and often close a sale.

Think about your current phone script. Do you ask for the appointment? the address? the sale? How might you improve your relationship with existing customers? How might you establish a rapport with new prospects?

? FYI

- Handle customer objections in a reasonable, positive way
- Increase the likelihood of a sale

CONTACTING BY PHONE

5.12 Overcoming Resistance

Two immediate objections come up when you use the phone as a means to contact prospects; they object to taking the phone call, and they object to granting an appointment.

To deal with the first objection, be sensitive to their needs. "If I caught you at a bad time, Mrs. Smith, I can call back at another time." Handle the second objection by reassuring the prospect that an appointment will only take a short time and that your purpose is simply to introduce your product/service to see if there might be some basis for doing business together. "Mr. Green, there are some people that this service can help and others who do not need it. I don't know which you are, but after ten minutes with you, we'll both know. If it's not for you, I'll be the first to tell you."

How do you currently respond to customer objections? Can you think of ways to overcome them consistently?

? F Y I

CONTACTING BY PHONE

5.13 Keeping it Brief

- Move the sale forward
- Increase the likelihood of a sale
- Identify customer needs and concerns

Taken together, the five or six elements that follow in your script should take up no more than three-quarters of a page, double-spaced. That's about 30-45 seconds. You should never talk that long before giving the prospect something to respond to. As a rule of thumb, ask the prospect a question every ten seconds or so.

Are you long-winded? Do you take too much of your prospect's time? Think about ways to cut your phone script to the bare essentials. You may lose customers if you don't.

WORKSHEET

CONTACTING BY PHONE

5.14 Your Telephone Script

Using the following guidelines, write out several ideas that will help you write the first draft of your script. You can edit and change things later. Right now, brainstorm. (You may want to refer to the seven previous FYIs.)

- Develop a plan that will increase your prospecting and sales success on the phone
- Identify the greatest possible number of issues for your script

1. A two-sentence introduction of yourself and your company:

   _____

2. A short statement that takes the pressure off the call:

   _____

3. The purpose of your call (two sentences maximum):

   _____

4. A statement that will capture interest (no more than three sentences):

   _____

5. How you would like the prospect to respond (two sentences):

   _____

6. Two ways to answer your most common objections:

   _____

7. One additional way to keep it short, and keep the prospect actively involved in the conversation:

   _____

WORKSHEET

- Organize and make the most of each sales call

CONTACTING BY PHONE

5.15 The Telephone Planning Sheet

Fill in the following information *before* you call.

Industry segment:

_____

Company:

_____

Name:

_____

Primary purpose of call

_____

Best time to call:

_____

Opening statement:

_____

Key points to cover:

_____

Information to ask for:

_____

Commitment to ask for:

_____

Key phrases (if any):

_____

WORKSHEET

- Keep track of your calls and remember their outcomes

CONTACTING BY PHONE

5.16 The Telephone Log

Activity Log							
Sales Professional _____ **Date** _____							
Company	**Contact**	**Type of Call**	**Rating (A, B, C)**	**Comments–Outcome**		**Time In**	**Time Out**

Type of Call   PA = Phone Appointment   P = Presentation   V = Appointment (Visit)
I = Incoming Call   S = Status/Follow-up   CC = Cold Call   L = Lunch

❓FYI

- Place your calls when prospects and customers are most receptive

CONTACTING BY PHONE

5.17 The Best Times to Call

Type of People	Best Time to Call
Executives/Business Owners	After 10:30 am
Physicians	11:00 am, 1:00 – 3:00 pm, 7:00 – 9:00 pm
CPAs	Anytime other than tax season
Publishers/Printers	After 3:00 pm
Engineers/Chemists	4:00 – 5:00 pm
Contractors/Builders	Before 9:00 am, after 5:00 pm
Clergymen	Between Tuesday & Friday
Dentists	Before 9:30 am
Druggists	1:00 – 3;00 pm
Attorneys	11:00 am – 2:00 pm, after 5:00 pm
Homemakers	11:00 – noon; 2:00 – 4:30 pm
Professors/Teachers	At home, 7:00 – 9:00 pm
Butchers/Grocers	Before 9:00 am; 1:00 – 2:30 pm

? F Y I

CONTACTING BY PHONE

5.18 Playing by the Numbers

Most salespeople dislike record-keeping. It's just one more thing to do during the day. Record-keeping is a necessary part of your job, however. Without it, you would be in the dark about your performance and ways to improve it. This is especially true for telephone work. You have to keep track of everything during the sales process, from the number of calls you make to the sales you confirm.

Calls (a.k.a. dials) per day . . . shows the effort you are making.

Contacts (a.k.a. reaches) per day . . . shows whether you are calling at the right time. Are you reaching your goal each day?

Appointments set per day . . . shows how good your telephone skills are. You may have a goal set for this as well.

Meetings (actual appointments kept) . . . show how many of your appointments are cancelled versus kept.

Number of sales shows how good your presentation and sales skills are.

Referrals . . . show you the number and quality of this source of prospects.

At the end of each month, do some simple math with the month's figures.

Number of reaches ÷ Number of dials. The closer this ratio is to one, the better you are at finding your prospects in when you call.

Number of appointments set ÷ number of reaches. This ratio will show you how many calls you have to make to get an appointment.

Number of appointments ÷ number of actual meetings. If this ratio is low, you are getting a lot of cancellations. You may be manipulating your prospects into saying yes.

Number of sales ÷ number of meetings. If this ratio is low, you need to hone your presentation or sales skills.

These ratios will indicate two major things: 1) the areas in which you still need training or coaching, and 2) your sales ratios. For example, at your present skill level, you may need to make 20 calls to get five appointments to make one sale. That's a valuable ratio to know!

CONTACTING BY PHONE

5.19 Key Telephone Skills

Work on these skills to make your phone contacts more productive.

1. Arrange a set time each day to make calls.

2. Determine the specific number of calls to be made, and stick to that number.

3. Establish call objectives before picking up the phone.

4. Fine-tune your script until it is perfect.

5. Internalize your script so you won't have to rely on it and to make it sound natural.

6. Develop a pleasing voice, which comes with a pleasing attitude.

7. Exude confidence and competence over the phone. Think positively about phone calls, so they won't become exhausting.

8. Match the vocal pace and task priorities of your prospect.

9. Be sure you know who the decision makers are.

10. Get useful information about decision makers from subordinates.

11. Be polite and you will turn the decision maker's secretary into an *ally*. Use humor if you can. Find out her name and use it.

12. If necessary, sell the decision maker's secretary on your product/service. She may be the one who makes appointments for the boss.

13. Find the right times to call people to increase your chances of getting through.

14. Have your notes and objectives in order before making phone calls.

15. Don't let interruptions break up your phone-calling sessions.

16. Keep thorough records. You can't improve without the insight they provide.

17. Keep yourself motivated and enthusiastic. Aim for at least one small success every day.

18. Make phone calls during the time of day that you are most alert and energetic. Mornings work best for most people.

19. No matter where you are in your telephone session, follow up a success with another phone call. Success breeds success.

20. Be sure you are pronouncing people's names correctly. When in doubt, ask.

21. Be courteous, no matter what. Ask permission to launch into your script. Say thank you. Be sure you are not calling at a bad time.

22. Realize that *any* time you call you are interrupting, so make your calls brief.

? FYI

- Learn to write a good letter of introduction

CONTACTING BY LETTER

5.20 How to Write a Personal Letter of Introduction

It's always awkward when a prospect asks, "Who are you?" when you call on the phone. Letters can help you avoid that.

Writing a letter is not unlike writing a telephone script. Keep it brief. Use a typewriter or computer printer and high quality stationery and break up the text so it reads easily. Follow these basic guidelines to ensure that your letter is effective.

1. Refer to your prospect by name. Look like you've done your homework, and personalize the letter.

2. Identify yourself and your company.

3. Mention who referred you, if possible.

4. State the purpose of the letter. Get to the point quickly.

5. Make your claim. Use benefits, service offers, guarantees.

6. Identify an area of probable interest. In your pre-call planning you should have uncovered a possible need.

7. Sound like an insider. Use the jargon of your prospect's industry.

8. Give some reasons why your customer should see you. Tie the benefits to your prospect's specific situation.

9. Include a brochure. Prospects, especially in technical fields, like to read impressive documents and see pictures of products.

10. Specify a follow-up time. Indicate when you will call or stop by, so your call will be expected and received.

? F Y I

- Learn to write a good
  form letter

CONTACTING BY LETTER

5.21 How to Write a Form Letter

You can use a form letter to contact prospects, but the rate of return (if a reply is requested) or level of interest upon follow-up will be significantly lower than it would be with a personal letter. The following questions will help you focus your letter and make it as effective as possible.

1. Does your lead-in immediately create interest?

2. Is your lead-in no more than two or three sentences in length?

3. Do you promise benefits to the reader up front? Don't wait too long to do so.

4. Have you fired your biggest gun first? Have you got another one for the end of the letter?

5. Is there a big idea behind your proposal? Do you have something that the reader can get excited about?

6. Are your thoughts arranged logically? Have you asked others to read and critique your letter?

7. Are your claims believable, in addition to being true?

8. Have you clarified what you want your prospect to do and did you ask him/her to do it? This is *very* important.

9. If there is an order form included with the letter, is it referred to in the body of the letter?

10. Does the letter *speak to* your reader rather than go on and on about you, your product, or your company?

11. Have you written with an easy, conversational tone? Write as if you were talking by phone, but avoid being overly friendly or cute. Remember, this is a business letter, good buddy.

12. How many words in your copy have five or more letter? They should not exceed 30 percent of the total word count. This is not the place to use high falutin' words.

13. Are there any sentences where you can avoid starting with "a", "an," or "the"?

14. Did you let the letter sit for a week and ripen before reading and editing it again for clarity and impact?

15. Has a customer read your letter and given you feedback?

16. Visually, does your letter conform to the following?

    - No paragraphs longer than six sentences.

    - Letter centered on page.

    - Indentations and a couple of paragraph headings to break up the text.

    - Underlining, boldface, italics and uppercase letters used very sparingly. You don't want to produce a gaudy, amateurish letter.

Finally, review the tips on letter writing that we discussed in FYI 4.12: Letters That Make Impressions.

WORKSHEET

CONTACTING IN PERSON

• Learn to convey to your prospects the benefits of meeting with you

5.22 Initial Benefit Statements

It is important to start a meeting off on the right foot. Nonmanipulative salespeople go into a meeting with the attitude, "I don't know if I can help you, so I'm here to find out. If my product/service is not what you need, I'll be the first to tell you. If it is what you need, we'll work together to make the sales process a mutually satisfying experience."

Although you don't want to state that attitude verbatim, you do want to convey your flexibility and nonmanipulative M.O. You also want to give your prospect a good idea of what's in it for him. An initial benefits statement tells your prospect why he or she might gain by taking the time to meet with you. For example, "Mr. Jones, I don't know yet if we have a fit between what you need and what I have to offer, but I can tell you that clients who have used my service saved over 50 percent on their photocopy and fax bills. Can we talk about your business for a couple of minutes to see what we might save for you?"

Think of three current customers or prospects with whom you have upcoming appointments. For each appointment, determine the purpose of the call and write an initial benefits statement.

Customer 1: _____

Customer 2: _____

Customer 3: _____

? F Y I

- Gain an awareness of the subtle do's and don'ts of meeting with prospects

CONTACTING IN PERSON

5.23 In-Person Do's and Don'ts

Do

Relax
Be yourself
Smile
Maintain eye contact
Be confident
Be friendly and real
Be proud of your company
Be sure you are dealing with the decision maker
Be sure you've asked for enough time for your presentation

Focus on fulfilling genuine needs
Be flexible in every way
Be patient with the sales process
Maintain the initiative
Gear benefits to client's needs
Be aware of client's time constraints
Be sincerely interested
Remember your call objective
Be enthusiastic and credible
Be prepared for resistance

Don't

Be pushy
Be cocky
Be demanding
Be manipulative
Be rushed into cutting your presentation short
Focus on the sale to the exclusion of your prospect's needs

Exaggerate or lie
Rush the sales process
Try to close the sale in your opening statement
Get drawn into an argument
Recite a canned presentation
Get defensive
Be too polished

CONTACTING IN PERSON

5.24 Contacting by Style

As Section 6 explains, people can be differentiated by their behavioral style. Each style is associated with a type of personality. Knowing the personality type of a potential customer can increase your chances for a sale because you will be able to approach that person in a way that best suits his or her personality. (These behavioral styles are described at greater length in Section 6.)

Relater

Letters should be soft, pleasant and specific. Mention person who referred you. Phone calls should also be anchored to a referral. Tell the relater how your product or service benefited his/her friend. Strive to be polite and easily liked. In person, relax and talk warmly and informally. Ask questions about his/her family and co-workers. Focus on feelings, relationships and building trust.

Socializer

Letters should have an upbeat, hip, friendly and faster pace. Initial benefits statement should emphasize status, recognition or being the first on the block to have a so and so. Phone calls should be upbeat and friendly as well. Flatter him/her and promise new greatness with your product or service.

In person, pretend he/she is running for office. Show great interest. Let him/her set pace and priority. Let him/her talk by asking, "How did you get into this business?" Socializers want to be friends first, so plan to have as many meetings as necessary to build the relationship.

In letters, give details and data to support your claims. On the phone, be considerate of his/her time constraints. Tell him/her what you'll cover in the meeting so he/she will know what to expect. In person, show logical proof, statistics, data, etc. that document your quality, track record and value. Verify your credentials on paper.

Speak slowly and succinctly. Get to the point. Don't bother to be sociable, be courteous and task-oriented.

When you write, call or meet with a director, be formal, business-like and task-oriented. Don't socialize. Get right to the point by showing that you've done your homework and can deliver bottom-line results. Always show a director what he/she has to gain by making an investment.

To get a meeting with a director, you have to provide sufficient information and enough of an incentive to deserve the meeting. That information and incentive will have to spell out what you propose and plant the seed that may grow into interest. Directors take pride in being incredibly busy, so you will have to let them call the shots about a meeting time.

Thinker

Director

Understanding behavioral styles

WHAT'S IN IT FOR YOU

- Greatly increase your understanding of human nature
- Increase your insight into your own behavioral preferences
- Minimize personality conflicts with people
- Change your behavior in subtle ways to make your prospects more comfortable

Vive La Difference!

Everyone is different. Conflicts between different personality types can ruin potential business relationships. Part of being compatible with people is a willingness to treat them the way *they* want to be treated, not the way *you* want to treat them. By recognizing personal styles (including your own), you can adapt your behavior to fit others. These *Relationship Strategies* will give you the insight needed to quickly get on the same wavelength with virtually anyone.

The first step in understanding behavioral styles is to determine your style. Next, you will think about the styles of people with whom you live and work. In subsequent sections, you will learn how to specifically change your behaviors to conform to the different styles you meet while selling.

WORKSHEET

TYPES OF BEHAVIORAL STYLES

6.1 Behavioral Styles Self-Test (Part I)

Read the descriptions on the left side of the page and circle the ones that fit you most of the time. Judging by the number of circled items, determine where you fall on a scale of one through four.

SUPPORTING

SUPPORTING
Relaxed and Warm
Opinion Oriented
Supportive
Flexible About Time
Relationship Oriented
Share Feelings Freely
Sensitive

4 VERY SUPPORTING

3 SOMEWHAT SUPPORTING

CONTROLLING
Formal and Proper
Fact Oriented
Controlling
Time Disciplined
Task Oriented
Keeps Feelings To Self
Thinking Oriented

2 SOMEWHAT CONTROLLING

1 VERY CONTROLLING

CONTROLLING

WORKSHEET

TYPES OF BEHAVIORAL STYLES

6.2 Behavioral Styles Self-Test (Part II)

Read the following descriptions and circle the ones that fit you most of the time. Judging by the number of circled items, determine where you fall on a scale of A through D.

INDIRECT	DIRECT
Avoids Risk	Takes Risks
Slow Decision - Maker	Swift Decisions
Passive	Aggressive
Easygoing	Impatient
Listens Well	Talkative
Reserved	Outgoing
Shy	Expresses Opinions
Keeps Opinions To Self	Readily

⟵——————————————————————⟶

A	B	C	D
VERY INDIRECT	**SOMEWHAT INDIRECT**	**SOMEWHAT DIRECT**	**VERY DIRECT**

✏ WORKSHEET

TYPES OF BEHAVIORAL STYLES

6.3 Combining the Scales

Now that you have a letter and number that represent where you stand on the two scales, circle the quadrant below that corresponds to your style.

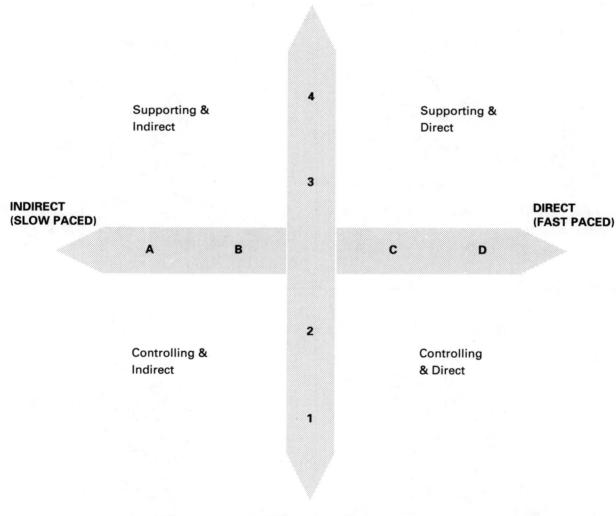

SUPPORTING
(RELATIONSHIP ORIENTED)

Supporting &
Indirect

4

Supporting &
Direct

3

INDIRECT
(SLOW PACED)

A   B   C   D

DIRECT
(FAST PACED)

2

Controlling &
Indirect

Controlling
& Direct

1

CONTROLLING
(TASK ORIENTED)

TYPES OF BEHAVIORAL STYLES

6.4 Meet the Styles

Now that you know the quadrant in which you fall, you can see whether you are a Relater, a Socializer, a Thinker, or a Director. It is important to realize that there are no "good" or "bad" personal styles. Each has its positive and negative aspects. In addition, we are all combinations of styles, but each of us has a dominant style that describes our behavior most of the time.

**(Relationship oriented)
SUPPORTING**

The Relater

The Socializer

INDIRECT (Slow pace) ——————————————— **(Fast pace) DIRECT**

The Thinker

The Director

**CONTROLLING
(Task oriented)**

TYPES OF BEHAVIORAL STYLES

6.5 Summary of Behaviors (Part I)

The following generalizations will help you understand and appreciate the different behavioral styles. You will find some of them amusing. See if you can relate them to people you know.

	Relater	Thinker	Director	Socializer
BEHAVIOR PATTERN:	Supporting and indirect	Controlling and indirect	Controlling and direct	Supporting and direct
PACE:	Slow/relaxed	Slow/systematic	Fast/decisive	Fast/spontaneous
PRIORITY:	The relationship/ communication	The task or process	The task or results	The relationship and interaction
APPEARANCE:	Casual Conforming	Formal Functional	Business-like Powerful	Stylish, sometimes outrageous
WORKPLACE:	Personal Relaxed Friendly	Structured Functional Formal	Busy Efficient Structured	Stimulating Personal Cluttered
SOURCE OF SECURITY:	Friendship Cooperation	Preparation Thoroughness	Control Leadership	Playfulness Other's approval
FEARS:	Sudden change	Criticism of their work	Being taken advantage of	Loss of Prestige
MEASURES PERSONAL WORTH BY:	Compatibility w/ others and depth of relationships	Precision Accuracy Activity	Results Track Record Progress	Recognition Status Number of friends
INTERNAL MOTIVATOR:	Involvement Being needed	The process competence	Winning/ control	The chase Being Included
CELEBRITIES:	Mary Tyler Moore Jane Pauley	Mr. Spock Sgt. Joe Friday	Lee Iacocca Margaret Thatcher	Carol Burnett Alan Alda (MASH)
STRENGTHS:	Listening Teamwork Follow-through	Planning & org. Systematizing Numbers	Delegating Leadership Inspiring Others	Persuading Enthusiasm Entertaining
WEAKNESSES:	Oversensitive Slow to start Goal setting	Perfectionist Critical Slow decisions	Insensitive Impatient Dislikes details	Restless Ignores details No time discipline
TYPICAL JOBS:	Psychologist Social worker Teacher	Engineer Accountant Librarian	CEO/President Military Leader High Administrator	Sales Entertainer Bartender
ANIMAL	Dove/koala	Owl	Bull/eagle	Chimp/peacock
IRRITATIONS:	Insensitivity Impatience	Disorganization Unpredictability	Inefficiency Indecision	Routine Perfectionism
UNDER STRESS:	Submissive Indecisive	Withdraws Headstrong	Dictatorial Critical	Sarcastic Superficial
DECISIONS ARE:	Made with others	Well thought-out	Decisive	Spontaneous
SEEKS:	Acceptance	Accuracy and information	Productivity/ bottom-line results	Recognition and fun

TYPES OF BEHAVIORAL STYLES

6.6 Summary of Behaviors (Part II)

The Relater Style

Slow at taking action and making decisions
Likes close, personal relationships
Dislikes interpersonal conflict
Supports and "actively" listens to others
Weak at goal setting and self direction
Has excellent ability to gain suport from others
Works slowly and cohesively with others
Seeks security and belongingness
Good counseling skills

The Socializer Style

Spontaneous actions and decisions
Likes involvement
Dislikes being alone
Exaggerates and generalizes
Tends to dream and gets others caught up
in his dreams
Jumps from one activity to another
Works quickly and excitedly with others
Seeks esteem and acknowledgement
Good persuasive skills

The Thinker Style

Cautious actions and decisions
Likes organization and structure
Dislikes involvement
Asks many questions about specific details
Prefers objective, task-oriented, intellectual
work environment
Wantst o be right, to can be overly reliant
on data collection
Works slowly and precisely alone
Good problem solving skills

The Director Style

Decisive actions and decisions
Likes control, dislikes inaction
Prefers maximum freedom to manage
himself and others
Cool, independent, and competitive
Low tolerance for feelings, attitudes, and
advice of others
Works quickly and impressively alone
Good administrative skills

WORKSHEET

TYPES OF BEHAVIORAL STYLES

6.7 Identify Styles of the People You Know

With selected family members, people at work, and customers in mind, review the Supporting/Controlling and Direct/Indirect Scales and the summary of behaviors. Determine the styles of people with whom you work, live, and play.

Family member _____ Style _____

Behavioral preferences _____ Style _____

Family member _____ Style _____

Behavioral preferences _____ Style _____

Family member _____ Style _____

Behavioral preferences _____ Style _____

Someone at work_____ Style _____

Behavioral preferences _____ Style _____

Someone at work_____ Style _____

Behavioral preferences _____ Style _____

Someone at work_____ Style _____

Behavioral preferences _____ Style _____

A customer _____ Style _____

Behavioral preferences _____ Style _____

A customer _____ Style _____

Behavioral preferences _____ Style _____

A customer _____ Style _____

Behavioral preferences _____ Style _____

❓ F Y I

TYPES OF BEHAVIORAL STYLES

- Discover the paces and priorities valued by each behavioral style

6.8 Pace and Priority Differences

Sometimes the most obvious differences between people are pace and priority preferences. Pace relates to how quickly you like to do things. Priority relates to your preference for getting down to work (task-oriented) versus socializing (relationship-oriented).

Tension develops when people of different styles fail to conform to each other's pace and/or priority. The diagram below suggests the types of adjustments that need to be made between different behavioral styles. For example, Relaters and Socializers have different paces, but the same priority. Relaters and Directors have pace *and* priority differences.

To adjust to another person's style, follow the guidelines given in FYI 14.14, "Prescriptions For Flexibility" and in the five "Selling By Style" FYI's (one each under Contacting Prospects, Studying Needs, Proposing Solutions, Confirming the Sale, and Following Up).

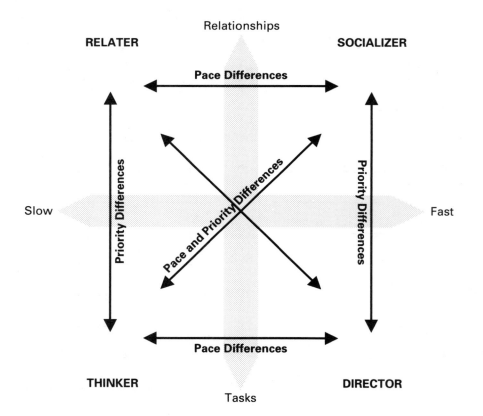

TYPES OF BEHAVIORAL STYLES

6.9 Observable Traits

	Verbal	**Vocal**	**Visual**
	(words)	(tone of voice)	(body lanquage)
THE RELATER	Asks more than tells Listens (more than talks) Reserves opinions Less verbal communication	Steady, warm delivery Less forceful tone Lower volume Slower speech	Intermittent eye contact Gentle handshake Exhibits patience Slower moving
THE THINKER	Fact and task-oriented Limited sharing of feelings More formal and proper Focused conversation	Little inflection Few pitch variations Less variety in vocal quality Steady, monotone delivery Low volume, slow speech	Few facial expressions Non-contact oriented Few gestures
THE DIRECTOR	Tells more than asks Talks more than listens Lots of verbal communication Makes emphatic statements Blunt and to the point	More vocal variety More forceful tone Communicates readily High volume, faster speech Challenging voice intonation	Firm handshake Steady eye contact Gestures to emphasize points Displays impatience Fast moving
THE SOCIALIZER	Tells stories, anecdotes Shares personal feelings Informal speech Expresses opinions readily Flexible time perspective Digresses from conversation	Lots of inflection More pitch variation More variety in vocal quality Dramatic High volume Fast speech	Animated facial expressions Much hand/body movement Contact oriented Spontaneous actions

BODY LANGUAGE

6.10 The Universal Language

Without speaking a word, people convey a tremendous amount of information about themselves and their attitude toward you. Body language is a universal language that goes beyond the intellect and the spoken word to reveal the depths of people's feelings. Once you have become a skilled body language observer, you can use your knowledge to 1) pick up people's nuances and gestures; 2) respond to them in ways that will put them at ease; and 3) consciously use body language to make your communication more effective.

What to Look For

The feelings conveyed by body language are fleeting. They go by like the frames of a movie. Fortunately, they are easy to spot and are generally repeated often.

Observing body language is second nature for most people. But to use it to your advantage, you must make the observation conscious, which means concentrating on the person you're talking to. Of course, you do this anyway if you are practicing active listening, which you are, aren't you?

The areas to watch are the hands, arms, face, eyes, legs, and the combinations of movements between these areas. Facial expressions convey a lot, as do posture and eye contact.

Clusters Are the Key

Observing one gesture is almost *meaningless*. Someone rubbing his eyes can simply have itchy eyes. The key to interpreting body language is to observe clusters of gestures. If someone is rubbing his eyes, pulling an ear, tapping a foot, looking around the room, and shifting uneasily in his chair, there's a good chance he is bored, nervous or frustrated. Careful observation will make the difference. When you do notice these clusters, it's time for you to do *something* different.

What to Do with What You See

First, ask yourself how the observed clusters compare to this person's usual way of behaving. Some people always have poor eye contact. Some people always act aloof. Try not to jump to conclusions. You have to either observe people for a while or know them well before you can interpret their body language infallibly.

Second, get feedback on your hunches. If someone's behavior has changed, ask a nonthreatening question to find out if you are the reason. You might say, "I hear you saying yes, but I get the impression that something else is on your mind. Would you mind sharing it with me?"

Last, remember what causes people to be comfortable. Some customers may get nervous until you reassure them that they are doing the right thing. Others react negatively to too much enthusiasm. You have to know when to tone it down and be more subtle.

? F Y I

BODY LANGUAGE

6.11 What Different Attitudes Look Like (Part I)

Openness	Enthusiasm
Open hands	Small upper or inward smile
Unbuttoned shirt collar	Erect body stance
Taking coat off	Hands open, arms extended
Moving closer	Eyes wide and alert
Leaning forward in chair	Lively and bouncy
Uncrossed legs and arms	

Defensiveness	Anger
Rigid body	Body rigid
Arms or legs crossed tightly	Fists clenched
Minimal eye contact with occasional sideways or darting glances	Lips closed and held in a tight thin line
Pursed lips	Continued eye contact
Head down with chin against chest	Squinting of eyes (sometimes)
Fists clenched	Shallow breathing
Leaning back in chair	Flaring of nostrils

Readiness	Evaluation
Leaning forward in a chair in an open posture	Sitting in front of chair with upper torso projected forward
Hands possibly placed mid-thigh	Slightly tilted head
Relaxed, but alive, facial expression	Hand to cheek gesture; head is often supported by the hand
Standing with hands on hips, feet slightly spread	Stroking the chin or pulling on beard

Nervousness	Critical Evaluation
Clearing throat	Body drawn back
Hand-to-mouth movements	One hand on cheek
Covering mouth when speaking	Chin in palm with index finger along side of nose or face and remaining fingers under mouth
Darting eyes or little eye contact	
Twitching lips or face	
Shifting weight while standing	
Tapping fingers	
Plucking at collar or ringing neck with finger inside shirt collar	
Incongruent laugh	
Pacing	
Jingling money in pockets	

BODY LANGUAGE

6.12 What Different Attitudes Look Like (Part II)

Suspicion and Secrecy

Failing to make eye contact or resisting glances
Glancing sideways at you by turning the body slightly away
Rubbing or touching the nose
Squinting or peering over glasses

Rejection and Doubt

Touching and rubbing nose
Squinting or rubbing eyes
Arms and legs crossed
Body withdrawn
Clearing throat
Hand rubbing or ear tugging
Raising an eyebrow

Confidence and Authority

Steepling (the higher the hands, the greater the confidence)
Resting feet on the desk
Leaning back with hands together behind back with chin thrust forward
Proud, erect body stance
Continuing eye contact
Smiling inwardly
Tipping back in chair

Reassurance

Pinching the fleshy part of the hands
Gently rubbing or caressing some personal object such as a ring, watch or necklace

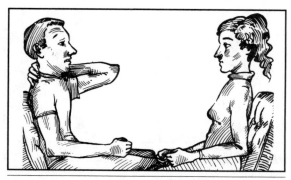

Frustration

Tightly clenched hands
Hand wringing
Rubbing back of neck
Controlled, short breathing
Blind staring
Running hands through hair
Tightly closed lips
Stamping a foot
Pacing

Self-Control

Wrists gripped behind the back
Crossed and locked ankles
Fists clenched
Pupils contracted
Lips closed or pursed

Boredom and Indifference

Head in hand
Drooping eyelids
Slouching
Tapping of foot or fingers
Feet swinging
Blank stares, little eye contact
Doodling
Slack lips
Posture aimed at exit

Acceptance

Spreading hands held to chest (for men)
Moving closer to the other person

? FYI

VOCAL QUALITY

6.13 How People Say What They Feel

Vocal quality is the flip side of body language. Although it deals with the spoken word which is a product of the intellect, vocal quality is determined by emotions. For this reason, it, too, is a window to the emotions. How people say things reveals as much about how they feel as it does about what they think.

Vocal qualities come in three flavors: rhythm, pitch and volume. Like body language, the key is to first note the person's normal way of speaking. We all speak with our own blend of rhythm, pitch and volume. After observing the norm, look for changes in these patterns. The changes are what give you clues about the person's feelings.

Rhythm. Despite popular belief, everybody's got rhythm. Rhythm refers to speed and inflection. How quickly a person speaks is a part of his or her personal style. You can expect Socializers and Directors to speak quickly. Thinkers and Relaters tend to speak at a slower pace.

Voice inflection—the natural expressiveness of the voice—also varies. Directors and Thinkers tend to have less drama in their voices than Relaters and Socializers.

Pitch. This refers to the high or low tonal quality of the voice. Again, it is not where the pitch starts, but how it changes that tells you something.

Volume. Some people naturally speak louder than others. Directors and Socializers are more likely to speak louder than Relaters and Thinkers.

What the Changes Mean

You should always verify your hunches about changes in vocal quality by asking questions or observing more closely. There are, however, some generalizations to remember.

Upward changes in volume and rhythm usually indicate excitement or enthusiasm. Anger is also accompanied by these changes, but we'll assume that you would never do anything to get a customer this mad.

Downward changes in volume and rhythm indicate boredom, fatigue, frustration, and sadness. Sometimes these changes, if accompanied by an increase in pitch, can mean the person is content. So be careful and check it out.

Increases in pitch indicate that the person is impatient or annoyed. Anger usually reveals itself with an increase in rhythm and volume as well.

? FYI

VOCAL QUALITY

- Increase your effectiveness by using your vocal qualities to your advantage

6.14 How Do *You* Say What You Feel?

The guidelines in the previous section helped you interpret other peoples' vocal qualities a little more accurately. When you communicate, you can increase your effectiveness if you pay attention to your vocal qualities. Professionalism takes awareness, practice and control. You can help yourself achieve a strong image by speaking with the following vocal qualities:

- You will appear confident if, *without shouting,* you project your voice in a full, strong manner.

- Intelligent people speak clearly and distinctly, enunciating and pronouncing their words properly. The rain in Spain falls mainly on the plain.

- Enthusiasm is one of the greatest assets that a salesperson can possess. It's part of what you sell Convey your enthusiasm by increasing your pitch and rhythm, *when appropriate.* There's nothing worse than inappropriate, hollow enthusiasm.

- Place emphasis and punctuation in your sentences by changing your vocal qualities. Stress importance by slowing down. Pause to let an important point sink in. Raise your volume slightly for enthusiasm and lower your volume to convey importance, confidentiality, or concern.

- Be an interesting speaker. Avoid—like the plague (and sales slumps)—monotonous speech. If you speak monotonously, do something to change. Hire a speech coach, take an acting class, or drink a strong cup of coffee.

- You will gain trust only when you speak with your natural vocal qualities. If you look like you are acting, you will quickly undermine your credibility. The key is to relax and be yourself, while keeping your "techniques" at hand to use if appropriate.

- As you do on the telephone, try to match the pace of your customer. If your customer is slow low-keyed, and quiet, be the same.

- An important part of being effective is matching your vocal style to the personal style of your customer. Even though you want to use vocal qualities to enhance your words, be careful to choose qualities that will be well received by the listener. Thinkers and Directors are less comfortable with enthusiasm than Relaters and Socializers. At all times, remember to adapt your style to your customer.

If you doubt the importance of being aware of your vocal qualities, consider the differences in the meanings in the following sentences when the emphasis is moved around.

"*I* **didn't say she stole the money.**"

"**I didn't** *say* **she stole the money.**"

"**I didn't say** *she* **stole the money.**"

"**I didn't say she** *stole* **the money.**"

"**I didn't say she stole the** *money.*"

NEUROLINGUISTIC PROGRAMMING

6.15 Introduction to NLP

Another valuable tool for helping you quickly establish rapport with people is NLP. This study of human behavior was pioneered by linguist John Grinder and psychologist Richard Bandler. They studied ways in which therapists and clients developed an intuitive sense of each other and, thereby, produced outstanding results in psychotherapy. These observations led to a theory of how the human mind works.

According to NLP, everyone has a dominant mode of perceiving and understanding the world. The three modes are auditory, visual, and kinesthetic.

Auditory. Some people are oriented to sounds and language. They learn more quickly by listening than by reading or seeing. They are the type of people who prefer to be *told* how much they are appreciated rather than *shown*. If you wanted to enhance your relationship with a client who is "auditory," you would be better off saying, "I really appreciate working with you" than sending a gift.

People who are auditory tend to say things such as, "I hear what you are saying," "That sounds good to me," and other hearing-oriented phrases.

Visual. Some people perceive the world primarily through sight. To them, a picture is worth a thousand words. They learn more easily by seeing or visualizing rather than by hearing or feeling. Demonstrations work better than descriptions for people who are visual. Flowers and scenic restaurants are the way to a visual romantic's heart, not solely sweet words of endearment.

People who are visual reveal themselves by saying things such as, "I see what you mean," "I get the picture," or "I'll believe it when I see it."

Kinesthetic. Some people are touchers. They like to be hugged or stroked. They experience the world through feeling, which often includes an acute sense of smell or taste. These are people who have to *do* something to learn it—a description or demonstration won't suffice. Kinesthetic individuals will respond to loving strokes or a home-cooked gourmet meal more than to a dozen roses or compliments on their appearance.

Phrases used by kinesthetic people include, "It just doesn't feel right to me," "If it feels good, do it," "How do you feel about that?" "This is heating up."

- Use eye cues to determine whether someone is auditory, visual, or kinesthetic

NEUROLINGUISTIC PROGRAMMING

6.16 The Eyes Have It

Grinder and Bandler noted that the movement of one's eyes reveals whether a person is accessing information visually, auditorially or kinesthetically. Eye movements in people are quite similar and the following generalizations are often true

Visual perception	Looking up and left	Visualizing (remembering) from the past; picturing the past mentally
	Looking up and right	Visually constructing an image to see what it would eventually look like
Kinesthetic perception	Looking down and right	Remembering past feelings
Auditory perception	Looking sideways to left	Hearing sounds or voices from the past (remembering)
	Looking sideways to right	Constructing a future conversation; thinking of the right words to use
	Looking down to left	Holding an internal dialogue with oneself; trying out how something sounds

A few left-handed people reverse the normal right and left eye cues; therefore, eye cues can be used only as clues to be confirmed by further observation.

Eye cues indicating thought processes

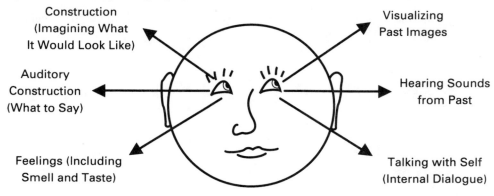

Construction
(Imagining What
It Would Look Like)

Visualizing
Past Images

Auditory
Construction
(What to Say)

Hearing Sounds
from Past

Feelings (Including
Smell and Taste)

Talking with Self
(Internal Dialogue)

William G. Nickels, Robert F. Everett, and Ronald Klein, "Rapport Building for Salespeople: A Neuro-Linguistic Approach, *Journal of Personal Selling & Sales Management* (November 1983), p. 1.

? F Y I

NEUROLINGUISTIC PROGRAMMING

6.17 Words That Tell

Among the clusters of behaviors you should observe are the words that people choose to express themselves. Along with eye movements, words speak volumes about our modes of perception. Individual words are less important than the general flavor of what a person is saying. Don't jump to conclusions based on one or two words. Take your time. Look for themes and style. The patterns below will give you a start in using NLP to create rapport.

Visual		Auditory		Kinesthetic	
analyze	look	announce	oral	active	lukewarm
angle	notice	articulate	proclaim	affected	motion
appear	obscure	audible	pronounce	bearable	muddled
clarity	observe	communicate	remark	charge	panicky
cognizant	obvious	converse	report	concrete	pressure
conspicious	perception	discuss	roar	emotional	sensitive
demonstrate	perspective	dissonant	rumor	feel	set
dream	picture	divulge	say	firm	shallow
examine	scene	earshot	shrill	flow	softly
focus	see	enunciate	silence	foundation	solid
foresee	sight	gossip	sound	grasp	structured
glance	sketchy	hear	squeal	grip	support
hindsight	survey	hush	state	hanging	tension
horizon	vague	inquire	talk	hassle	tied
idea	view	interview	tell	heated	touch
illusion	vision	listen	tone	hold	unbearable
image	watch	mention	vocal	hustle	unsettled
inspect	witness	noise	voice	intuition	whipped

William G. Nickels, Robert F. Everett, and Robert Klein, "Rapport Building for Salespeople: A Neurolinguistic Approach," *Journal of Personal Selling & Sales Management* (November 1983), p.2.

Note: This has been a very basic introduction to the power of NLP. For more detailed discussion, refer to *Beyond Selling: How to Maximize Your Personal Influence*, by Bagley and Reese.

?FYI

PACING

6.18 Types of Pacing

In sales, pacing means "being where the customer is" It is alignment on multiple levels. The proper pacing of your customer can be very helpful in truly building rapport with them. The following are the most common ways you can align or get "in sync" with where the customer is. Each method is a form of pacing.

1. **Emotional Pacing.** Another term for emotional pacing is empathy, or understanding and appreciating the other person's feelings. We've all had our good and bad days. That goes for customers as well. If you can "tune in" to a customer's mood—to see things from his or her perspective—you will let that customer know that you are on their wave length. If some customer is very enthusiastic and energetic, align with that mood by pacing or acting as if you were in the same mood.

2. **Posture Pacing.** Adopt the posture and general behavioral style of your customer. This does not mean mimicking the person you are speaking to. Rather, your body language and posture should subtly reflect the customer's body language and posture. For example, if your customer sits and talks with arms and legs crossed—a traditionally defensive posture—the worst thing you can do is lean forward and become more adamant—or enthusiastic—or charming. Your posture would be "out of sync" with that of your customer. Remember, you will be building rapport if you assume the same or similar posture and gestures of the person you are communicating with.

3. **Tone and Tempo Pacing.** Match the tone and tempo of your customer's speech as closely as possible without mimicking them. The best example can be seen in regional speech variations. People in some parts of the country are known for a rapid-fire, get-to-the-point style of speech. Others are more "laid-back," slower, indirect, and use softer tones. Whichever it is, you will build rapport more quickly by using the general tone and tempo of your customer.

4. **Language Pacing.** One form of language pacing is using the buzzwords that your customer uses. Be certain to use these key words and phrases appropriately. Overusing or misusing these words will only get the opposite of the results you are seeking. Another form of language pacing is matching their patterns for processing information and expressing themselves. The three most common are: visual (see), auditory (hear), and kinesthetic (feel). If a customer talks in one of these distinct patterns, you should phrase your comments in similar patterns. The majority of people are visually oriented. Using words that are visually oriented with visuals will assist in building rapport. Noting someone with an auditory or kinesthetic pattern will create an opportunity to align with them quickly and easily.

Other methods of pacing include values, beliefs, cultural, and content pacing.

WORKSHEET

- Build higher levels of rapport with people
- Learn how to match and mirror the posture of clients

PACING

6.19 Types of Pacing—Posture Pacing (Part I)

Practice matching and mirroring the physiology and posture of someone you are *not* communicating with. For example, in a restaurant or office, find someone sitting across the room and match the way they are sitting, moving, leaning, crossing arms, crossing legs, gesturing, etc.

Try this over a period of time. The challenge is being subtle. Do not pace this person in a way that will draw conscious attention to what your are doing. Slowly and naturally shift into the way they are sitting, standing, walking, etc.

Below is a list that will help you learn how to pace an individual's posture. Use the list as a beginning point for matching the posture of someone you want to build rapport with.

Leans forward _____

Leans backward _____

Stand stiff and erect _____

Hunches _____

Rocking motion _____

Head tilts _____

Head nods _____

Crosses legs _____

Crosses arms _____

Holds pen _____

Points _____

Pounds fist _____

WORKSHEET

- Build higher-level rapport with business associates
- Improve your posture pacing with people you communicate with regularly

PACING

6.20 Types of Pacing—Posture Pacing (Part II)

Apply your posture pacing skills in meetings and with people you communicate with regularly. Pick one person and match his/her general posture and physical movements and gestures. Notice what happens over time to your level of rapport and influence as you add this dimension to your communication.

Write down some of the key posture patterns of this individual.

Leans forward _____

Leans backward _____

Stand stiff and erect _____

Hunches _____

Rocking motion _____

Head tilts _____

Head nods _____

Crosses legs _____

Crosses arms _____

Holds pen _____

Points _____

Pounds fist _____

WORKSHEET

PACING

6.21 Types of Pacing—Voice Tempo

Practice adjusting your rate of speech to the speed of the person you are communicating with. This form of pacing can be very powerful but very difficult to do without practice. It's important to practice in a "safe" environment. Try this initially with friends or family or, maybe, with a waiter or waitress before attempting to use this powerful tool in your business dealings.

The list below will help you identify and categorize important aspects of the tempo of the person you are communicating with. Check the appropriate items.

Very slow _____

Slow _____

Moderate _____

Fast _____

Very fast _____

Rhythmic _____

Arhythmic _____

WORKSHEET

WHAT'S IN IT FOR YOU

- Build higher levels of rapport with business associates
- Develop the tone of your communication to that of the person you are communicating with

PACING

6.22 Types of Pacing—Voice Tone Pacing

Practice adjusting the tone of your speech to that of the person you are communicating with. This kind of pacing can be very powerful but subtle. Before using it in a business environment, practice it in a safe environment, such as with family or friends.

The list below will help you identify important aspects of the tone of the person you are communicating with. Check the appropriate items.

Pitch:

Low _____

Medium _____

High _____

Apologetic _____

Confidential _____

Monotone _____

Condescending _____

Demanding _____

WORKSHEET

VERBAL PATTERNS

6.23 Language Patterns

Individuals organize and express their experience in three primary categories; visual (picture images), auditory (listening images), and kinesthetic (feeling images) patterns. Listen to the radio or television or practice with an interested group of people.

Write the sensory-specific words you hear in the appropriate column below. Next to or below the term you list, write a word that would be an appropriate response to the speaker's verbal pattern.

Language Patterns

Visual	Auditory	Kinesthetic
see	hear	touch
look	listen	handle
focus	tell	grasp
show	talk to me	rough
scan	speak	smooth
stare	ask	excited
preview	rings true	impact
short-sighted	sounds like/good	hit on
clarify	rattle	move
graphic	tune in	grab
color	sing	stroke
dress up	voice	get the point
frame	harmonize	sad
visualize	harmony	scared
appearance	amplify	angry
cloud	tempo	cold
dark	volume	tough
fantasize	all ears	solid
	say nothing	irritate

WORKSHEET

VERBAL PATTERNS

6.24 Verbal Pattern Identification

Individuals organize and express their experience in three primary categories: visual (picture images), auditory (listening images), and kinesthetic (feeling images) patterns. Listen to the radio or television or practice with an interested group of people.

Put a check in the appropriate column when an individual uses words in that pattern.

Exercise: Verbal Pattern Identification

First example, person A:

Visual	Auditory	Kinesthetic	Unspecified

Person B:

Visual	Auditory	Kinesthetic	Unspecified

Communicating for results

WHAT'S IN IT FOR YOU

- Increase your understanding of communication in general

- Gain insight into communication skills such as questioning, listening, feedback, body language, vocal quality, and Neurolinguistic Programming

- Learn about behavioral styles—including your own—and discover how this knowledge will increase sales

The information-gathering phase of the sales process is where you make or break the sale. Up to this point you've done your homework, targeted the right prospects, contacted them, and set up appointments. Now that you are meeting face to face to find out what makes them tick, your all-important communication skills come into play.

Communication skills include questioning, active listening, feedback, the observation and use of body language and vocal qualities, and behavioral flexibility.

The cornerstone of good communication is sensitivity to the needs of the other person. All of the skills that follow will help you achieve that. If you have had *any* success as a salesperson, you probably possess good communication skills. The FYI's and Worksheets that follow may seem simple to you, but study them anyway. They will strengthen the skills that you use unconsciously and teach you new ones to use consciously.

COMMUNICATE BETTER AND SELL MORE

7.1 The Communication Process

The following diagram shows you the process of communication for you as both a speaker and a listener. They key is to make yourself understood, verbally and nonverbally. The speaker (sender) wants (intends) to send a message to a listener (receiver). In order to succeed, the speaker must use the proper verbal and non-verbal cues to cut through "noise" (verbal and nonverbal distractions in the world that might distort the receiver's perceptions).

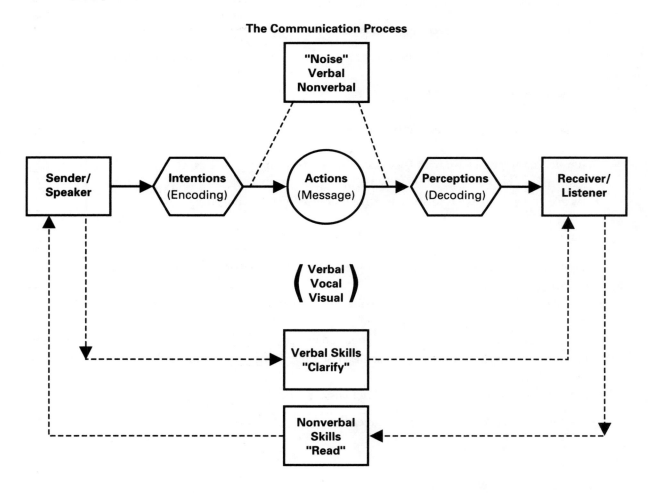

The Communication Process

COMMUNICATE BETTER AND SELL MORE

7.2 The Nuances of Asking Questions

Types of Questions

Open-Ended Questions begin with who, what, where, why, when and how. They—

- let the other person speak in narrative form

- increase the other person's involvement in conversation

- encourage people to discover things on their own

- create an unstructured dialogue in which the person's behavioral style can be revealed.

"Tell me about your business."

"Tell me how you presently advertise your services."

"What do you hope to gain with this new addition to your computer system?"

"How are you going to define and measure increased productivity?"

"What benefits are you seeking to derive from a service such as ours?"

Developmental Questions start with a narrow focus and lead to more specific questions. "Tell me about your customer service training."

Clarifying Questions seek feedback, an explanation, or more details. "What exactly do you mean by 'close tolerance'?"

Third-Party Questions make a statement about other people's feelings or experience and ask for feedback. *"Consumer Reports* rated our laptop as the best value in its price range. Is this the price you had in mind?"

Close-ended Questions seek a yes, no, or brief answer. They—

- Serve as a form of feedback or seek agreement

- Direct the conversation

"How many employees do you have?"

"Do you have a pension plan?"

"Do you know anything about Local Area Networks or compilers?"

"Have you ever worked with a voice-mail system before?"

COMMUNICATE BETTER AND SELL MORE

7.3 Ten Tips for More Effective Questioning

1. **Ask permission.** In some situations it is understood that you are there to gather information. In other situations, it is appropriate to show respect by asking permission to ask questions. "May I ask you some questions about your business?" may be a rhetorical question, but it is worth asking anyway.

2. **Start broad, then get specific.** Broad, open-ended questions are a good way to start gathering information. They put your prospect at ease because they allow any type of response. "Could you tell me about your business?" is a nonthreatening way to begin. Listen to what your prospect *says* and what she *omits* Both will suggest areas to explore in greater depth, such as, "Could you tell me more about how absenteeism impacts your bottom line?"

3. **Build on previous responses.** Any good interviewer knows that the most logical source of questions comes from the interviewee's responses. Dovetail your questions with the responses by listening for key words. For example:

   "I own six flower shops that specialize in large event decorating."

   "You specialize in large events. Why did you choose that niche?"

   "Lower overhead. I can work out of a warehouse rather than a storefront. I don't have to maintain perishable stock; I order in large quantities only when needed, which keeps my prices down."

   "What do you mean by large events? How would you define that? What are the minimum orders?"

4. **Use the prospect's industry vernacular, if appropriate.** If you are talking to an expert, show your expertise by sounding as if you've spent your whole life in his industry. If you are talking to a neophyte, don't embarrass him with your technical jargon. This is especially true in retail sales in which customers look to salespeople for guidance, not confusion.

5. **Keep questions simple.** If you want useful answers, ask useful questions. Convoluted or two-part questions should be avoided. Ask straightforward questions that cover one topic at a time.

6. **Use a logical sequence for your questions.** Prospects like to know where your questions are headed. If they can't tell, they may suspect you are manipulating them. By following key words and asking questions in a logical order, you will keep your intent clear and build trust.

7. **Keep questions nonthreatening.** Start off safe, general and nonthreatening. That means asking open-ended questions that do not touch on sensitive subjects. Later, after you have built up trust—and when it is appropriate—you can ask about financial ability, business stability, credit rating, religion, sex, politics . . . anything relevant.

8. **If a question is sensitive, explain its relevance.** It makes sense to justify a sensitive question to your prospect. After all, she has a right to know why you are asking.

9. **Focus on desired benefits.** Not all prospects are experts in their field. Many need to be educated, especially about your product's features and benefits. So ask what they hope to achieve, not necessarily how they hope to achieve it. That will put you in the position of being able to show how your product or service will fulfill those needs.

10. **Maintain a consultative attitude.** Ask questions in a way that will yield the most information with the least strain. Be prepared. Ask questions in a relaxed manner and patiently wait for responses. Investing a little time now will save a lot of time later.

LEARNING TO LISTEN

7.4 Three Types of Listening

When people listen to each other, they don't always do a good job. There are three types of listening dynamics that come into play, only one of which is acceptable in important relationships, business or personal.

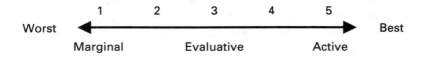

Marginal Listening. This level of listening can get you into trouble very quickly. Marginal listeners are guilty of many things:

Preoccupation with their own thoughts or feelings

Staring blankly at the speaker or into space

Distracting the speaker with nervous mannerisms

Conveying a self-centered attitude

Insulting the speaker with indifference

Misunderstanding more than half of what is said

Here's an example of marginal listening:

Customer: "You want me to take a whole day off from work so I can sit at home *all day* waiting for your repairman to show up?"

Customer Service Rep: "I'm sorry, but that is our scheduling policy. The first available day is two weeks from Monday." (Meanwhile, the CSR is thinking, "Just a half-hour to go before lunch.")

Evaluative Listening. Although better than marginal listeners, evaluative listeners still are not fully present. They are guilty of:

Categorizing or evaluating what is said rather than trying to listen and understand

Concentrating on composing a response

Making quick judgments about the speaker

Finishing the speaker's sentences for him or her

Getting distracted by emotionally loaded words

Rushing through a conversation

Marginal listening sounds like this:

Customer: You want me to take a whole day off from work so I can sit at home *all day* waiting for your repairman to show up?"

Customer Service Rep: (defensively) "This is our busiest time of the year and there's nothing I can do about it."

Active Listening. Active listening takes a concerted effort, but it is the only way to truly get on the same wavelength with someone. Active listeners are:

Concentrating on what people are saying

Controlling their impulse to finish people's sentences

Making an effort to see the speaker's point of view

Giving feedback to the speaker

Active listening leads to a sincere response:

Customer: "You want me to take a whole day off from work so I can sit at home *all day* waiting for your repairman to show up?"

Customer Service Rep: "I can see that would be a major inconvenience for you. Unfortunately, this is our busiest time of the year and qualified technicians are hard to come by. Could you arrange for a neighbor to let our serviceman in?"

LEARNING TO LISTEN

7.5 Ten Keys to Active Listening

1. **Resist distractions.** Ignore external noises while you focus on what the other person is saying verbally and nonverbally. Also ignore the internal noise that we all have going on.

2. **Take notes.** Most people remember about 50 percent of what they hear, so take enough notes to help you recall the full content of the conversation later.

3. **Let people tell their story.** When getting to know someone and his or her business—or when listening to a customer's problem—let that person tell the story the way he or she sees it. A great deal of valuable information is revealed in a person's narrative. Save your developmental and clarifying questions for later.

4. **Offer verbal feedback.** Let your prospect know that you are paying close attention by giving verbal cues ("Uh-huh," "Yeah," "OK," "Sure," "I understand"). These are also called passive listening techniques.

5. **Listen selectively.** Read between the lines. Look for the important messages that people convey in the *way* they say things. Sometimes what they mean to say is contained in what they leave out.

6. **Relax.** Create a relaxed environment in which your prospect will feel comfortable telling his story. Don't chime in with your two cents worth at every opportunity.

7. **Listen with your entire body.** Show that you are listening by leaning forward in your chair. Keep your arms uncrossed, at your sides or on the table. Use good eye contact and nod in agreement when appropriate. Try not to react to negative things that are said.

8. **Be aware of "personal space."** If you are in your prospect's office, don't play with his trophies or fondle his paperweight. If you are standing next to someone, don't stand right in his or her face. Give people their space; and remember, that space is different for different cultures. Do your homework before you meet with a customer, especially if you are going to a foreign country.

9. **Ask questions.** Gently ask the types of questions that will help you help your prospect, as we discussed previously.

10. **Care about your prospect.** If you do not sincerely care about people, you will have a hard time being a good listener. Remember, there is no such thing as an uninterested speaker, only uninterested listeners.

✏ WORKSHEET

LEARNING TO LISTEN

7.6 Other People's Listening Habits

One of the easiest ways to change your behaviors is to see them in someone else. Below, list the five most important things you like to see another person do when listening to you:

1.

2.

3.

4.

5.

Now list five of the biggest turn offs—things that people do that you dislike:

1.

2.

3.

4.

5.

Which of the above are you guilty of?

WHAT'S IN IT FOR YOU

- Increase your awareness
  of other peoples' poor
  listening habits

LEARNING TO LISTEN

7.7 Irritating Listening Habits

Listed below are 23 listening habits of superiors that have been distinctly irritating to one or more of their subordinates. Check the numbers of the habits listed that irritate you because they are practiced by your immediate superior or a co-worker on your level. Then identify the five listening habits that to you are the worst.

_____ 1. He does all the talking; I go in with a problem and never get a chance to open my mouth.

_____ 2. She interrupts me when I talk.

_____ 3. He never looks at me when I talk. I'm not sure he's listening.

_____ 4. She continually toys with a pencil, paper or some other item while I'm talking; I wonder if he's listening.

_____ 5. His poker face keeps me guessing whether he understands me or is even listening to me.

_____ 6. She never smiles—I'm afraid to talk to her.

_____ 7. He changes what I say by putting words into my mouth that I didn't mean.

_____ 8. She puts me on the defensive when I ask a question.

_____ 9. Occasionally he asks a question about what I have just told him that shows he wasn't listening.

_____ 10. She argues with everything I say—even before I have a chance to finish my case.

_____ 11. Everything I say reminds him of an experience he's either had or heard of. I get frustrated when he interrupts, saying "That reminds me . . ."

_____ 12. When I am talking, she finishes sentences for me.

_____ 13. He acts as if he is just waiting for me to finish so he can interject something of his own.

_____ 14. All the time I'm talking, she's looking out the window.

_____ 15. He looks at me as if he is trying to stare me down.

_____ 16. She looks as if she's appraising me . . . I begin to wonder if I have a smudge on my face, a tear in my coat, etc.

_____ 17. He looks as if he is constantly thinking "No" or questioning the truthfulness or value of what I'm saying.

_____ 18. She overdoes showing she's following what I'm saying . . . too many nods of her head, or "mm-hm's" and "uh-huh's".

_____ 19. He sits too close to me.

_____ 20. She frequently looks at her watch or the clock while I am talking.

_____ 21. He is completely withdrawn and distant when I'm talking.

_____ 22. She acts as if she is doing me a favor in seeing me.

_____ 23. He acts as if he knows it all, frequently relating incidents in which he was the hero.

WORKSHEET

LEARNING TO LISTEN

7.8 Listening Action Plan

Answering the following questions will help you make a *commitment* to improving your listening skills.

1. I listen most effectively when _____

    _____

    _____

2. I tend not to listen effectively when _____

    _____

    _____

3. The three listening areas in which I am strongest are _____

    _____

    _____

4. My three areas of listening that need the most improvement are _____

    _____

    _____

5. I will practice good listening skills with the following people:

    a) _____

    b) _____

    c) _____

6. I will practice good listening skills in these situations:_____

    a) _____

    b) _____

    c) _____

7. I will know I have become a better listener when: _____

    _____

    _____

    _____

? FYI

USING FEEDBACK

7.9 Verbal Feedback

Are you always sure you know what someone is saying? Of course not. Misunderstandings are common, especially when you don't know the other person well. In a sales situation, you cannot afford misunderstandings—they're amateurish. For this reason, you must make it a habit to use feedback to ensure crystal-clear communication.

There are many reasons to use verbal feedback.

Confirming the Agenda. You may want to start information-gathering when your prospect wants to socialize more; or you may want to confirm the sale when your prospect still has questions to ask. The only way to know if you are focusing on the right thing is to ask. "I'd like to ask you some questions about your business. Would that be ok?" "I'd like to write up an order. Did you have any more questions to ask me?"

Setting Pace and Priority. You will increase trust and build stronger relationships if you remain sensitive to your customers' needs and behavioral styles. Stop now and then to ask, "Do you want me to slow down or go over anything I've already discussed?" or "Let me know if I should skip over these details and get right to the bottom line for you." You can test the priority waters by asking, "How would you like to start this meeting?" (See FYI 6.8)

Understanding Vague Statements. Language is an inexact form of communication. What does someone mean when he says, "It's too expensive"? The only way to know is to ask, "What exactly do you mean by . . . ?" (See Worksheet 10.10 "It's too expensive".)

Increasing and Maintaining Interest. Few sales situations are ideal, so prospects may get distracted, bored, or lose interest. To keep them involved, ask questions now and then such as, "How do you think this would solve your problem?"

"You seem puzzled. Can I explain something a little better for you?"

"Can we talk about this issue a bit more?"

Verbal feedback requests information. There are several phrases that can help you elicit feedback:

"Let me be sure I understand your major concerns."

"Let me summarize the key points we've discussed."

"So what I hear you saying is . . . "

"Did I understand you correctly?"

"Is that what you meant by . . . ?"

"I'm not sure what you meant by . . . , could you put that in different words?"

Be a stickler for accuracy and understanding while always being sensitive to the priority and pace needs of your customers.

✏️ WORKSHEET

- Become aware of nonverbal feedback and learn to control it

USING FEEDBACK

7.10 Nonverbal Feedback

Nonverbal feedback is basically comprised of body language and vocal quality. Both convey messages and should be used consciously to build the relationship. A skilled salesperson pays attention to others' feedback, and uses nonverbal feedback to keep the lines of communication open and enthusiastic. Start by observing the feedback of others, and becoming aware of your own. Later, you can strive to control it.

How do you react in the following situations?

1. On the telephone, a secretary or receptionist refuses to put you through to a prospect. How does your vocal quality change?

2. In person, a prospect brushes you off by saying he's too busy to see you. What happens to your body language?

3. You walk into a prospect's office. How do you carry yourself and what does it say about you?

4. During information-gathering, your prospect becomes bored or distracted. What does your facial expression reveal?

5. During a presentation, how does your body language reflect your enthusiasm and sincerity?

6. If, during a presentation, your prospect seems to be closed down, how does your body language or vocal tone change? How *should* it change?

7. When asking for the sale and your prospect is doubtful, what does your body language say about your disappointment?

8 Studying needs

WHAT'S IN IT FOR YOU

- Increase your understanding of the "need gap"
- Determine the information required to uncover your prospects' needs
- Learn how to ask questions unintrusively
- Gain insight into the various roles of the people you will encounter in prospects' companies
- Understand and appreciate the value of the needs summary and success criteria

You are your customers' problem-solver. That might be your most important role. And the only way you can fill that role is to know your customers' problems and needs. This section gives you tips on how to determine a prospect's needs—how to identify basic issues, how to ask probing questions that you can use to uncover unstated needs, and how to match your company's product benefits to those needs.

WHAT'S IN IT FOR YOU

- Understand the importance of the need gap
- Determine which to discuss first—the prospect's current situation or future goals

IDENTIFYING CUSTOMER NEEDS

8.1 The "Need Gap"

A need gap is simply a discrepancy between what a person or company wants and what they have at present. It's the difference between the ideal situation and the actual situation. Studying needs is a process of gathering information by asking questions, doing research and making observations. It culminates in an understanding of your prospect's business that lets you identify need gaps that you may be able to close.

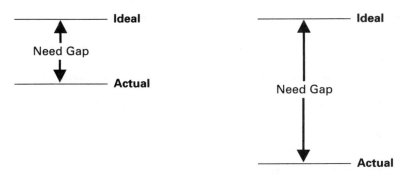

Current Situation Versus Goals

Your prospect's current situation and future goals are the two primary areas you should investigate. Which should you study first? Believe it or not, the order is important. Goals are abstract ideas that pertain to the future. The current situation is a concrete topic that deals with the present. Some people prefer to talk about one over the other. Using your knowledge of relationship strategies, you should gear your conversations accordingly.

As you learned in Section 6, Socializers and Directors are pie-in-the-sky dreamers who focus on goals and future objectives. Relaters and Thinkers, on the other hand, are more grounded and focused on the present. To more quickly establish a rapport, discuss goals first with Socializers and Directors. Discuss the here and now of the current situation first with Relaters and Thinkers.

Many salespeople think they can create a need in their prospect's mind for the product or service being sold. That is not how ethical, nonmanipulative sales are conducted. You cannot create needs. They either exist, or they don't. An ethical, consultative salesperson gathers information to determine if there is a need gap. If there is and it can be filled with your product or service, that's great. If there is no need gap or it requires a different solution, then the ethical salesperson admits this and does not try to force the sale. Instead, the salesperson would contact the prospect again in six months to see if his or her situation has changed.

WORKSHEET

WHAT'S IN IT FOR YOU

- Determine the information and the documents you will request from prospects
- Formulate specific questions to ask prospects

IDENTIFYING CUSTOMER NEEDS

8.2 How to Uncover the Need Gap

Begin researching your prospect's need gap by determining the information you will need and planning questions that will help you thoroughly probe the gap.

1. What information do you need to determine your prospect's need gap?

   a. _____

   b. _____

   c. _____

2. What are six specific questions you can ask to uncover the above information?

   Three open-ended questions:

   a. _____

   b. _____

   c. _____

   Three closed-ended questions:

   a. _____

   b. _____

   c. _____

3. Documents/data to ask for:

   a. _____

   b. _____

   c. _____

4. Other sources (e.g. publications/people/company records) of information:

   a. _____

   b. _____

   c. _____

?FYI

IDENTIFYING CUSTOMER NEEDS

8.3 Topics to Study

The process of studying needs depends on many factors, including the nature of your product or service, the behavioral style of your prospect, your relationship with your prospect and the typical sales cycle in your industry. Your information gathering could be highly structured—with you asking a lot of questions and taking copious notes—or more informal: you might simply get to know your prospect and develop trust and rapport.

When you choose the structured approach, you need to know what to study. The more complicated the sale, the more important the following areas will become to you:

1. **Current situation versus goals = need gap.** What they need now versus what they are getting. What they hope for versus where they are now.

2. **Psychological factors.** Try to discover if your prospect is buying for prestige, love, imitation, fear, variety or purely practical reasons.

3. **Prospect's point of view.** How does your prospect feel about this purchase? Is she afraid to spend the money? Is her reputation on the line? What are the personal risks and rewards associated with this sale?

4. **Key decision makers.** You've got to know the cast of characters and their input into the decision-making process. Otherwise you may spend too much time with the wrong person.

5. **Buying urgency.** Is your prospect shopping around leisurely or getting bids or is he in a hurry to make a deal?

6. **Buying criteria.** What characteristics of your product or service are most important to your prospect? Is she buying, for example, quality, price, service or the ability to customize?

7. **Political influences.** You may be bidding against your prospect's brother-in-law. Knowing this will help you form your strategy and determine the amount of time you devote to this account.

8. **Bad experiences.** It is not uncommon for salespeople to find accounts who have had bad experiences with their companies. The ideal solution, if possible, is to resolve the problem, change the prospect's attitude to a positive one, and move on.

9. **Product service demands.** If you are penetrating a new industry, you must find out as soon as possible whether your product or service will have to meet some standard of quality, performance, or certification.

10. **Monetary constraints.** Part of qualifying a prospect is determining buying power, but that changes over time. Keep your understanding of buying ability current by asking questions. If the situation sours, don't lose hope. Sometimes prospects can borrow or take money from other departments to pay for your product or service. It's your job to show how borrowing that money will be a wise move.

IDENTIFYING CUSTOMER NEEDS

8.4 How to Ask the Right Questions

A direct, tactful approach to questioning prospects will help you uncover needs, build rapport, and customize your presentation. Use open-ended questions to stimulate discussion. Use other questioning tactics to draw out your prospects before moving on to the next subject. The order of the following questions is unimportant.

To determine: Sales potential and buying cycle
Ask: "How much and how often do you buy?"

To determine: Buyer's needs
Ask: "What problems have you been having with _____?"

To determine: Current supplier
Ask: "What company is now supplying you with _____?"

To determine: Long-term potential
Ask: "What are your company's long-term goals? Paint a picture of your company for me as you see it three to five years from now."

To determine: When the sale may be confirmed
Ask: "Would you walk me through the decision-making process for a purchase such as this?" "How is a decision like this typically made?"

To determine: New prospects or markets
Ask: "Who is the end-user? Where and how will this product/service be used?"

To determine: The ultimate decision maker
Ask: "Besides yourself, who else will be involved in the decision-making process?"

To determine: Your prospect's buying authority
Ask: "What is your role or responsibility for this purchase?"

To determine: The quality of service provided by present supplier
Ask: "Typically, how long does it take to get a quote/delivery/service from your present vendor?"

To determine: Other problems with present supplier
Ask: "How do you think they could improve? What have you been striving for, but unable to attain?"

To determine: Knowledge of your product/service (this provides an opportunity to talk about benefits)
Ask: "What do you know about my company's product/service?"

To determine: Expectations of quality and price
Ask: "What kind of quality do you need? How important is price versus value? What is your price range or budget for this?"

To determine: Referrals
Ask: "Who do you know here or elsewhere who might have a similar need for my product/service?"

To determine: Other needs or expectations
Ask: "What else do you look for in a top-notch supplier?"

IDENTIFYING CUSTOMER NEEDS

8.5 And Yet More Questions

These questions will help you learn more about your prospects' needs, and customize your presentation to address them.

What are your short-term goals? Long-term goals?

What does this purchase mean to you personally? What does it mean to your company?

What do you perceive as your greatest strength? Weakness?

How do you perceive my company? Its strengths? Its weaknesses?

How is the potential of new products or services evaluated?

Who has your business now? How did they get it? How can I get it?

What are your buying criteria and success criteria?

Where would you put the emphasis regarding price, quality and service?

What level of service are you willing to pay for?

What do you like best about your present supplier? What don't you like?

What do you look for in the companies you do business with?

What might cause you to change suppliers?

What do you like best about your current system? What would you like to see changed?

What do you perceive your needs to be? How important are they to you?

If you were me, how would you proceed?

Which trade associations do you belong to?

Which trade/professional journals do you read?

What will it take for us to do business?

How soon can we begin?

Can you tell me why you decided against us?

What is my best shot for getting back the account?

What did we do in the last sale that impressed you most?

What do you look for in your relationship with a supplier?

Who was the best salesperson who ever called on you?

When would be the best time for me to call you back?

What else can I do for you?

?FYI

IDENTIFYING CUSTOMER NEEDS

8.6 Understand the Cast of Characters

Many people in your prospect's organization may play a role in making a purchase. To make a sale, you have to distinguish the major characters from the minor, and make sure you meet everyone who will influence the decision.

Role	Description
Users	As the name implies, these are the personnel who will be using the product in question. Users may have anywhere from an inconsequential to an extremely important influence on the purchase decision. In some cases, the users initiate the purchase by requesting the product. They may even develop the product specifications.
Gatekeepers	Gatekeepers control information to be reviewed by other members of the buying center. They may control the dissemination of printed information or advertisements, or determine which salesperson will speak to which individuals in the buying center. For example, the purchasing agent might perform this screening role by opening the gate to the buying center for some sales personnel and closing it to others.
Influencers	Although Influencers are not Users, Deciders, or Buyers, and can only say no but not yes, they have important relationships with Deciders or Buyers because they filter information in a way that exerts significant impact on the decision-making process and the sale.
Deciders	Deciders are the individuals who actually make the buying decision, whether or not they have the formal authority to do so. The identity of the decider is the most difficult role to determine: buyers may have formal authority to buy, but the president of the firm may actually make the decision. A decider could be a design engineer who develops a set of specifications that only one vendor can meet.
Buyers	The buyer has formal authority for selecting the supplier and implementing all procedures connected with securing the product. The power of the buyer is often usurped by more powerful members of the organization. Often the buyer's role is assumed by the purchasing agent, who executes the clerical functions associated with a purchase order.

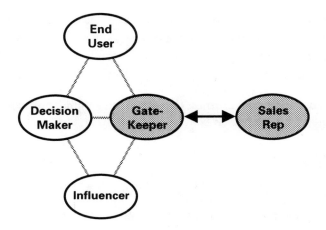

?FYI

IDENTIFYING CUSTOMER NEEDS

• Know the different ways
key players interact in the
purchasing process

8.7 Understand the Interactions of Key Players

For a purchase that is relatively simple, the purchasing agent will function as gatekeeper, influencer and, quite often, the decision maker.

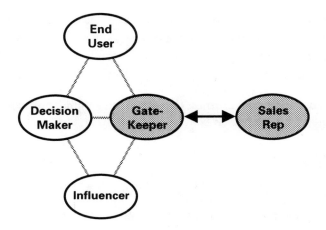

For purchases that involve a great deal of financial, personal and organizational risk, the buyer-seller relationships might be paired off as follows:

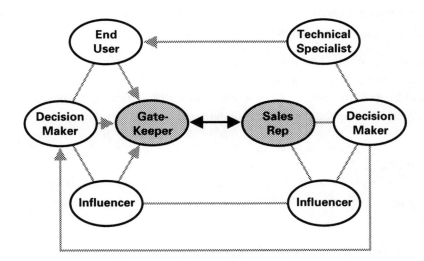

?FYI

IDENTIFYING CUSTOMER NEEDS

8.8 The Needs Summary

When you have finished studying your prospect's needs, it is time to present a needs summary. This is a formal summary of your prospect's needs presented in their order of importance. This presentation—like any—should be well organized, well documented, and professionally delivered. Keep in mind these tips:

1. **Seek agreement and feedback.** If you have been communicating well with your prospect and asking the right questions, your assessment of his business situation should be accurate. However, you should always confirm your findings by asking for feedback and agreement. That way you can fine-tune your summary and eliminate any potentially embarrassing mistakes.

2. **Categorize problems and opportunities.** Organize your summary by categorizing your findings into six categories:

   a. Problems for which you have the solution

   b. Opportunities that should be pursued immediately, with which you can help

   c. Problems that are unimportant to your prospect and can be ignored

   d. Opportunities that are worth considering, but belong on the back burner

   e. Problems that need to be fixed for which you have no solutions, but hopefully can provide suggestions or referrals

   f. Opportunities that should be pursued, but that you have no way of helping him capitalize on. Again, give suggestions or referrals

3. **Conduct situational triage.** When you uncover many need gaps, never attempt to solve them all at once, unless they are *all* related to the benefits that your product or service can provide. Conduct a situational triage to determine which problems or opportunities should be tackled first and which can wait. As a salesperson and consultant, you will gain credibility this way.

4. **Don't oversell.** If you try to solve all your prospect's problems with one huge solution, you run the risk of overselling. Overselling often scares prospects away. It is better to break problems down into manageable increments and solve them slowly, comfortably, and affordably over time. Make it clear to your prospect that you see the big picture and plan to solve the balance of the problems in a timely manner.

5. **Propose solutions.** By now you know who to meet with, what materials you will need, what specific needs you will address, and how your prospect regards you and your company. The next logical step is to move on to proposing solutions. Set an appointment for a presentation, if appropriate.

❓ FYI

IDENTIFYING CUSTOMER NEEDS

8.9 Establish Success Criteria

WHAT'S IN IT FOR YOU

- Find out how your product/ service will be evaluated after the sale
- Use the evaluation criteria to add credibility to your presentation

The only way to determine if your product or service will truly be the solution to your prospect's needs is to discuss success criteria when you are studying needs. There are several ways to approach this. You could ask, "What are you going to measure to determine if this worked for you?" Or you could say, "Imagine you are looking back on this purchase six months from now. What criteria will you use to judge the success of my product/service?"

Establishing success criteria early in the sales process serves many purposes. The most obvious is that you will have a *concrete, measurable* basis with which to track performance and judge success or failure after the sale.

As a presentation tool, success criteria will help you customize your solution and directly address your prospect's needs. In addition, they will allow you to put features, benefits and price in the proper perspective. It's valuable to be able to say, "For the level of performance you demand, you will need the Model XYZ. If you were willing to settle for a lower level of performance, you could spend less and get Model ABC, but I wouldn't recommend it, based on what you've told me."

Discussing success criteria during the studying phase of the sale will show you how realistic your prospect is and whether his or her expectations can be met by your company. It may be appropriate for you to size up the prospect's situation and try to lower his or her performance expectations. There are times when prospects want more than they really need or are willing to pay for. Part of your job is to paint a more realistic picture.

When discussing success criteria, take notes. Later, after you have confirmed the sale, again bring up the subject of success criteria. This time, put everything in writing and give your customer a copy. As part of the follow-up process, help your customer track your product/service's performance. This process will keep you in touch, strengthen your relationship, and show both of you how good (or bad) your product or service is.

IDENTIFYING CUSTOMER NEEDS

8.10 Studying Needs by Style

Relater

When interviewing a relater, talk warmly and informally. Ask gentle, open-ended questions and be sensitive about their feelings and privacy.

Relaters avoid saying negative things about people and situations. They also tend to tell you what they think you want to hear. It becomes a matter of diplomacy to extract from them accurate information about your competitors.

Socializer

Socializers love to talk about themselves. You must, therefore, give them sufficient time to do so before asking business-oriented questions. In the beginning, your business questions should be sprinkled throughout with personal/social questions. As you get to know them better, they will be willing to talk business more quickly.

Socializers can be very open and may tell you their life stories and fondest dreams. If you can demonstrate how your product or service ties in with their dreams, socializers will sell themselves. That's the slam-dunk we all love in sales.

Thinkers like to answer questions that reveal their expertise. Ask fact-oriented rather than feeling-oriented questions. Phrase your questions to elicit the right information–"How many . . ., "How often . . .," "What problems do you foresee . . .? " and that sort of thing. Let them show you how much they know.

When answering their questions, make your responses short and to the point. Leave your feelings out of it. Be left-brained, analytical, scientific, and factual. If you do not know the answer to a question, don't fake it. Tell them you will find the answer and get back to them by a specific time. Then do it.

Thinkers are very time-conscious, so be sensitive to their time constraints.

Thinker

Directors tend to be impatient, so you have to alternately ask interesting questions and give information. They want to know where your questions are leading. Aim your questions at the heart of the issue and only ask about those things that cannot be uncovered via other sources. In other words, don't waste a director's time.

As mentioned before, you must appear to have done your homework. This will be reflected in the level of information that you pursue and the way you ask questions. "In the last four years you have brought your company from number 15 to number 3 in the industry. What happens now?"

Director

176

WORKSHEET

• Get your client to identify priorities and, thus, be able to meet his/her needs better

DENTIFYING CUSTOMER NEEDS

8.11 Getting Agreement on Cost, Quality, and Time

Ask your client the following questions to help define Cost, Quality, and Time.

- What does quality mean to you?

- How would you define quality?

- How do you define time? Is it delivery date, responsiveness, or something else?

- What specifics do you include when you think about cost?

- In what context do you think about cost? Is it in terms of price of product? terms? alternatives?

Show your client the diagram below. Ask, "Where would you place the dot to indicate your priorities for this purchase?"

Examples

Indicates Price Buyer

Indicates Quality and Time top priorities – willing to pay for Quality and Time

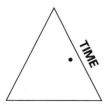

A Buyer who will pay for responsiveness

A Buyer who is willing to wait for the right Quality and Price

Note: Adapted from *Beyond Selling: How to Maximize Your Personal Influence* by Bagley and Reese.

✎ WORKSHEET

IDENTIFYING CUSTOMER NEEDS

8.12 Criteria-Sorting Grid

- Help set and identify the customer's decision-making criteria
- Use the criteria to create compelling presentations

Use the following grid to rank-order your customer's priorities.

Criteria Sorting Grid

Customer_____ Company_____

Style_____

Date_____ Phone_____

Sorts	**Prioritize**
Problem Avoidance/Goal Orientation	Weak · · · · · Strong
___Problem Avoidance	
___Goal Orientation	
Past Assurances/Future Possibilities	
___Past Assurances	
___Future Possibilities	
Authority Sort	
___Self	
___Others	
___Data	
General/Specific Sort	
___General	
___Specific	
Cost/Convenience Sort	
___Cost	
___Convenience	
___(a) Time	
___(b) Quality	
Believability Sort	
___Visual	
___Auditory	
___Kinesthetic	

How many times? or How Long?_____

Key influences on this person:

1._____ 2._____

9 Proposing solutions

WHAT'S IN IT FOR YOU

- Increase your understanding of the theory and practice of giving presentations
- Learn to speak in terms of benefits rather than features
- Learn how to plan effective presentations
- Discover how to modify your presentations to complement the behavioral styles of your prospects

Lots of people can find problems. It's the one who proposes the right solution who gets the sale. Often that is a matter of how you make your presentation. This section focuses on how you can present your products' benefits in ways that will enable you to make the sale.

? FYI

PRESENTATIONS THAT SELL

9.1 The Structure of Presentations

Although many salespeople like to wing it rather than prepare a structured presentation, by far the majority of professionals rely on an outline. Whether you speak well extemporaneously or depend on copious notes, you still must give a logical flow to your ideas. In your presentation, cover five general areas.

The Claim. You are making a presentation because you offer the promise of some benefit. That benefit may be increased sales, fewer sick days, less paperwork, fewer mechanical breakdowns . . . it doesn't matter. Whatever the claim, it must be related to your prospect's need gap.

The Need Gap. Over half of your work as a salesperson is uncovering and diagnosing a prospect's need gap. During a presentation, you must keep him or her aware of that gap and continually relate your product's benefits to that need.

The Solution. Your product or service must genuinely be able to solve your prospect's problem. You must be able to present a clear, concise statement of how your product will do so. Your proposal may include specific, measurable criteria by which the success of the solution will be judged. This may be a point of negotiation and will ultimately reflect the guarantee that comes with your product/service.

Documentation. How can you prove your claims? Document successes. Offer testimonial letters with lots of specifics. Give an impressive demonstration. Break out the slides and show pictures, graphs, data, and other proof.

A Call to Action. You've got to ask for the sale. Too many salespeople fail to do this. It's a natural thing to ask for feedback on your presentation and your product/service and then to ask for your prospect's business.

PRESENTATIONS THAT SELL

9.2 Toward More Effective Presentations

During a presentation, you not only sell your product or service, you sell yourself and the presentation process. You cannot hope to make a sale with an excellent product, a good rapport with your prospect, and an inept presentation.

Entertain Your Prospect. Capture your prospect's attention 100 percent of the time. That means *be interesting*. Vary the pace of your speech, involve your prospect with questions, use visual aids, add humor, and present data in ways that are clear and easily understood.

Remember Murphy's Law. Precisely those things that you cannot prepare for, you must prepare for. Anything can happen: interruptions, equipment failures, unexpected time constraints, and other snafus. During your presentation, recover from an interruption by summarizing what has recently transpired and moving on unflustered.

Play Off of Needs. Keep your prospect aware of his or her need gap and continually relate your proposal to the closing of that gap.

Keep It Relevant. Customize your presentation. Follow a structure. If you have a canned presentation, be sure to tailor it to the prospect. Always adapt to the situation. If your product has 42 features, *only* discuss the ones most important to your prospect. To discuss all 42 would be a boring, foolish, waste of time. Failing to customize shows that you have failed to get to know your prospect and her needs.

Be Ethical. Avoid the temptation to exaggerate. Tell the truth. If you do not know the answer to a question, be honest and tell the person you will find out.

Build Perceived Value. Again, customize by putting your product or service's price, quality, performance, delivery, service, and other factors into the perspective that your prospect will appreciate. By the time you propose a solution, you should know your prospect's buying criteria and success criteria. Be sure you address both, especially when they are different, which they should *not* be.

Differentiate Yourself From the Competition. Nothing is worse than trying to sell a commodity. If you are, you can only compete on price, which is a never-ending, no-win battle. You must find ways to make yourself, your company, and your product/service different; and those differences play a large part in your presentation.

Be Confident. Rehearse your presentation until you have lost the fear that you may forget what to say. Relax, control your pace, make eye contact, stay tuned in to your prospect.

Share Your Enthusiasm. Enthusiasm is a big part of what you are selling. It shows confidence in your product/service.

Stay Sensitive To Your Prospect's Needs. Although most salespeople would rather reschedule an appointment than condense their presentation, you may not have a choice. Some prospects are difficult to catch, so make the most of the time you're given. When you are forced to condense your presentation, pare away the extras and concentrate on the relevant benefits.

Being sensitive also means giving your prospect the floor when she seems to have a question or some resistance. Look for signs that something is on her mind.

Create Descriptive, Carefully Worded Phrases. Be able to describe your product or service quickly and clearly with phrases that have an impact. By repeating these phrases throughout your presentation, you will reinforce your message; but be sure to vary the phrases slightly to avoid monotony.

Slow down after presenting an important point. Slowing down creates an emphasis and allows the idea to sink in.

Present Simple Concepts First, Complex Later. The simple ideas will help prospects understand the complex ideas. Avoid concepts that are too detailed for prospects to understand. It's better to hand out supplemental material to be read later than make prospects feel ignorant.

Customize Your Presentation To the Prospect's Behavioral Style. Vary the amount of statistics, figures, graphs, computer read outs, spreadsheets, and other numbers you present depending on your prospect's behavioral style. Thinkers want lots of numbers. Directors just want bottom-line figures. Socializers and Relaters want fewer numbers still. Shape your presentation according to the guidelines given in 9.8, "Proposing Solutions by Style."

Ask for Feedback. Make sure everything you say is understood. Leave no room for confusion or misunderstanding. There are practical and legal implications to this piece of advice.

Involve Your Prospect. Use questions and hands-on participation (if appropriate). The earlier in a presentation a prospect asks questions, the less chance there will be for unanswered questions to become objections later.

Believe In Yourself and Your Product/Service. It will show and be contagious.

WORKSHEET

PRESENTATIONS THAT SELL

9.3 Comparisons with the Competition

Selling's first rule of thumb is: *Don't knock the competition.* It's terribly amateurish and potentially unethical. A better approach is to know your competition well and compare yourself with them fairly, but only after your prospect has asked you to do so. The worksheet below can be filled out in advance or you can work on it with your prospect. In either case, it is a valuable selling tool.

Comparing Your Products and Service and Your Company with Competitors				
Product or Service	**Yours**	**Competitor A**	**Competitor B**	**Competitor C**
Specifications				
_____	_____	_____	_____	_____
_____	_____	_____	_____	_____
_____	_____	_____	_____	_____
_____	_____	_____	_____	_____
_____	_____	_____	_____	_____
Features				
_____	_____	_____	_____	_____
_____	_____	_____	_____	_____
_____	_____	_____	_____	_____
_____	_____	_____	_____	_____
_____	_____	_____	_____	_____
Benefits				
_____	_____	_____	_____	_____
_____	_____	_____	_____	_____
_____	_____	_____	_____	_____
Service	_____	_____	_____	_____
Delivery	_____	_____	_____	_____
Price	_____	_____	_____	_____
Terms	_____	_____	_____	_____
THE COMPANY				
_____	_____	_____	_____	_____
_____	_____	_____	_____	_____
_____	_____	_____	_____	_____
OTHER				
_____	_____	_____	_____	_____
_____	_____	_____	_____	_____

?FYI

PRESENTATIONS THAT SELL

9.4 Speak the Language of Benefits

New salespeople are often confused by the difference between features and benefits and the role each plays in a presentation. A feature is an aspect of the product or service that exists regardless of the customer's need for it. A benefit is the use or advantage that a customer derives from a feature. For example, a customer who is shopping for a truck may not care about four-wheel drive. It is a feature, but an irrelevant one to some people. However, when an off-road enthusiast walks up to the truck, that feature suddenly becomes a benefit.

A benefit, then, is a feature in action. Most customers, especially end-users on the retail level, think in terms of benefits. They don't care what features make something work. They are only concerned with the end result—the benefits they can derive from the purchase.

During a presentation, you must know what kind of person you are dealing with. If you are selling to an engineer, you must discuss features as well as benefits. Most of the time, however, you will not have to cover features in such detail. In fact, most final decision makers only care about the bottom line, which is how they will benefit from the purchase.

Concentrate on speaking the language of benefits. This means addressing your prospect's problems or needs one at a time and showing how your product/service will solve *each specific* problem. Get your prospect involved by using the Feature-Feedback-Benefit (FFB) method. Present a feature and ask for feedback.

Salesperson: "This computer has 60 Megabyte hard disk. How important is that to you?"

Customer: "I don't know. Is that enough to store at least 200,000 names for a mailing list?"

The customer has done two things: 1) revealed a lack of knowledge and need for consultative help; and 2) described an important benefit that must be provided by the product. Later in your presentation, you would come back to this benefit and make a point of showing how it will be provided.

Keep in mind that a feature can provide more than one benefit. Similarly, a desired benefit can be accomplished with more than one feature. For example, a fireplace can provide more than heat. The benefit of recreation can be derived from a swimming pool, a big backyard, a finished basement or proximity to a park.

During your presentation, be sure to point out all the possibilities, especially if flexibility and diversity are desired benefits. In addition, use the following question—or similar ones—to uncover other desired benefits.

"How do you see this fitting into your current or future situation?"

"Have I missed any advantages that this may provide you? What might they be?"

"This is how my product/service can be used in (situation A); can you see ways that it will help you with (situation B)?"

"How do you see this addressing the problem/opportunity we discussed earlier?" (Be specific.)

"Does this look like it will meet your needs?"

If the answer is no, say, "I'm sorry, I must have missed something. What were you looking to accomplish that I have overlooked?"

WORKSHEET

WHAT'S IN IT FOR YOU

- Increase your knowledge of your products' or services' features and benefits

PRESENTATIONS THAT SELL

9.5 Features/Benefits Identification

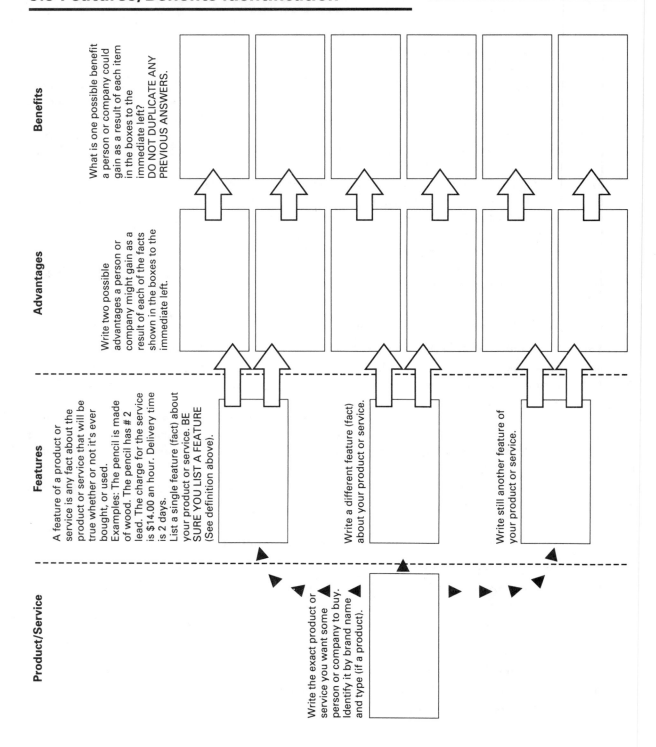

Benefits

What is one possible benefit a person or company could gain as a result of each item in the boxes to the immediate left? DO NOT DUPLICATE ANY PREVIOUS ANSWERS.

Advantages

Write two possible advantages a person or company might gain as a result of each of the facts shown in the boxes to the immediate left.

Features

A feature of a product or service is any fact about the product or service that will be true whether or not it's ever bought, or used. Examples: The pencil is made of wood. The pencil has # 2 lead. The charge for the service is $14.00 an hour. Delivery time is 2 days.
List a single feature (fact) about your product or service. BE SURE YOU LIST A FEATURE (See definition above).

Write a different feature (fact) about your product or service.

Write still another feature of your product or service.

Product/Service

Write the exact product or service you want some person or company to buy. Identify it by brand name and type (if a product).

186

✎ WORKSHEET

PRESENTATIONS THAT SELL

9.6 Presentation Planning Guide

Prepare the following worksheet in advance to help you with your presentations.

Company: _____   Buyer's name: _____

Industry: _____   Phone: _____

Address: _____   Appointment date: _____

Prospect's behavioral style: _____

Call objectives: _____
_____

1. Introduction to use:

2. Initial questions to ask:

3. Initial summary or statement to make:

4. Questions to ask to further explore need gap:

5. Needs to address:

6. Features and benefits to emphasize:

7. Benefits to seek agreement on:

8. Plan for presentation:

9. A/V aids to use and equipment needed:

10. Testimonial letters to bring:

11. How to get prospect involved:

12. Feedback questions to ask:

13. Possible resistance and how to handle it:

14. Key points in summary of presentation:

15. How to ask for the sale:

16. Outcome of presentation:

17. Suggestions for improvements:

ⓘ F Y I

PRESENTATIONS THAT SELL

- Effectively use demonstrations to help prospects visualize your product/service's success

9.7 Fine Points for Presentations

We all know that a picture is worth a thousand words and that a demonstration is worth 1,000 pictures, models, descriptions, and testimonials. A well-done demonstration will catch your prospect's attention, emphasize your main points, help prospects understand complex concepts, combine seeing and hearing to aid memory, stimulate your own enthusiasm, reduce the amount of resistance that arises, and help you achieve the purpose of the proposal!

The key is to have your prospect visualize the success of your product/service for himself. To achieve this, remember these fine points when preparing or presenting your demonstration.

1. Keep visuals simple. Use words, graphics, or both to reinforce or explain your main points.

2. Limit text to 40 characters. Most people can grasp this much at a glance. Never put your entire presentation on slides and read it to a prospect.

3. Slides with text should be written in phrases, not complete sentences. You will fill in the details and clarify any unclear phrases.

4. Use upper- and lower-case letters. All caps are difficult to read.

5. Give the text room to breathe on the slide or page and situate it in a similar location from page to page or slide to slide.

6. Keep it simple, sweetheart. Graphs or charts should present only one idea at a time to increase comprehension.

7. Line charts are best used to show how one or more variables changed over time.

8. Bar graphs are best used to show the relationship between two or more variables.

9. Pie charts show the relationship between parts within a whole.

10. Tables and charts with complex data should only be used with groups that will understand them, and only when the group plans to study the graphics closely. In the average sales proposal, complex concepts should be simplified and explained.

11. Spend the money to make slides colorful, but not gaudy. Red should be used very sparingly. Bright colors are OK for main points, while shading, arrows and highlighting add interesting dimensions to the slide.

12. Always have a duplicate videotape, audiotape, slide set, or whatever A/V medium you are using.

13. Learn to be your own repair person. If possible, carry along a kit that contains critical items you need most often, such as:

projector bulbs	electrical tape	head cleaner
duct tape	Pressurized air	pliers, knife
3-prong adapter plugs	flashlight	projector trays

Also, call ahead to ensure that critical items are available.

14. Use a room that is larger than necessary rather than one that is just right or too small. People don't like feeling crowded.

15. Arrange the chairs so that there are aisles on the sides rather than down the middle. That way, late comers will not walk in front of the projector.

16. Always rehearse your demonstration, including the slides, video, or other aids you plan to use.

PRESENTATIONS THAT SELL

9.8 Proposing Solutions by Style

WHAT'S IN IT FOR YOU

- Learn how to gear your presentations to people of different behavioral styles

Relater

Relaters are relationship-oriented, so you need to show them how your solution will support, enhance or stabilize the people side of business. They are also resistant to change, so present changes in a way that is nonthreatening. Assure them that daily operations will remain pretty much the same, with any changes implemented slowly and for the benefit of all.

Concentrate on security, relationships, harmony, steadiness, and concrete benefits. Involve relaters in your presentation by asking for their opinoins and feeling.

Socializer

Socializers are the group with whom you should sell the sizzle more than the steak. They are dramatic people who want to see how your product/service will increase their prestige, recognition or image.

High entertainment value is essential when dealing with socializers. Incorporate as many senses as possible in your presentation. Get your prospect involved. Back up your claims with testimonials and success stories about highprofile people they know and respect.

Socializers like to jump on the band wagon, so celebrity or executive endorsements work well. In fact, if you can find one person your prospect highly respects who uses your product/service, chances are good that your prospect will buy without hesitation.

The cornerstones of a presentation to a thinker are logic, accurate information, perceived value, quality, and reliability. Honesty is important as well, which is why you should be upfront about any short-comings. Thinkers are analytical people who look for the bugs in systems, so point them out yourself and you will gain credibility.

Back up your claims with documents, data, slides, computer printouts, etc. Always have copies of these support materials for them to keep. Testimonials from other technically minded people will carry a lot of weight, especially if your prospect knows and respects those people.

Your presentation should be as stream-lined as possible and pack a lot of technological punch.

Thinker

A director's priorities are usually making money saving time, and becoming more efficient. Gear your presentation accordingly. Use quick benefit statements to show her how she can become more successful.

Due to their time crunch, directors want you to have done all the analyses. Simply present them with the results of your research and give them choices to make.

There will be times when you need to give a detailed presentation. Write the details and make a professional-looking proposal out of it. Give it to your prospect for future reference. Hit the main points in your presentation if she asks about the details, provide them.

Directors, like thinkers, are time-disciplined, so make your presentation short and to the point.

Director

10 Handling customer resistance

WHAT'S IN IT FOR YOU

- Gain insight into the reasons customers resist
- Learn to more effectively handle resistance
- Understand the traditional and nontraditional forms of customer resistance
- Learn how to handle the common excuse, "It's too expensive"

Most parents will tell you that the first word their children learned to say was "No." It makes sense—it's a short word, easy to say, and it ends all further need for discussion or decision-making—at least as far as the speaker is concerned. This principle is similarly true for adults, including customers. "It's too expensive." "It's too big." "It's too small." "It's too complicated." "It's not complicated enough." All of these—and a lot more—are the kinds of resistance you face everyday. Some of these objections point to real customer needs and concerns, and you will need to address them in an appropriate manner. But some of these kinds of objections are parts of other agendas, and you need to be able to determine the source of these kinds of resistance in order to overcome them. This section gives you tips on how to do that.

❓ F Y I

USING CUSTOMER RESISTANCE

10.1 Resistance Is Feedback.

Inexperienced salespeople see customer resistance as potholes or stop signs on the road to a sale. Experienced salespeople realize that customer resistance is a normal, natural, and necessary part of the sales process. Resistance is not a stop sign, it is an arrow pointing in the right direction. When a customer brings up some resistance, it does not mean, "I'm not going to buy;" it just means, "I'm not sold yet." Big difference.

Let's face it, very few sales proceed from start to finish with the customer agreeing 100 percent on every point. If that happened, you would be in shock. Similarly, few customers disagree with 100 percent of what you say. So most sales fall in between these two extremes. Part of the give and take of the sales process is getting feedback from your prospect.

You will have a much healthier attitude if you expect and welcome resistance rather than fear it. Fearing resistance may make you resent your prospect for making your job more difficult. Welcoming resistance as a form of feedback puts you in a helpful and understanding frame of mind.

Inexperienced salespeople fear customer resistance because they find themselves at a loss for answers. Only experience (which includes role-playing) and study will calm your nerves and prepare you for your most common objections. The ideas that follow will show you how to get a handle on one of the most common stumbling blocks in sales.

WORKSHEET

USING CUSTOMER RESISTANCE

10.2 What You Do Now

1. Recall a recent unsuccessful sale in which you handled a prospect's resistance poorly.

   a. What was your customer's concern? _____

   b. What was your response? _____

   c. How could you have answered more effectively? _____

2. When a prospect tells you that your price is too high, how do you respond?_____

3. When a prospect has doubts about the quality of your product or your company's reputation, what do you say?_____

4. On a scale of one to ten, rate yourself on the qualities that are needed when dealing with customer resistance:

   a. Confidence in yourself _____

   b. Confidence in your company/product _____

   c. Product knowledge _____

   d. Industry knowledge _____

   e. Knowledge of human nature_____

   f. Patience_____

   g. Ability to avoid arguments _____

   h. Calmness under stress_____

   i. Ability to be diplomatic _____

? FYI

USING CUSTOMER RESISTANCE

- Increase your understanding of the reasons for customer resistance

10.3 Why Customers Resist

Resistance can take many forms, but there is a finite number of reasons why customers resist. It is your job to tactfully, patiently, and empathically find out the reason(s). The reasons fall into five broad categories: Need, Relationship, Ability, Product/Service, and Price.

Need. There are times when a prospect's need has decreased since the last time you contacted him or her. Markets change, sometimes overnight. The problem may also be perceived need. You may have failed to show your prospect the extent of his or her need and exactly how your product or service will be the solution. It's time to do more information gathering, research, and custom-tailoring of your presentation.

Relationship. People do business with people they like. Your customer may be resisting because something went wrong with your relationship. There may be a lack of trust, confidence, or comfort with you personally. If that is the case, either work to improve the relationship or turn over the account to someone else.

Ability. Your prospect may not be the final decision maker. You should have found this out earlier, during your information gathering. An inability to buy may also be due to high interest rates, a lack of space, or seasonal fluctuations in business.

Product. The worst reason for a prospect to resist the sale is that your product is inferior or your company has a bad reputation. If true, these are difficult issues to overcome. The best way to deal with them is to present concrete evidence that things are improving. Assure your customers that the past will not adversely affect their future satisfaction.

Price. Not everyone can afford to buy what they want or truly need. An important part of prospecting and information gathering is qualifying your prospects. However, not all salespeople do a thorough job of this. It is conceivable that you will ask for the sale from someone who truly cannot afford what you are selling.

It is also conceivable that the issue of price is a cover-up. It is easy to use "It costs too much" as an excuse for some other problem. It is your job to not only build perceived value (so you can justify your prices), but find out the real reasons your customer is resisting.

USING CUSTOMER RESISTANCE

10.4 Types of Resistance

Resistance is valid when the questions or statements have a logical basis. Invalid resistance is an insincere excuse used to stall or hide a valid issue.

Valid resistance is always legitimate. It does not mean the sale is doomed, and should always be addressed directly. Some resistance sounds as if it would stop the sale instantly, but further probing reveals that is usually not the case. An example of valid resistance that would stop a sale is the inability to deliver on time. Your prospect may need the product in 90 days, but you cannot deliver in less than 180 days. There's no way out of that bind.

Most resistance really hides a desire for more details. By finding fault with something, your customer may actually be looking for assurance regarding quality, guarantees, or warranties. "That metal looks awfully thin" can be interpreted as "What assurances can you give me that it will stand up to my intended use?"

"I don't need any more at this time" could mean "I haven't had the time to think about this" or "Show me how your product is different from what I'm now carrying."

"My boss isn't going to go for this" can mean "You should give me some collateral material to help me sell this to my boss." It could also mean, "I'm afraid to make this decision on my own."

When that happens, either make the decision-making easier, or try to meet with the boss.

Invalid resistance sometimes masquerades as valid resistance. That is why you have to be able to recognize the difference. Invalid resistance presents a stall or put-off—a way for your customer to say, "I don't want to think about this now because I'd be forced into making a decision." Invalid resistance has many sounds to it:

"I have to leave in fifteen minutes."

"I'll be out of town next week."

"Leave your material with me and I'll look it over when I get a chance."

"I have to discuss this with my partner/wife/boss."

All of these excuses seem valid, so it may require careful judgment to determine if they are genuine or not. Through observation and knowledge of your customer you will know whether you are hearing the truth or a stall.

Invalid objections pose a challenge to your attitude. Your positive attitude must be conveyed as you handle the resistance. For example, you could say,

"I understand that you are busy, may I see you this afternoon or tomorrow morning?" "I don't mind leaving some materials with you, but I get the impression that you are still unclear on some aspect of what we have just discussed. Is there some point that I could explain better?" "I don't blame you for wanting to involve your partner/wife/boss in this decision. Let's ask her to join us now for a few minutes and we'll bring her up to speed."

With other types of invalid resistance, the prospect's statements don't even make sense. The change in attitude may be sudden and without cause. When this happens, you have to find out what the invalid resistance is hiding. Beneath the surface there is a problem either with the prospect's need, your relationship, the customer's ability to make a decision, your product or service, or its price.

To find out the real reason behind an invalid resistance, use the four-step process in the following FYI.

? F Y I

USING CUSTOMER RESISTANCE

10.5 A Four-Step Plan for Handling Resistance

Every prospect and every sales situation is different, but handling resistance can follow some general rules. Keep these in mind:

1. **Listen carefully.** Never interrupt someone. You may have heard all the common resistances, but your customer has the right (and the need) to speak his mind. Take the time to note your customer's body language, vocal inflections, and other buying signals.

2. **Check your understanding with feedback.** You can get feedback in the form of a question or a statement. Either way, you should put the prospect's concern in your own words and turn it into an issue you can address.

   Never argue with a customer. Don't try to win a battle of logic. Simply turn their issue into a question you can answer.

3. **Address the issue effectively.** This means using a method that is direct and convincing. Sometimes prospects cannot see their own business dilemmas. It is your job to clarify issues and help them overcome their fear of spending money, making decisions, change, or whatever is bogging them down.

Worksheet 10.6 will cover valuable methods for addressing resistance. Study and practice them.

4. **Confirm acceptance.** If you handled the resistance well, it should no longer be an issue. How will you know? You have to ask point-blank, "Are you completely satisfied with that answer?" or "Have I put your concerns to rest regarding this matter?" Be sure to consider the person's behavioral style when asking this question. Try to use the word *think* with Directors and Thinkers and *feel* with Relaters and Socializers.

Once you have dealt with the resistance, you may be in position to ask for the sale. The closer you are to the end of your presentation, the more appropriate it will be to ask for the sale or at least test the waters, depending on the buying signals you pick up.

WORKSHEET

USING CUSTOMER RESISTANCE

10.6 When to Respond to Resistance

When should you respond to a customer's resistance? There are only three good choices: Before the issue comes up; immediately; and later, after postponing.

Before the Issue Comes Up. Every product and service has its strengths and weaknesses. Knowing a weakness and building an answer to it into your presentation is a smart practice. It handles the resistance before it ever comes up. Doing this also allows you to discuss the weakness, put it in perspective and possibly lessen its severity. In addition, honesty builds credibility and trust.

List three common issues that customers bring up about your product or service. What could you say about them in advance to eliminate these sources of resistance?

1. _____
2. _____
3. _____

Immediately. Customers do not like to be ignored, so the safest bet is to answer questions when they are asked. Unless you have a logical reason to postpone your answer, handle the resistance immediately. Professionalism dictates that you are always sensitive to what is going on with your customer. Immediate responses convey respect, empathy, and good communication skills.

List three common objections that you must answer immediately.

1. _____
2. _____
3. _____

Later, after postponing. Some issues are better off postponed. Perhaps you plan to cover an issue later and your prospect has jumped the gun. The most common question that comes up prematurely is price. (For ways to handle the price issue, see FYI 11.6, "Timing and Perceived Value.") Prospects always want to know how much something is going to cost before they know what it is and how it will solve their problem. This is natural, so be prepared for it. The way to handle the price issue is to postpone it:

> **"That's a good question, but one I'd like to cover in a few minutes, if you don't mind. I want to put my product in perspective so the price will have some meaning to you. Is that OK?"**

This postponing method acknowledges the value of the question, gives an honest reason for delaying, and shows respect by asking (twice) for the prospect's permission to postpone the answer.

Think of three common resistances that you can postpone answering and what you will say to do so.

1. _____
2. _____
3. _____

USING CUSTOMER RESISTANCE

10.7 Methods of Handling Resistance

After you have listened to your prospect's resistance and clarified it with feedback, you must respond in a way that makes sense. Only you can determine the best method for the situation, but having some options will enable you to remain calm.

Feel, Felt, Found. This method conveys understanding, assures your prospect that he is not alone, and reassures him that this common misgiving becomes unimportant when additional information is considered. This ties into a person's need to be appreciated, accepted, informed, and in control.

You're probably familiar with this method. You say, "I can understand how you *feel* about . . . . I have had other customers who *felt* the same way until they *found* out that . . . ."

Use The Balancing Act. There are times when a product or service has a definite weakness, but is a good buy for a prospect anyway. When someone points out a valid disadvantage, the only thing you can honestly do is admit it. Agree with your prospect on this point and you will maintain whatever credibility you presently have. Then show her all the reasons your product/service is still a good buy. Point out all the ways that the benefits compensate for a minor weakness.

> **"I understand that this computer system will require more room than you anticipated, but based on the needs we've discussed and your projected expansion, it is a system you will soon grow into."**

If appropriate, use testimonial letters, case histories, or statistics to help your case.

The Ben Franklin Balance Sheet. The Ben Franklin Balance Sheet is an exercise in logic. Here's how to do it *right:* Vertically divide a sheet of paper in two. On one side, list the reasons to buy; on the other side, list the reasons not to buy. Some salespeople only help with the positives. Nonmanipulative salespeople are fair; they help with both sides. Don't stop there. Since no two reasons are equal, it is important to give weight to each. For both columns, have your prospect prioritize the entries by dividing 100 points among them. So one reason may deserve 25 points, another may only deserve ten points, and so on. Then add up the points and divide by the number of reasons. This will give you a weighted average—a more accurate picture of which way to go.

Get Clarification. Often resistance is vague or generalized. A statement such as "Your service won't work for us" is impossible to respond to unless you ask for clarification. Ask simple, open-ended questions to uncover the root of the problem.

> **Salesperson: "Can you tell me what you mean when you say it won't work?"**
>
> **Customer: "The response time is too slow."**
>
> **Salesperson: "I can easily upgrade the system to double or triple the response time. Which of those would be fast enough for you?"**
>
> **Customer: "Triple will work fine. Can I give you my order now?"**

Deny and Correct. There are times when a prospect is misinformed. Someone might have given him inaccurate information or he might have misunderstood something you said. In either case, you have to gently set him straight. The way to do this is to say something like, "It may be my fault, but it seems you have gotten the wrong impression. Please, let me set the record straight." Of course there are other things you could say. Whatever you say, it has to 1) sound real, not canned; 2) be diplomatic; and 3) set the stage for a correction.

Compare Apples With Apples. To win an argument, you have to be fairly well versed in the rules of logic. Along the same lines, logic dictates that, when you make a comparison, you compare apples with apples. Resistant prospects do not always follow a logical train of thought. It's up to you to keep the logic train on track.

> **Customer: "This laser printer won't print 15 pages per minute."**

> **Salesperson: "When we first talked, you said your highest priority was high-resolution print quality. Is that still your first priority? If not, let's rank your priorities so I will know what to recommend."**

Put the Ball Back in Their Court. This is also called the Boomerang method. There are times when a customer's reason for not buying is the precise reason he should buy. This is the perfect example of a customer not being able to see the forest for the trees.

> **Customer: "I can't afford an 800 number."**

> **Salesperson: "You can't afford *not* to have an 800 number! The business that a toll-free number will generate will more than pay for the service."**

To make your argument completely sound, back it up with hard evidence. Use charts, graphs, statistics, case studies, and testimonials to show how much time or money will be saved or earned with your product or service. The Boomerang method works well when your customer lacks some information or fails to see the big picture.

- Learn to increase your credibility with effective proof of your claims
- Identify people and companies that can support you in your sales effort
- Determine ways to improve your company's warranty

USING CUSTOMER RESISTANCE

10.8 Types of Evidence That Support Claims

No matter what method you use to deal with resistance, you must produce evidence to prove what you are saying. That's part of your job. Simply knowing what to say to change a prospect's perspective is not enough. The proof you offer can take many forms.

Make a Comparison. Different customers have different buying criteria. If your prospect is mentally comparing your product/service with another, it is essential to help with that process. You can use a system such as the Ben Franklin Balance Sheet (or Worksheet 9.3, "Comparisons with the Competition") to list advantages and disadvantages of yours versus theirs. The method of comparison that you use will depend on what you are selling. The higher the cost, the longer the sales cycle, and the more high-tech your industry, the more you will have to use sophisticated comparison techniques. These may include computer data analyses, slide shows, tours of manufacturing plants or other locations, presentations by engineers, and so on.

List three ways that you can make a convincing comparison between your product/service and a competitor's.

1. _____
2. _____
3. _____

Present Testimonials or Case Histories. One of the most convincing forms of proof is to present a company in a similar situation and show how your product/service solved their problem.

This can be done with testimonial letters or the presentation of a case history, which can take the form of a slide show. The combination of the two is very powerful.

List three companies that can serve as case histories to bolster your presentation.

1. _____
2. _____
3. _____

List three people from whom you can get testimonial letters.

1. _____ Company: _____
2. _____ Company: _____
3. _____ Company: _____

Demonstrate. This was covered in detail in FYI 9.7

Present Warranties or Guarantees. Unconditional guarantees are a very powerful way to make the buying decision safe and easy for your customer. Even conditional guarantees can be very effective. What they say about the product/service and company is: "We believe in the quality of what we are selling and have the integrity to stand behind it." Of course, a strong reputation and long history in the business helps as well.

How effective is your company's warranty or guarantee? List three ways it could be improved.

1. _____

2. _____

3. _____

Calculate the Cost of Waiting. Customers often agree that a purchase is in their best interest, but then want to wait awhile before making a final decision. If you can honestly show how delaying will cost them money, prospects will be motivated to decide now. In your calculations, include rising interest rates, price increases, changes in the market, potential decreases in the customer's market share, and so on. Your knowledge of the industry plus an understanding of the economic, political, technical, and other factors affecting it will add to your credibility.

What are some of the factors that might increase your customer's cost if he or she delays action?

1. _____

2. _____

3. _____

WORKSHEET

USING CUSTOMER RESISTANCE

- Specify ways that you will apply what you have learned in this section to future customer resistance

10.9 Handling Future Resistance

To improve the way you handle resistance, list the most common resistance you encounter at different phases of the sale, what type it is, and how you will deal with it in the future:

1. Resistance upon contact: _____

   Type: _____

   Your new response: _____

2. Resistance when setting up an appointment: _____

   Type: _____

   Your new response: _____

3. Resistance when information gathering: _____

   Type: _____

   Your new response: _____

4. Resistance at the beginning of your presentation: _____

   Type: _____

   Your new response: _____

5. Resistance during your presentation: _____

   Type: _____

   Your new response: _____

6. Resistance upon asking for the sale: _____

   Type: _____

   Your new response: _____

✎ WORKSHEET

- Learn a better way to respond to resistance

USING CUSTOMER RESISTANCE

10.10 "It's Too Expensive"

How do you handle this objection?

"It's too expensive" can mean several things. It can mean:

1. Your product costs more than I have in my budget. My budget is $5,000, your product is $7,500."

2. "I don't think your product is worth the price. I have $7,500, but I wouldn't spend it on your product."

3. "Your product is worth what you're asking and I have that amount, but I don't need to spend that much—it's more than my needs require."

The key is to find out which of the three meanings apply to the objection, "It's too expensive." Think of three questions you could ask to uncover the real meaning.

1. _____

2. _____

3. _____

Customer: "I like your product, but it's too expensive."
Your First Response _____
Another Response: _____
A Third Response: _____

Our Solutions

Once you have clarified your prospect's meaning, you have several options.

If your prospect does not have the money in the budget, work with him to 1) see if funds can be shifted from other sources; 2) try to work out financing; 3) sell someone higher in the company so that additional funds can be allocated.

If your prospect does not think your product or service is worth the asking price, you need to increase the *perceived value*. To do so, you can: 1) add value with additional services or add-on products; 2) compare every facet of your product to your competitors—show how your product is better in terms of quality, service, reputation, warranty, etc; 3) negotiate a lower price, if your company routinely does this.

If your prospect tells you that you are trying to sell him more than he needs, sell him less. If your product line does not include something with fewer features that is less expensive, then refer him to another company.

Point out the difference between buying criteria and success criteria. Your customer is basing his buying decision on price, but later will evaluate the success of your product/service on different criteria. The key is to show your prospect that his buying decision should be based on the same criteria that he'll later use to judge success. This is how you build perceived value.

Your Solutions

What are some things you can say to address the three meanings of "It's too expensive"?

1. _____

2. _____

3. _____

11 Confirming the sale

WHAT'S IN IT FOR YOU

- Understand the difference between manipulative and nonmanipulative confirmation
- Learn to recognize confirming opportunities and the importance of the benefit summary
- Learn or review some traditional confirmation techniques that have been given our unique twist

Manipulative salespeople study closing techniques as a way of building up their arsenal of weapons for the sales battle. Nonmanipulative salespeople see the sales process as a cooperative effort. They study closing techniques to give themselves various options to use with different types of people in different situations. Part of maintaining a smooth working relationship is selling to someone the way they want to be sold; in other words, making the buying process easy for the customer.

Confirmations come in many shapes and sizes. Your customer's behavioral style, the length of your relationship, their interest level and other factors will dictate the best way to ask for the sale. Only you can determine which confirmation is best in a given situation. Keep the following options in mind.

?FYI

CLOSING VERSUS CONFIRMING

11.1 Confirming Versus Closing the Sale

Traditional salespeople think of "the close" as a series of techniques used at the end of a presentation. These techniques are designed to get the prospect to say yes and give an order, even if he doesn't want what is being sold.

The traditional view is passé. Consultative salespeople take a more enlightened view of confirming the sale. To nonmanipulative salespeople, confirming the sale is a natural process—the logical outcome of involving the customer in every step of the sales process. there are two ways to involve a prospect: the manipulative way and the nonmanipulative way. Traditional salespeople often ask questions that give the prospect frequent opportunities to say either yes or no. Some people believe that a prospect is more likely to say yes to the sale if she has gotten into the habit of answering yes to all the previous questions. It's a twisted game of logic in which the salesperson wins agreement throughout, hoping that the final answer will also be yes. The problem is that the prospect answers yes to simple, superficial questions that don't build an argument in favor of the sale.

Other salespeople think prospects have a need to say no. By giving them the opportunity to say no to a lot of questions, the thinking goes, the prospect will have the no's out of his system and be ready to say yes when the salesperson asks for the sale.

Both tactics are silly. The real way to involve a prospect is to make sure the two of you are on the same wavelength at all times. This means that from the very beginning, you must gather enough information to determine that the two of you really have a basis for doing business. The ideal sales process is a *mutual* journey of uncovering a need, working on a solution and confirming a sale. When the journey is mutual, confirming the sale is a matter of *when,* not *if.* When the journey is not mutual, salespeople spend their time trying to convince prospects that they need what's being sold. The sales process can become precisely the type of unethical, pushy, arm-twisting, foot-in-the-door, manipulative hustle that everyone loathes.

For the nonmanipulative salesperson, the sale *begins* when the customer says yes. It's not a close but an opening, the start of an ongoing business relationship. An analogy can be drawn between the confirming process and asking someone to marry you. If you were worried about the answer, you wouldn't ask. Obviously, the question would be premature. The decision to marry is the outcome of a mutually developed relationship. Usually the issue has been discussed before the question is formally asked. When it is asked, it is a rhetorical question that simply serves to crystallize (and romanticize) already understood feelings.

？FYI

CLOSING VERSUS CONFIRMING

11.2 The Benefit Summary

Traditionally, the benefit summary has been regarded as an integral part of most confirmation techniques. The enlightened salesperson, however, sees the benefit summary as a part of every sales process. No presentation—no matter how abbreviated—is complete without a benefit summary.

In a benefit summary, you summarize the points to which your prospect has responded positively. Be sure to go over benefits, not features. There is a big difference. This is especially important when your prospect is going to take the information back to another decision maker. When this is the case, your prospect becomes your salesperson, so you must prepare him well to represent you and your company. Leave as little to his memory as possible, which means putting everything in writing and providing collateral materials.

You will know which benefits to emphasize by 1) your prospect's reactions during your presentation and 2) the data you gathered during your information gathering.

One way to involve your prospect in your presentation is to have him create his own list of benefits. Get him to imagine how he would use your product/service and then ask him to come up with his own list of benefits. As he does this, he will sell himself.

You can accomplish this by asking how your product/service will help him with a specific problem. After he tells you the benefit, ask, "What other problems could this solve for you?"

The benefit summary puts into capsule form the highlights of your presentation. It is an opportunity to ask for feedback and a way to help your prospect retain the most important points. When you present your benefit summary, list the most important items first and last. They are the ones that stick the most.

At the end of your summary, give your prospect the opportunity to agree, disagree, or ask questions. Once agreement has been expressed, the buying signals should turn green.

The language of a benefit summary is simple: "Mr. Rush, we've talked about many things in the last hour. Let me summarize what I see as the key benefits for you. You're looking for a car that will bring you prestige. You're looking for something that will outrun the police and will evade radar. You mentioned that you want something small for easy parking. It is also important for you to be the first person on your block to have one. Based on all those things, I would strongly recommend the Acura NSX as the perfect car for you."

Follow up with an open question with direction, such as, "Mr. Rush, how would you like to proceed?" or "Where do we go from here?"

CLOSING VERSUS CONFIRMING

11.3 Confirming Opportunities

The key to recognizing confirming opportunities is to know your prospect. By the time you get to the proposal and confirmation stages, you should be familiar with the person's behavioral style and other personality traits. This knowledge will help you understand the signals he or she is sending.

Always be sensitive to your prospect's needs. If you are in the middle of a presentation and you get cues that it is time to ask for the sale, do so. Make sure, however, that you have created sufficient perceived value in your prospect's mind. Condense your presentation, but do not end it abruptly. Give a benefit summary and ask for the sale. Conversely, if you get the message that your prospect needs more information, don't ask for the sale. Find out what is needed and provide it.

It helps to be able to recognize a prospect's verbal and nonverbal buying signals. Buying signals come in three shades: red (negative or stop), green (positive or go), and yellow (neutral or caution).

Listen for the questions that your prospect asks. They are good indicators of his or her mind-set. Interpret questions and comments within the context of your proposal and relative to your prospect's other characteristics (behavioral style, body language, etc.). Some typical questions are:

1. Could I try this one more time? (+)

2. Is it possible to install this on a trial basis? (+)

3. What kind of warranty/service contract is available? (+)

4. What sort of credit terms do you offer? (+)

5. How soon can you deliver? (+)

6. This system is more reliable than mine? (0)

7. This is interesting. What else can you tell me? (0)

8. Can you leave some catalog sheets with me so I can go over them with my colleagues? (0)

9. I can't consider this with interest rates so high. (−)

10. Will these prices still be good in six months? (−)

11. I'm overstocked now. Where am I going to put more merchandise? (−)

Yellow (neutral) buying signals indicate that the person is still undecided. Perhaps you haven't presented enough information or the right kind of information; or perhaps the person is a slow decision maker. If that is the case, try helping with the Ben Franklin Balance Sheet. (See FYI 10.7 "Methods of Handling Resistance.")

When the buying signals are red, it is time to back up a step or two. Give a benefit summary (always your best transition) and politely ask an open-ended question with direction, such as "Where do we go from here?", "What's our next step?", or "How do we proceed?"

Above and beyond these specific suggestions, remember to always stay tuned to what is happening in your prospect's mind. Remember the body language cues discussed in FYI 6.11 and 6.12:

1. A prospect who sits with open arms is receptive; one who sits with arms crossed tightly is defensive. For the latter, find out what's wrong. Work on the relationship.

2. Interest is conveyed by leaning forward, listening carefully and nodding in agreement.

3. A prospect who is supporting his head with one hand and gazing off has lost interest.

4. People relax when they decide to buy. A tense posture is a sign that all is not well. Find out why.

5. Happy, animated facial expressions show that a prospect is relating well to you.

❓ F Y I

TYPES OF CONFIRMATION

11.4 The Tentative Confirmation

The Tentative Confirmation is a useful option when a prospect is interested, but hesitant to make a commitment. It offers the flexibility of a "way out" and, at the same time, puts an end to shopping. There are several scenarios in which the tentative confirmation works well.

Airlines, hotels, and car rental agencies use the tentative confirmation all the time. Imagine a car rental clerk giving a travel agent some information about a car. It is available on a specific date, but the travel agent has to check with her client before confirming. The reservationist usually says, "It is not uncommon for all our cars to be out on the weekends. I'd hate for you to call back and find this car unavailable. Why don't we go ahead and reserve the car for you? If your client says OK, then your work is done. If your client changes his mind, just call back and we'll cancel."

The tentative close begins the commitment process. It's ideal for customers who need a little push before they will commit themselves. Some personal styles will sit on the fence forever until they are pushed gently one way or another. What little commitment is gained is not very strong—but in these cases, a small commitment is sometimes better than none.

Most people do not have the time or inclination to exhaustively comparison shop to find the best deal possible. That's why the tentative confirmation also puts an end to or slows down the shopping process. The customer's mind-set usually changes from "I'm still uncertain" to "I've made a decision."

The tentative confirmation is not a trick or a manipulative technique, but an option that may work for some customers. It is appropriate for the person who wants what you are selling, not the customer who is uninterested. It is commonly used in sales in which the customer needs to arrange financing or other details. Imagine these situations:

> **"It's going to be six weeks before your order is delivered anyway. In that time, if you decide you don't want it, just call me and I'll allocate that shipment to another customer."**

> **"For our publication, the deadline for camera-ready art is the tenth of the month. Occasionally we run house ads. Why don't I reserve a space for your ad? If you decide by the ninth that you don't want to run it, we'll just insert a house ad."**

With the tentative confirmation, you are saying, in effect, "To make it easy for you, I'm willing to let you have your cake and eat it too." This type of confirmation creates a commitment that is not legally binding, but has a powerful psychological effect.

TYPES OF CONFIRMATION

11.5 The Pilot

The Pilot—also known as the puppy dog close—is a valuable service that is often misused. It works when used to assure customer satisfaction as an adjunct to a commitment. It fails when used to confirm a sale.

Some salespeople misuse the pilot by trying to gain commitment when no commitment is present. The salesperson says, "Look, I can see you're undecided. Why don't you take six gross and see how you like them. If you like them, we'll do business. If you don't like them, I'll take them back." The problem is, without a genuine commitment, your customer is going to take the product, look for all the things that are wrong with it and find reasons *not* to buy. The lack of commitment combined with having the product forced upon her will create a negative selective perception. It's human nature.

The right way to use the pilot confirmation is to assure customer satisfaction when a commitment exists. When a customer says to you, in essence, "If everything you have said is true, then I want to buy," offering a trial run or sample can help you back up your claims. It's an easy way to help a customer become comfortable with the commitment she has already made. In this situation, selective perception will be positive— your customer will look for things that are right. This is why the pilot is a powerful tool for assuring customer satisfaction, not for confirming the sale.

?FYI

TYPES OF CONFIRMATION

11.6 Timing and Perceived Value

Salespeople often ask, "If I'm in the middle of my presentation and my prospect gives strong buying signals, should I stop and ask for the sale?" The answer is yes, but no.

Yes, you don't want to continue to the end of your presentation and risk boring your customer. But no, you can't drop everything and ask for the sale. Why? You have to create a perceived value in the prospect's mind by furnishing relevant features and benefits that put everything in the proper perspective. The key is to speed up your presentation and cut out any unnecessary parts. Get to the most relevant points quickly, and *then* ask for the sale.

When should prices be revealed? Ideally, only after the perceived value of the product or service is high. If, in the middle of your presentation, you are asked, "How much is it?", you should tactfully avoid giving the price. To give the price at that point would risk presenting a lopsided view of the product (and, therefore, an unreasonable price). Finish your presentation and then give the price. That way it will have more meaning and a higher probability of being accepted.

There are many ways to avoid giving prices. The most honest way is to say, "With all due respect, a price without a context is meaningless and unfair to both of us. If you don't mind, I'd like to tell you more about my product before getting to the price." You can also say, "There are a number of different plans (or variables) possible. I'd like to give you a better feel for our product/service and then see which plan suits you best. At that point, I will tell you exactly what the price is for *your* plan." If you sense that this is acceptable to your prospect, you could continue by asking more information-gathering questions, if necessary.

If your prospect asks again, offer a range of prices. If you are asked a third time, give the price. It is better to risk a misunderstanding (lack of perceived value) than to risk making your prospect angry.

Giving a price before creating a sense of value in the customer's mind is a disservice to the salesperson and the customer. In a sense, the customer is misled because he does not know what he is getting for the price, which makes the price meaningless. He is more apt to reject the product or service based on inadequate information. At the same time, the salesperson is hindered from accurately presenting his product or service and loses sales from customers' lack of understanding. Both should be avoided.

? FYI

TYPES OF CONFIRMATION

11.7 Assumptive Confirmations

WHAT'S IN IT FOR YOU

- Use assumptive confirmations to respectfully and tactfully determine whether your prospect is ready to buy

Assumptive Confirmations are generally abused by traditional, manipulative salespeople. They are taught to use this "closing technique" as a way to force the sale. The basic premise is, if you don't give your prospect the choice of saying no, you will make the sale.

Nonmanipulative salespeople use these confirmations differently. They use them as *trial confirmations*—questions that determine whether a prospect is ready to make a commitment. The assumption is not that you are going to force the sale, but that you and your prospect have been and continue to be on the same wavelength. The sale, therefore, is a given. Even so, assumptive confirmations must be used respectfully.

The Alternate-Choice Confirmation. This is a common traditional confirmation in which the prospect is given the choice between two positive alternatives. The manipulative use of this option seeks to replace the yes or no choice that most prospects want with a pressured "yes or yes" choice.

The alternate-choice confirmation is used by nonmanipulative salespeople when the prospect's buying signals are green. The customer is saying, verbally or nonverbally, "Yes, I'm buying." It would be unnecessary to ask for the sale. In this situation, it is perfectly acceptable to give your customer the choice of two positives.

> **"Do you want delivery made to your New York warehouse or your New Jersey distribution center?"**

> **"Do you want special terms or is our standard 2 percent 30 days good enough for you?"**

> **"Do you want the standard service contract or would you like more comprehensive coverage?"**

Another nonmanipulative way to use the alternate-choice confirmation is to test the waters. If a prospect's buying signals are unclear, you could ask, "Would you want the modular office system or the custom-designed layout?" Notice that the nonmanipulative way of asking is to state the question hypothetically, saying "Would you . . . ?" rather than "Do you . . . ?"

The Minor Point. Another assumptive closing technique used by the manipulative school of selling is the minor point. It seeks to get a prospect to answer a question about some minor detail of the product or service. If the question is answered, the assumption is that the sale is made. It's not a very safe assumption, unless the buying signals are clearly positive.

Nonmanipulative salespeople can use minor points as stepping stones to confirming the sale, but with a slight twist. The questions are asked not with the assumption of the sale being made, but as a way to get the prospect to visualize and mentally own the product/service. This is part of information-gathering and is an effective way to get someone involved in the sales process. Again, the questions are asked hypothetically, with the premise being, "If you were to buy . . . " or "Imagine yourself using this product/service . . . " Some examples:

> **"Would you use your cellular phone in just one car or would you want a portable that can be moved?"**

> **"Do you want to train your entire staff simultaneously or one at a time?"**

> **"Do you want your VIPs picked up at the airport in a limousine or a shuttle bus?"**

We all know that a picture is worth a thousand words. When you get your prospect to visualize the use of your product/service, you smooth the way for his or her acceptance of it.

Physical Action or Order-Blank Confirmation. Here again, the assumption for a traditional salesperson is, "If I just act as though the sale were made, my prospect may not object." To accomplish this, the salesperson begins filling out an order form without first asking for the sale. As we discussed previously, the nonmanipulative salesperson would only use an assumptive confirmation like this if the prospect's buying signals were clearly green. It is rude, insensitive, and absurd to ignore yellow or red buying signals by acting as if all is well.

❓ F Y I

TYPES OF CONFIRMATION

11.8 The Direct Confirmation

There is nothing wrong with being straightforward and confidently asking for the sale. It is the natural thing to do after you have studied the prospect's needs, proposed a solution, and covered the relevant benefits. Yet the majority of salespeople fail to ask for an order. Every year corporate surveys are conducted to determine the shortcomings of salespeople. Without fail, corporate buyers report that salespeople flop by being poor listeners and failing to ask for the sale.

Fear of rejection is the only reason someone would fail to ask for an order. If you have conducted the sales process in a consultative, nonmanipulative way, you have nothing to fear. The lines of communication are open. You have sought your prospect's agreement every step of the way. Now that it is time to ask for the sale, it's an easy step, especially if you have been observing buying signals.

Many buyers appreciate a no-nonsense approach to confirming the sale. There's nothing wrong with asking, "May I have your business?" It is direct and polite. But be careful who you use it with. While directors and socializers may appreciate it, relaters and thinkers may be put off.

Whatever you do, avoid asking for the sale in a negative say, such as "Why don't we write up an order?" That's an invitation to rejection, and it sounds terribly wishy-washy. Exude confidence in yourself and your product/service. Try:

"Let's set up your account next week so you can start using the service as soon as possible."

"I have a truck coming into this part of town on Thursday, and I'd love to put your order on it."

"I know you're going to be happy with this system. Can I turn in your order today?"

Automobile salespeople use the direct approach all the time. They ask their prospects, "What will it take to get you to buy today?" If they get a decent answer, they'll know what is important to the customer and what aspects of the sale need to be emphasized (price, monthly payments, trade-in, etc.). Then they think to themselves, "Let the games begin."

TYPES OF CONFIRMATION

- Understand when to motivate a prospect with a promotional special or an impending price increase

11.9 The "Act Now" Confirmation

Nonmanipulative salespeople don't rush or pressure their prospects into making commitments. Nevertheless, there are times when a price or quantity will only be honored for a limited time. Telling your prospect about price increases or promotional specials can motivate an undecided buyer by creating a sense of urgency.

> **"My company has announced that prices will go up by 5 percent next month due to supplier increases. If I can write up your order now, you can stock up before the increase takes effect."**

The "Act Now" Confirmation must only be used when it is based in fact. It should never be used deceptively. There is no denying that some people—primarily thinkers and relaters—are slow decision makers. Sometimes they need to be motivated to get off the fence. When you are selling something that a prospect truly needs, there is nothing wrong with urging him or her to act now to save time or money or avoid inconvenience.

The "Act Now" Confirmation can create wonders for your reputation. You will be a hero any time you prevent a customer from running short of inventory or paying higher prices.

TYPES OF CONFIRMATION

11.10 The Call-Back Confirmation

Most sales are not confirmed on the first attempt. In fact, statistics show that many salespeople need to ask for the sale an average of four to six times. That means a lot of people are going to say no before they say yes. Every salesperson leaves presentations empty handed now and then. Don't get discouraged and write off those accounts. Find valid reasons to call them back.

When you call back, make it clear that you have a new reason for calling. No one is going to meet with you again if you plan to repeat yourself verbatim and hope for a different outcome.

A common reason for a call-back is to provide requested information or new data that will interest your customer. For example, "Mr. Smith, after I left the other day I became aware of a company that is using our system for the same application you have in mind. I've got some of their data on the system's effectiveness and was hoping to bring it by to show you."

When you return for the call-back, give a concise review of your presentation. Be sensitive to your prospect's time constraints, but try to review all the salient benefits discussed in the original presentation. While the last meeting may be fresh in your mind because you took notes, your customer will remember only a small fraction of what was said. For this reason, use reassuring phrases such as "you remember . . . ", "we agreed last time that . . . ", and "you may recall that . . . "

There's no guarantee that a call-back will help you make a sale. But it does guarantee that you will be face-to-face with your prospect—and *that* is the only way a sale is possible.

TYPES OF CONFIRMATION

11.11 Confirming by Style

Relater

Relators don't rush into decisions. They often solicit other people's opinoins and then make up their minds. To help with the decision-making process, lay out a clear action plan and spell out the safest, most logical course of action that you are recommending. Relaters like guarantees because they minimize risk.

A relater who says, "I have to think about it" may be avoiding the discomfort of saying no. Find out the truth and work with it. It is not wise to rush a relater. You may, however, have to give a gentle nudge. This is done by acting as a consultant. You can say something like, "We both agree that this (solution) will solve your (problem), so why don't we go ahead and implement it now?"

Another gentle prod is, "Jean, I recommend you implement this plan. I would't say that if I didn't really mean it."

Socializer

By the time you get to the confirming phase of the sale with a socializer, he's your friend. So ask directly, "Where do we go from here?" or "What's our next step?"

Capitalize on the enthusiasm that socializers exude, but don't throw cold water on the sale by getting very technical or insisting on filling out paperwork.

If you normally draw up a letter of commitment, have it prepared in advance and go over it quickly with your new customer. You can also send it as a follow-up to the confirmation. If there is someone other than your prospect who can work on the details, find that person and fill out the order forms with him. If your prospect must do it, make it quick. Socializers hate paperwork and details.

Like directors, thinkers like logical options that are backed up with proof. Unlike directors and socializers, thinkers are not comfortable with snap decisions. In fact, if given the time, some will analyze a decision to death.

Thinkers are researchers and will compare your product/service to the competition. You can suggest features that your prospect should look for when making comparisons. Point out your company's strong points. You can even do a cost-benefit analysis for your prospect, but expect him to verify it before making a decision.

Thinkers, like relaters, may need to be pushed gently. Do this the same way you would nudge a relater.

Thinker

You can be direct with directors. Ask, "Based on what we've just discussed, are you interested in . . . " Often they will tell you yes or no. Some will put you off as if they have not yet decided, when, in fact, they aren't even thinking about your proposal. If a director is too busy or does not have enough information, your proposal will not sink in and make an impression.

Give directors options with probable outcomes. Include information on price versus quality. Include benefits that she cares about and leave out the irrelevant.

You must let a director make her own decision. Remember, she has a need for power and that need cannot be ignored by a pushy sales-person.

Director

⬤12 Making the transition to management

WHAT'S IN IT FOR YOU

- Understand and begin to develop the skills required of sales managers
- Increase your knowledge of the many techniques used to motivate a sales team
- Learn to conduct sales contests
- Learn to run effective sales meetings
- Learn to manage people the way they want to be managed—according to their behavioral style

Does this scenario sound familiar?

You're a top producer. One day you walk into the office and hear the boss wants to see you. You go into the boss's office and are told, "You're being promoted to sales manager! Congratulations!" You find out later that you'll be making less for a while, but your responsibilities will increase. That's a shock: you'd rather stay out in the field making more money with less responsibility.

Like it or not, it's the way of the world. Almost every company takes its best and puts them in the position of passing their expertise on to others. Is it a good idea? No, but that doesn't seem to change things.

The skills needed to be a top salesperson are not necessarily the same skills required to be a good manager. In fact, many are almost directly opposite. Most salespeople, by nature, are social animals with little interest in organizational skills and even less inclination to become more organized. Most good managers, on the other hand, are methodical, systems-oriented people who get their paperwork done on time. They also possess many other skills, as you will see in FYI 12.2.

Most newly promoted sales managers are over their heads . . . and they know it. Fortunately, upper management also knows it, so there is a grace period during which new managers can stumble while they learn.

Being a manager is a complex position. You have to learn it quickly, and do the best job you can. Some of the ideas in this section will help you get your feet wet . . . and then some.

[1] The authors would like to thank Rick Barrera for many of his ideas on this subject. A sales, customer service and sales management consultant and trainer, Rick can be reached in California at (619) 456-4050.

?FYI

BUILDING ON YOUR PAST SUCCESS

12.1 The New Sales Manager Syndrome

Mistake Number One: Overcontrol

Most sales managers begin by trying to overcontrol their sales team. They do this out of habit. As a salesperson, everything you did to be the best was under your control. You planned your territory, decided how many customers to call on, and honed your selling skills. Now, things are different. Your performance is judged by the performance of your sales team. The key to your success has more variables, most of which are out of your direct control. The natural reaction is to try to engineer your success by overcontrolling your sales team.

Mistake Number Two: Mistaking Activity For Accomplishment

As a salesperson, you thrived on activity that had an immediate outcome. At the end of the day you could look back and count the number of customers you contacted, letters you wrote, meetings you attended, and orders you wrote. Your schedule was filled with activity.

Now, you've been put in an office and told to run the ship. There is nothing concrete to do. Your tasks aren't neatly laid out before you. At this point, most people jump into activities that appear productive but are actually just time-consuming. If this impulse isn't checked, they begin calling on accounts themselves or shuffling territories. The mess gets worse—unless old habits are changed.

Solution: Manage People, Not Things

First, resist the temptation to accomplish everything yourself. Your role as sales manager is not unlike the role of a Hollywood director. Film directors coach their actors from behind the scenes. They never insult their talented people by acting for them. If guidance is needed, the director steps in to provide it. The actor, however, is responsible for the final performance.

By managing people and not things we mean that you should forget about balancing territories, opening new accounts, and reaching quotas. Instead, concentrate on nurturing your team into a committed, high-energy unit. If you work on the people side of managing, everything else will fall into place. This means creating a positive, supportive work environment and providing on going training, coaching, and feedback.

Skills Needed. At first, the most important skills will be the people skills that you mastered as a top salesperson: Listening, questioning, feedback, body language, and relationship strategies. Later you will have to work on and master management skills: recruiting and selecting, settling policy, facilitating growth, evaluating performance, setting budgets and understanding accounting, along with promotion and legal and disciplinary details.

As if all that weren't enough, you need to possess sales and leadership skills: the ability to motivate people, structure rewards, create a positive ambience, manage territories, give performance feedback, run a sales meeting, and coach new hires.

How To Get What You Want. Of the three major skills required of sales managers—people, management and sales/leadership skills—which do you think will get you the performance that you want? *People skills*. The successful sales manager gets what he or she wants by being an effective communicator and supportive mentor.

To do all this, you must not only invest in your sales team, but in yourself as well.

BUILDING ON YOUR PAST SUCCESS

- Identify the many skills a successful sales manager must sharpen

12.2 The Skills of the Sales Manager

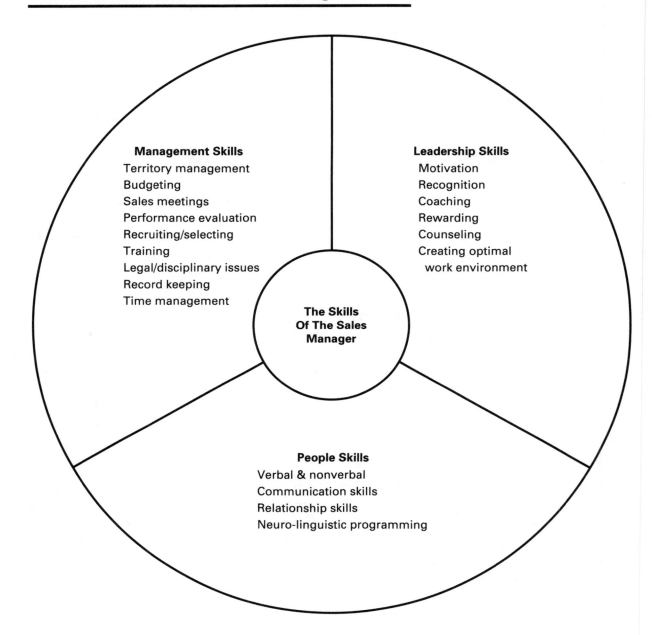

Management Skills
Territory management
Budgeting
Sales meetings
Performance evaluation
Recruiting/selecting
Training
Legal/disciplinary issues
Record keeping
Time management

Leadership Skills
Motivation
Recognition
Coaching
Rewarding
Counseling
Creating optimal
    work environment

**The Skills
Of The Sales
Manager**

People Skills
Verbal & nonverbal
Communication skills
Relationship skills
Neuro-linguistic programming

BUILDING ON YOUR PAST SUCCESS

12.3 Motivating Your Sales Team

Whether you are a new sales manager or a veteran, one of your most daunting tasks is the continual motivation of your sales team. Motivating people is one of those leadership skills that is not developed overnight, but the following pointers will help you get a handle on this fine art.

1. Be a *results* leader. Define job objectives and expected results with each of your salespeople.

2. Encourage participation in decision-making and goal-setting.

3. Encourage personal growth and provide opportunities for such.

4. Keep the job interesting and challenging.

5. Tie job satisfaction to level of productivity.

6. Reward beginners, even just for learning.

7. Keep lines of communication open.

8. Cater to every member of the sales team, not just top performers.

9. Solicit the team's input for contests and incentives.

10. Involve the CEO in motivation.

11. Design flexible incentive programs that give people things they really want.

12. Commend both long- and short-term sales goals, by rewarding follow-through that keeps long-term customers as well as opening new accounts.

13. Sell the benefits of incentive programs and quotas to your team. Remember the difference between convincing versus forcing and influencing versus controlling.

14. Never reward poor performance; coach, train and counsel instead.

Five Ways to Develop a High-Performance Team

1. Give them a shared sense of mission.

2. Give them clear and attainable goals.

3. Give them frequent, objective feedback and recognition.

4. Give them rewards for performance.

5. Give them timely support and help.

SALES CONTESTS

- Discover the rationale behind sales contests

12.4 Why Sales Contests?

Sales contests are popular, but do you really know why? As a sales manager, you should understand their purpose.

Purpose. To generate excitement, and motivate, reward, and recognize results.

Value. To increase revenue and profits, acquire new accounts, create a positive work environment, improve salespeople's knowledge of their territories, hone specific selling skills, promote specific products or services, increase off-season sales, improve collections, increase contacts per day, etc.

Reactions. Top performers excel without contests; bottom people are motivated by the desire to simply keep their jobs. Contests are designed to motivate the middle performers.

Requirements. To be fair, a contest must be efficient and equitable. *Efficient* means the contest will direct sales efforts to achieve specific goals with a minimum of wasted time or effort. *Equitable* means that both new and old salespeople have an equal opportunity to win.

Types of Contests. An open-ended contest pits each salesperson against his or her own past performance. A closed-end contest pits one group, territory, or company division against another.

   Individual quota (open-end) contests, because they are based on past performance, put people who have saturated their territories at a disadvantage. There are ways to use handicaps or structure the contest fairly. For example, the contest could be for the most orders, not the highest dollar amount.

   Multiple award contests spread awards among the greatest number of people. This type of contest can incorporate individual quotas as subcontests. For example, a quarterly contest could be divided into three monthly contests. People can win both categories. Or multiple achievement levels could be set and different prizes awarded for achieving 90 percent, 100 percent or 110 percent of individual quotas.

   Team award contests reward everyone on the team and can include individual quotas as subcontests. These team efforts can increase teamwork, charge the work environment, and even include inside salespeople, support staff and customer service reps. This can result in more rapid processing of orders, better customer service and improved interdepartmental communication.

SALES CONTESTS

12.5 Contest Themes, Timing and Rules

Theme. Contests should be built on a theme—athletic events or a simulated Olympics, financial metaphors, rising thermometers, treasure hunts, lotteries, mystery or detective themes, and so on. Keep two things in mind when devising a theme. First, make it familiar to everyone. Don't use a sports model that everyone will not understand or identify with. Second, try to link your theme to your company, to the goal of the contest, or to the grand prize, especially an expensive one.

Timing. Timing is crucial to any sales contest and is, therefore, often reflected in the theme. When the theme is related to time, it becomes a natural point on which to build the promotion of the contest. Timing opportunities might include seasonal downturns, a competitor's annual promotional campaign, holidays, community events, world events (e.g., America's Cup, Olympics, presidential campaign, Berlin Wall), introduction of a new product, and opening of a new branch.

The contest should be planned far in advance so that brochures, samples, and promotional items can be created before the big push. It should not, however, be announced until the last minute.

Selecting the correct time to announce the contest is critical to its success. A common criticism of sales contests is that they merely affect when sales are made; that is, salespeople hold back before the beginning of the contest and oversell before it is over. To avoid these problems:

1. Announce the contest immediately prior to the starting date.

2. Do not conduct contests at the same time each year. They become predictable.

3. Tie contest goals to company objectives such as gaining new customers, increasing follow-through, improving customer service, learning new sales skills, or developing better work habits.

4. Schedule contests to end just prior to a heavy selling season to eliminate post-contest slumps.

5. Set rules that specifically forbid holding customer orders and overstocking. *Also, deduct any returns from contest results for one month after the contest has concluded.*

6. Maintain the sales team's increased motivation after the contest by introducing something new—perhaps a new product to sell, new selling tools, or a new sales program.

Rules. Rules must be clear and disseminated in a way that prevents any misunderstandings. Your rules must include:

1. What must be accomplished to win

2. Starting and ending dates

3. How sales will be credited (by volume, number of orders, dollar amount)

4. How joint sales will be handled

5. How contest ties will be handled

6. Whether contest prizes are exchangeable

7. When contest prizes will be awarded

8. How canceled orders or denied credit will be handled.

SALES CONTESTS

12.6 Contest Promotion, Duration, Awards, Budget

Promotion. Effective sales contests require a dramatic kickoff, solid promotion, and an impressive finish and award ceremony. The sales manager plays an important role in its day-to-day promotion. Daily encouragement, weekly announcements of standings, and other upbeat news will motivate the sales team.

Surprise mini-contests are also useful for sustaining momentum. For example, if the grand prize is a vacation, mini-contests could award luggage, cameras, or typhoid shots.

Sales Contest Duration. How long should a contest run? Length is important to success. The perfect duration is difficult to pinpoint, but it should be determined by six factors:

- *Contest Goals*—Contest should be long enough to allow the accomplishment of its objectives.

- *Logical Calender Periods*—Sales contests should begin and end on dates that mark the changing of months, fiscal quarters, or some other logical division of the year.

- *Seasonal Nature of Products/Services*—Trying to stimulate off-season sales may be more frustrating than productive. No incentives will increase the sales of heaters in the summer and air conditioners in the winter. Be logical.

- *Complete Territory Coverage*—Allow enough time for salespeople to achieve maximum results.

- *Sales Team Morale*—Determining how long salespeople can sell at a sustained pace without losing enthusiasm is extremely important.

- *Award Budget*—The higher the value of the award, the longer the contest should last, so that sufficient sales can be generated to cover contest and awards expenses.

Types of Awards

The type and cost of the awards, especially the grand prize, should be consistent with the expected results of the contest. Cash, merchandise, travel, recognition and honor prizes (rings, membership in President's Club) are preferred in this order: travel, recognition, merchandise, cash. This order varies by industry, income, and the economic climate. To play it safe, select awards that your salespeople want, not what you want. Ask members of the sales team; give them several options to stimulate ideas. You can always allow the winners to select their prizes from a catalog.

Often salespeople will say they want money, but research has proven that cash prizes are the least effective motivators. Salespeople know that they will turn around and spend the money paying bills. The most effective motivator is a prize that they would not ordinarily buy themselves, such as an exotic vacation or merchandise.

Sales Contest Budget

There are a couple of generalizations to keep in mind when you develop a contest budget.

1. A contest should pay for itself.

2. The budget should be based on contest goals and the expected increase in profits and income.

3. Ten percent of the expected increase in sales should be spent on the contest.

4. Seventy-five percent of the contest budget should be spent on prizes, 25 percent on promotion.

5. Projecting what the contest will generate is difficult. Use past contests as guidelines.

SALES CONTESTS

12.7 Short Versus Long Contests

Short Contests

A short contest lasts one to six weeks. Its advantages are:

1. Less time for salespeople's interest to wane.

2. Contest goals appear more attainable to salespeople, assuring a high level of participation and motivation.

3. Salespeople have to get started immediately; there is no time to procrastinate.

4. The level of enthusiasm remains constant.

5. Appropriate for promoting specific products/services.

6. When combined with promotional discounts, they create a sense of urgency that motivates customers to buy.

There are some disadvantages to short sales contests, however.

1. Some new salespeople will not have sufficient time to get started and excel in their performance.

2. Short contests, with less expensive prizes, sometimes fail to generate enough interest among the sales team.

3. Although they can energize self-motivated salespeople, they often fail to motivate poor performers who find it difficult to produce under pressure.

Short contests are best employed when the contest objectives are limited and simple, and the monetary and psychological value of the awards is modest.

Long Contests

Long contests are two months to one year in length. Their advantages are:

1. Salespeople have sufficient time to produce far-reaching results.

2. More exciting, expensive awards can be given.

3. An entire product line or array of services can be promoted.

4. Year-round sales contests and incentive programs are common. The winners are generally recognized at the company's annual meeting or convention; prizes are significant cash awards, vacations, or membership in elite company "clubs."

The disadvantages of long-term sales contests are:

1. Because they tend to lose their novelty, their motivational impact decreases with time. This can be overcome by dividing year-long contests into quarterly programs with slightly different, but related themes.

2. The monetary value of awards must be sufficiently attractive to keep salespeople interested. This may prove difficult for small companies.

3. Rewards that are deferred for too long may lose their appeal to participants.

? F Y I

- Learn the key elements that make sales contests succeed

SALES CONTESTS

12.8 Contest Do's and Don'ts

Ineffective Contests Are Guilty Of:

- Rewarding only one winner

- Taking place at the same time each year

- Setting the same goals for the contest each year

- Awarding the same prizes each year

- Giving some salespeople or territories an advantage

- Leaving out sales support staff and other company employees

- Not being tied to specific, new training.

Make Your Sales Contests Succeed By:

- Appointing one person to administer the contest efficiently

- Setting realistic goals, attainable by everyone, thereby making the contest fair

- Analyzing current markets, sales programs and company goals before designing the contest

- Creating a catchy theme and never letting the contest grow monotonous

- Spelling out the rules so there are no misunderstandings

- Selecting exciting, top quality prizes

- Planning far in advance so all systems can support the extra effort

- Continually promoting the contest and the awards banquet

- Announcing the results soon after the contest ends

- Evaluating the effectiveness of the contest for future use.

? F Y I

WHAT'S IN IT FOR YOU

- Learn how to structure a relevant meeting that holds your
  sales team's attention

SALES MEETINGS

12.9 Start on the Right Foot

There are two things a manager must accomplish in every sales meeting. You must hold your salespeople's attention, and you must teach them something. If you fail to do both, you are wasting everyone's time. Well-run sales meetings can mean the difference between stimulating and enervating your team.

Sales meetings can be compared to a tune-up on a car. A periodic tune-up, performed properly, keeps your car running at maximum efficiency. A well-tuned car is fun to drive. A poorly done tune-up, no matter how frequently it is performed, does not improve the car's efficiency; in fact, it could make it worse. A car that is out of tune is sluggish and no fun to drive. Similarly, uninspired sales meetings rob the sales team of energy rather than giving it a lift.

Where Meetings Go Wrong. Sales meetings most often fail because they lack form and/or content. A lack of form means a meeting provides useful information, but in a way that reduces the chances that people will remember it. When you bore people, they doodle instead of listening and taking notes. Unfortunately, this is very common.

Your form may be good, but the meeting must also have content. As you hold their attention you must get them fired up *and* give them information they can immediately put to use in the field. The only exception is the meeting in which your primary goal is to raise spirits.

Be Careful What You Talk About. Sales meetings that become preoccupied with administrative details, logistics, paperwork, and record-keeping trivia are guaranteed to turn people off. Also, meetings should not discuss an individual's problem unless the problem is typical and its solution would be valuable to the entire team. For example, one team member may be having difficulty getting accounts to pay on time. This would be relevant to the team if others are having the same problem. If they are not, there is no sense wasting their time. The sales meeting is a time for group growth.

Keep It Relevant. A sales meeting can fail if its topic is irrelevant. Too many sales managers plan a meeting around a subject that is inappropriate to the sales team's needs or their marketing philosophy and practices. Instead of taking the time to discover their needs, the sales manager makes an assumption and the meeting turns out to be virtually useless. This is one of the many reasons why sales meetings should be tied in with an integrated, comprehensive sales program. If there is an overall picture, all the pieces of the puzzle will make sense.

? F Y I

SALES MEETINGS

12.10 Where, When, How Often and About What?

Where and How Often. Some companies have all the members of their sales team in one city; others are spread throughout the world. Where you hold your meetings—and how often you hold them—will depend on how spread out your sales team is. The ideal situation is to have everyone get together once a week; once or twice a month if people are spread out.

The frequency of your sales meetings will hinge on how efficiently and effectively your sales team is operating and the amount of new information or training you need to disseminate. If your team is a well-established, smoothly running machine, it needs less maintenance than a new, insecure team. A new team needs training, coaching, motivation, and support to be sure they get a handle on things.

When. The time and day of the week should be decided by consensus. Monday morning meetings will charge everyone up for the week, but they cut into selling time. To avoid interfering with the workweek, many managers choose Saturday mornings. If you do this, expect groans of resistance. If you insist on Saturday morning meetings, consider holding them less often.

Where. The best place to have a meeting is away from the office and all its distractions. Some companies rent meeting rooms in restaurants so they can combine business with pleasure. Buying the sales team breakfast or lunch is a nice gesture. It shows that the company values its people and doesn't mind spending money to make them happy.

If an outside meeting room is beyond the company's budget, any place within the company's offices will do if it is away from busy phones and co-workers who are trying to concentrate. Sales meetings can become loud when the team laughs, cheers, applauds, and interacts in dozens of other spirit-building ways. Their enthusiasm should not be squelched by the practicalities of an office full of workers.

What Meetings Can Be About. The answer is simple—anything that will improve the team's performance, directly or indirectly. Here is a partial list to get you started:

Industry knowledge	Product knowledge
Market/customer knowledge	Customer service
Cold calling	Finding and qualifying prospects
Studying customers' needs	Role-playing presentations
Handling resistance	Confirming the sale
Systematic follow-up	Building goodwill
Time management	Pricing and credit policies
Negotiation	Contests and special promotions.

❓ F Y I

SALES MEETINGS

12.11 Sales Meetings That Work

A sales meeting should be well organized and have a primary goal. Getting together for a "rap session" does not work and is a waste of time. Meetings should be held for one of five basic reasons.

1. **Train or retrain.** The more your salespeople know, the better they will perform. Most salespeople forget the majority of their training and use only those skills that help them get by. They may be meeting their quotas, but continued training will help them exceed their goals.

   Training should be more practical than theoretical. Information must be specific and useful in order to help your team. They should be able to leave the meeting and immediately implement what you have taught.

   Ongoing training should be consistent with an overall sales philosophy. For example, if your team's philosophy is nonmanipulative selling, don't hold a training session on high-pressure closing techniques. Strive for consistency.

   After the initial training, no matter how long it takes, retraining will be necessary. Sales meetings allow you to see weak spots in the team and to strengthen them before they cave in. They best way to manage crises is to avoid them.

2. **Improve communications.** Regardless of other goals, sales meetings should always improve communication. Salespeople are social animals who enjoy belonging to a family. The sales team is a family, and you are its mother and father. As such, an important part of your job is making all members of the team feel that they belong.

   One way to keep the lines of communication open is to be sure your people hear about policy changes *from you*. Hearing about something through the grapevine does not foster a sense of community. When there is good or bad news to share, tell everyone at once in a sales meeting.

3. **Motivate the team.** As sales manager, you are also a cheerleader. Keeping the team's morale high is one of those leadership skills that comes with the job. Raising that morale is a legitimate reason to have a sales meeting. In fact, if that is not the primary reason for the meeting, it should always be the secondary reason. *Your people should always leave a sales meeting feeling better than when they arrived.*

   One part of motivation is recognition. Salespeople thrive on recognition for their positive accomplishments. You should never publicly berate someone for poor performance. In fact, people learn by being told what to do, not what not to do. Use sales meetings as a time to give recognition to top performers and people who are improving.

4. **Solve problems.** You are also a trouble shooter. You have to spot the bugs in the sales machinery and work them out. A meeting can be devoted to discussing problems, but make sure they pertain to everyone. Again, this should not be a free-form rap session, but a structured meeting with a theme.

   Often, the best problem-solving sessions are conducted with the team broken up into small groups This gives each person a chance to have his or her problem addressed by the group members. *It's a well-known fact that salespeople learn most from each other.*

5. **Introduce new products or contests.** This is the best way to introduce a new product or a sales contest. And do it with a bang. Get everyone fired up and ready to roll. The importance of a new product or contest can be dramatically enhanced with an appearance by your CEO.

   Keep your finger on the pulse of your team, be perceptive enough to see what your people need to learn to excel, and you will circumvent major stumbling blocks.

SALES MEETINGS

12.12 Encourage Participation

When members of your sales team interact, they learn more than when they sit and listen to you. Spend as little time as possible in front of the group. Begin the meeting, take care of necessary business, introduce the meeting's theme or purpose, and then get your people involved in a learning experience as soon as possible. Having your audience participate assures you that they are paying attention and learning. Participation can be active or passive. Active participation might entail breaking the team into small groups to discuss a problem. Passive participation could mean asking everyone to answer a question in their own minds.

One way to encourage participation and learning is to ask people to take notes. Note-taking really does help people learn more quickly. It creates a triple impression—you hear, write, and see.

Another way to get people participating is to use your salespeople as trainers in those areas in which they excel. If you have someone who is particularly good on the phone, have him or her give a ten-minute how-to presentation. This boosts the presenter's ego and motivates others to excel so they can be the trainer another time.

There are many ways that participation pays off for you and your team. By building participation into each sales meeting, you will:

- *Tap everyone's creativity.* The sales team often has the answers to sales and service issues because they are in the field every day.

- *Create a team spirit.* Participation makes everyone feel a valued part of the team.

- *Stimulate interest.* Interacting with other salespeople encourages everyone to compare notes on methods, successes, and failures.

- *Reward and recognize.* Salespeople love recognition from each other. Participation increases recognition.

- *Hone skills.* Participating in role-playing and other forms of rehearsal helps salespeople grasp the application of a selling principle.

- *Increase motivation for self-improvement.* As time passes, your people will see improvements in themselves and others. Participating in this process will encourage them to continue working on themselves to be the best they can be.

- *Evaluate salespeople in-depth.* By observing salespeople while they interact, role-play, and discuss their problems, you will get a better idea of their abilities, shortcomings, and needs. This can't be done when everyone is simply sitting and listening to a speech.

- *Receive feedback on effectiveness of training.* After you have trained your team, you need to monitor their progress. The questions they ask, their concerns, and their performance in role-playing will give you a great deal of insight into the effectiveness of your training.

The sales manager's job is not to always solve his team members' problems. Often he or she is wiser to shed enough light for people to discover their own answers. Make yourself available to offer your insights, but only after they have done some thinking on their own. Remember the adage about teaching a man to fish rather than catching the fish for him.

SALES MEETINGS

12.13 It's Showtime!

An effective sales meeting leaves a lasting impression. It should be something special—not necessarily a high-budget production, but a memorable, effective tool that will have an impact on your sales team. There are many ways to achieve this goal, but the bottom line is to educate, entertain, and motivate your audience. Keep these basic ideas in mind when planning your meetings:

- Clearly define the purpose of the meeting.

- Make sure its objectives cannot be accomplished in a more effective manner, such as by phone, individual meetings, memos, or field coaching.

- Think of people outside your department—within and outside the company—who can enhance the meeting with a presentation.

- Make the meeting as short and powerful as possible.

- Prepare your materials well in advance.

- After the meeting, appraise the meeting's effectiveness with feedback from your sales team.

A sales meeting is very similar to a sales presentation. You must sell your team on something—a new skill, a certain attitude, a new product, a contest, or some other good reason to be away from the field. To do so, you will use some basic sales skills—discover needs, get attention, stimulate interest, make a presentation, create a desire, and stimulate action (using a variety of media). In short, put as much energy and imagination into "selling the troops" as you would into selling a customer.

? F Y I

SALES MEETINGS

12.14 What to Do in Sales Meetings

You've got approximately one hour to fill at every meeting. What are you doing to do?

Show Films and Videos. Even films or videos that were not produced specifically for your company can offer generic information in entertaining ways. More important than the video or film is the discussion that follows. Be sure to leave ample time for a thorough discussion.

Update Product Knowledge. It never hurts to review the features and benefits of your products or services. To do this, 1) Ask people in advance to prepare a *brief* presentation on *one* feature and benefit of your product/service; or 2) Call on people during the meeting to speak extemporaneously about a feature and its benefit.

Have Fun with Game Shows. To test product knowledge, create a meeting based on a TV game show. Use questions that test product, service, customer, and market knowledge. You can form teams or let people play individually. Keep the questions short and give a prize to the winning person or team.

Discuss Case Histories. Present an actual or hypothetical situation and tell the group how the problem was solved. Then present another case and ask the group to solve it themselves, either individually or—better yet—in small groups.

Lead Role-Playing. This is an extremely valuable and common activity in sales meetings. It is so important that we will devote the next FYI to it. Stay tuned.

Increase Competition Knowledge. Bringing the competition's product into the meeting will add impact to the discussion. If that isn't possible, consider making a field trip, or use drawings, slides, and models that may be available. Be sure to get brochures, price lists, and specification sheets on the competition as well.

When discussing the competition, it is essential to be honest with your people. If another company's product/service is better, say so. Then tell them how your company compensates for that fact.

Allow Show-Off Time. One meeting or a short segment of every meeting can feature your top performer. Give him or her the floor and let the rest of the sales team ask questions after a brief talk about a particularly difficult account. This opportunity to brag and share insights, attitudes, and techniques lets the star bask in recognition and encourages others to work hard so they too may one day be in the spotlight. Present this session in a way that will encourage people rather than make them feel dejected.

It's one thing to be in the limelight and quite another to make that time informative for the sales team. To make sure your superstar will be interesting, organized, and instructive, have him or her answer the following (with some preparation in advance);

The major obstacle I was up against was . . .
My approach to this situation was . . .
The needs I uncovered were . . .
My proposal covered these points . . .
What made this proposal different was . . .
The resistance I encountered was . . .
I handled that resistance by . . .
The most important factor in confirming the sale was . . .
My follow-up consisted of . . .
This is where I/we stand now with this customer . . .

Conduct Brainstorming Sessions. Brainstorming sessions should be used infrequently because they do not have a high entertainment/educational value. Be aware, however, that the synergism of motivated salespeople working on a common problem produces a very creative atmosphere. Their collective brainpower can be used to come up with ideas on virtually any problem or challenge.

? FYI

SALES MEETINGS

12.15 The Fine Points of Role-Playing

Role-playing is one of the most common and effective training tools. It is a valid form of practice . . . and practice makes perfect.

- Role-playing is an excellent test of your sales team's ability.

- It improves sales skills with the least investment of time and money.

- It is the best way to practice handling resistance.

- It develops a salesperson's ability to think quickly.

- It provides experience in a setting that is less threatening than an actual sales call.

To most people, role-playing is like medicine—highly beneficial, but tough to swallow. It presents a threat even in the relatively safe environment of a sales meeting. For the first time the salesperson's performance is going to be honestly critiqued. To decrease anxiety and increase the effectiveness of a role-playing session, keep these rules in mind.

1. Get everyone to relax. Assure them the role-playing will not be evaluated, if it won't be. Tell them it is just a way to practice situations and stimulate discussion.

2. If the session will be videotaped, have the camera set up before everyone enters the room. Get people acclimated to being on camera by playfully interviewing them about nonsensical things and playing the tape back for laughs.

3. Role-play in small increments. Begin by discussing a problem and soliciting possible solutions from the group. When you hear an answer that is reasonable, begin a brief role-play by acknowledging the person's contribution and then saying, "That would work well. Let's try it. I'll be the customer, you be yourself; let's see how it might work out."

4. Once you have introduced role-playing as a group exercise, break people up into small groups. It is too threatening to ask beginners to role-play in front of a large sales team. Let them get their feet wet in front of smaller groups.

5. It is important to give each participant in the role-playing as much information as possible about their role. Prepare cue sheets that provide background on the prospect, the call objectives, and other specifics that will allow each person to conduct the role-play intelligently. It is rarely productive to throw people into a situation with directions like, "OK, Joe, you're the prospect; Mary, you're going to try to sell Joe a Model 832." Too vague.

6. Much of the success of the role-play depends on the realistic responses of the buyer. If the buyer is too easy or too tough, the game will not be helpful. Buyers should be instructed to be realistic and reasonable. If possible, give the buyer a criterion on which he or she will base acceptance of the deal For example, the buyer could be instructed to say no until the salesperson gives a benefit summary and asks for the sale.

7. If the role-playing will be critiqued, some ground rules should be set in the beginning. Comments should be positive, impersonal, and constructive. The players in the game often feel better if they are allowed to critique themselves first. Regardless of the quality of the exercise, always end on a positive note.

8. Lastly, the role-playing can be stopped at any time for a discussion.

WHAT'S IN IT FOR YOU

• Adapt your management
techniques to fit the
personality styles on
your sales team

SALES MEETINGS

12.16 Managing by Style

	Relater	Thinker	Director	Socializer
MOTIVATION	Show how something will benefit their relationships and strengthen their position with others.	Appeal to their need to be accurate and to their logical approach to things.	Provide them with options and clearly describe the probabilities of success in achieving goals.	Offer them incentives and testimonials. Show them how they can look good in the eyes of others.
RECOGNITION	Their teamwork, the way they are regarded by other people, their relationship skills, and their ability to "get along" with others.	Their efficiency, thought processes, organization, persistence, and accuracy.	Their achievements, upward mobility, and leadership potential.	Their appearance, creative ideas, persuasiveness, and charisma.
COUNSELING	Allow plenty of time to explore their feelings and understand the emotional side of the situation. They express their feelings, but indirectly. Draw them out through questioning and listening techniques. Create a nonthreatening environment.	Describe the process that you plan to follow. Outline how that process will produce the results they seek. Ask questions to help them give you the right information. Let them show you how much they know.	Stick to the facts. Draw them out by talking about the desired results. Then discuss their concerns. Focus on tasks more than feelings. Ask them how they would solve the problem.	Allow them plenty of opportunity to talk about things that are bothering them. Listen for facts and feelings. Many times Socializers merely need to "get something off their chest" and talking may solve the problem.
COACHING	Reassure them that what you are seeking to correct is the behavior only. Don't blame or judge the person; keep things focused on the behavior and its appropriateness.	Specify the exact behavior that is indicated and outline how you would like to see it changed. Establish checkpoints and times.	Describe what results are desired. Show them the gap between actual and desired. Suggest clearly the improvement that is needed and establish a time when they will get back to you.	Specify exactly what the problem happens to be and what behavior is required to eliminate the problem. Be sure you confirm in writing the agreed-upon behavior changes.
DELEGATING	Make a personal appeal to their loyalty. Give them the task, state the deadlines that need to be met and explain why it's important to do it in that specific way.	Take time to answer all their questions about structure and guidance. The more they understand the details, the more likely they will be to complete the task properly. Be sure to establish deadlines.	Give them the bottom line and then get out of their way. So that they can be more efficient, give them parameters, guidelines, and deadlines.	Make sure you get clear agreement. Establish checkpoints so that there is not a long period of time between progress reports.

13 Ethical and legal aspects of selling

WHAT'S IN IT FOR YOU

- Honesty is still the best rapport-builder. It's just that simple. Your long-term success in sales will depend on it.

WORKSHEET

SETTING YOUR STANDARDS

- Increase your awareness of your ethical values

13.1 Your Ethical Values

Answer yes or no to the following questions. Answer according to how you act, not how you think you *should* act.

1. Do you ever make disparaging remarks about the competition to help you win a customer? If so, are they ever unfair or exagerated? ☐ yes ☐ no

    Explain _____

2. Do you see your sales activities as being separate from and independent of your company and its image? ☐ yes ☐ no

    Explain _____

3. Considering the wealth they amassed, can you condone the business practices of people such as Ivan Boesky and Michael Milken? ☐ yes ☐ no

    Explain _____

4. Do you think getting rich is worth taking high risks for, including a possible prison term? ☐ yes ☐ no

    Explain _____

5. Do you think right and wrong are more situational than absolute? ☐ yes ☐ no

    Explain _____

6. Do you feel pressured to meet your sales quotas at any cost, regardless of what it takes? ☐ yes ☐ no

    Explain _____

7. Is the unspoken rule in your company, "Profits first, details later"? ☐ yes ☐ no

    Explain _____

8. Do you take liberty with your expense account? Would you be nervous if your company performed an audit of your expense account ☐ yes ☐ no

    Explain _____

9. Do you ever exaggerate claims about a product or service in order to win an account? ☐ yes ☐ no

    Explain _____

10. Do you ever load-up customers with unnecessary products or do you oversell toward the end of the year? ☐ yes ☐ no

    Explain _____

11. Do you think you can afford to bend or break company ethical values because no job lasts forever? ☐ yes ☐ no

    Explain _____

12. Do you compare your standards of behavior to other people's? ☐ yes ☐ no

    Explain _____

13. Do you believe all is fair in love, war, and business? ☐ yes ☐ no

    Explain _____

14. Would you offer kickbacks or gifts to a buyer? ☐ yes ☐ no

    Explain _____

If you answered yes to any of these questions, your ethical standards are less than angelic . . . and may eventually get you in trouble.

WORKSHEET

SETTING YOUR STANDARDS

13.2 Ethical Decision-Making

There are some industries in which people are faced with ethical dilemmas every day. Having an immediate, internal sense of right and wrong is ideal, but, in lieu of that, it is helpful to have a set of questions that can help you make tough decisions. Keep the following questions in the back of your mind—or in the desk drawer—to refer to when your gut instinct doesn't give you much direction.

1. Who will be helped by this action? To what degree?

   _____

2. Who will be harmed by this action? To what degree?

   _____

To help you answer the first two questions, use the scales that follow to quantify the harm or help created by the action in question.

3. Would you want to see an article about you and your actions in tomorrow's local newspaper?

   _____

4. Would you want someone to do this to you?

   _____

5. How would you explain your actions to someone whose esteem you value?

   _____

6. What are the probable results of your actions and are they results you can be proud of?

   _____

Your Customer

HARMED ←————————————————————→ HELPED

1   2   3   4   5

Your Company

HARMED ←————————————————————→ HELPED

1   2   3   4   5

Your Competitors

HARMED ←————————————————————→ HELPED

1   2   3   4   5

Your Customer's Competitors

HARMED ←————————————————————→ HELPED

1   2   3   4   5

Your Customer's Customers

HARMED ←————————————————————→ HELPED

1   2   3   4   5

Yourself

HARMED ←————————————————————→ HELPED

1   2   3   4   5

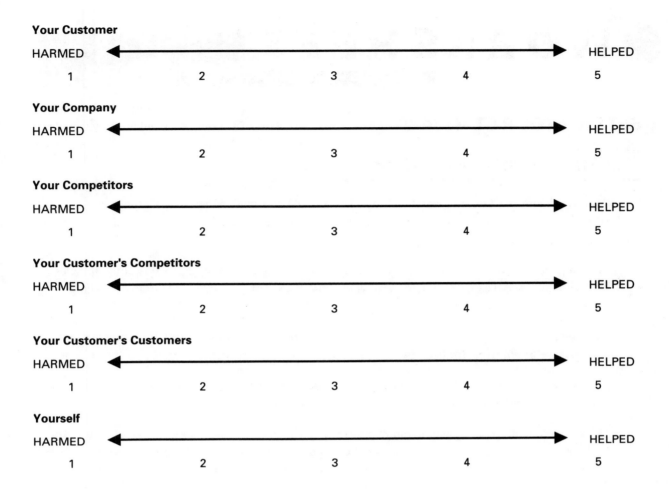

WORKSHEET

SETTING YOUR STANDARDS

13.3 Staying Out of Hot Water

Ethical standards are not the only standards to which salespeople must adhere. Don't forget the law. All kinds of laws govern business transactions. Because you cannot be expected to be aware of all of them, the following guidelines will serve you well.

1. Know the difference between "sales puffery" and specific statements of fact made during the sales presentation. Avoid exaggeration to make your story sound terrific. Stick to the truth, the whole truth, and nothing but the truth.

2. Thoroughly educate your customers on all aspects of your product or service before completing the sale. Leave no surprises for later. Be thorough.

3. Know everything there is to know about your product/service: technical specifications, capabilities, design characteristics, delivery/installation abilities, and so on.

4. Read carefully all promotional literature printed by your company on the products/services you are selling. If there are any inaccuracies, make them known to management. These inaccuracies are often unintentional, sometimes originating with overzealous advertising copywriters.

5. Study your company's terms of sale policies. If you overstate your authority to establish prices, your company can be legally bound.

6. Stay abreast of local and federal laws that affect your industry, especially those pertaining to warranties and guarantees.

7. Be careful how you state the capabilities of your product or service and check the accuracy of those statements that you routinely make.

8. *Never* be afraid to say, "I don't know. I'll have to get back to you about that."

Building customer satisfaction

WHAT'S IN IT FOR YOU

- Retain more customers.

- Increase your awareness of the importance of customers

- Learn the three R's of customer service

- Learn how to protect your current customers from competitors

- Increase your understanding of the role that company-wide service has on sales

- Enhance your reputation as a caring, conscientious sales consultant

- Discover the best way to handle customer complaints

- Learn the many ways to follow up after the sale to ensure customer satisfaction

- Discover effective, creative ways to improve service and, therefore, sales, in your company

? F Y I

WHAT'S IN IT FOR YOU

- Increase your awareness of the dimensions on which you are judged as a professional salesperson
- Determine professional areas in which you need improvement

INCREASING YOUR CUSTOMER AWARENESS

14.1 The Personal/Performance Model

Whenever you meet someone to do business, you are judged on two levels of service: personal and performance. Your customer's judgment process is unconscious, but it has a profound effect nonetheless.

The performance level of service includes all the things you do to give customers what they want: your product and industry knowledge, giving effective presentations and demonstrations, reliably following up on your promises, making sure orders are accurate, realistically promised, and delivered on time, and much more. You could think of the performance level as all the tasks in your job description, and then some.

The personal level of service is, in essence, your skill in communication: how well you listen, ask questions, give feedback, show empathy, build trust, create rapport, adapt to other people's behavioral styles, and so on.

Both levels are important and affect customers' opinions of you, your company, and your product/service. The performance and personal levels of professionalism do not always contribute equally to a buyer's decision-making process. The ratio varies from industry to industry. A life insurance agent is more likely to be judged on a personal level than a performance level. Conversely, the performance level probably plays a larger role for people who sell high-tech products or services.

1. Are you judged more on your personal or performance level in most selling situations in your industry? Use this chart to determine the percentage that each contributes.

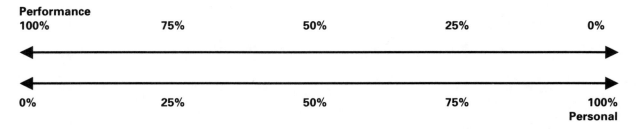

2. Now that you are aware of the personal/performance model, identify the areas in which you see room for improvement.

WORKSHEET

INCREASING YOUR CUSTOMER AWARENESS

14.2 What Are Your Service Standards?

1. Have you defined a level of service that you strive to deliver? If not, develop standards for the following:

   - How quickly you return phone calls

   - How closely you monitor the timely delivery of products or services

   - How often you keep in touch with customers and prospects

   - How frequently you solicit customer feedback on your products and service quality.

   What other aspects of service can you add to this list?

2. List three ways to make it easier for customers to do business with your company.

   a. _____

   b. _____

   c. _____

3. List three ways to streamline the problem-solving process for customers.

   a. _____

   b. _____

   c. _____

4. List three ways to reduce or eliminate any recurring problems that your customers experience with your products or services.

   a. _____

   b. _____

   c. _____

5. What opportunities are presented by the recurring problems that you listed in question four? How can you turn unhappy customers into loyal customers?

   _____

? **FYI**

WHAT'S IN IT FOR YOU

INCREASING YOUR CUSTOMER AWARENESS

• Learn to make service *measurable* and, therefore, similar to other goals

14.3 Build Service into Performance Evaluations

One of the keys to providing truly exceptional service is to practice goal-setting.

Make It Measurable. Service has to be specifically defined so it can be measured. For example, Blue Cross of California has defined several aspects of service as 1) Faster Claims Payment, 2) More Accurate Claims Payment, and 3) Prompt Response to Customer Telephone Calls.

The best way to define your company's service standards is to ask your customers what is important to them. Ask them informally or invite them to participate in focus groups. Avoid setting standards in a vacuum; that is, without customer input.

Develop A System For Keeping Track. You have to do more paperwork, but the end justifies the means. If you are going to measure service, you have to collect data. The paperwork can be simple and may require only a few seconds of time.

Set Goals For Performance. You must set performance objectives that will make customers happy. The goals must also be realistic to achieve. For example, if one of your company goals is to answer the phone before three rings, you must have the manpower to make that possible.

Keep Track And Analyze. Use the data to compare actual performance with objectives. A lot of insight can be gained from this data.

Many companies have become famous for defining their service standards and making them measurable. A couple of well-known examples are Federal Express (delivered by 10:00 am next morning) and Domino's Pizza (half-hour delivery).

INCREASING YOUR CUSTOMER AWARENESS

14.4 Anticipate Service Opportunities

Describe each of your products/services in the following terms. Spend the most time on the third category—the one that differentiates you and your company from the competition. Try to come up with additional ways to set your company apart.

1. **Tangible Product/Service** These are the features of what you sell. Tangibles are usually the same for you and your competitors.

2. **Expected Services** The second level of services includes delivery, installation, warranty, financing, and other things that customers normally expect. *How* you provide these services is as important as what you provide.

3. **Extra Services** These services are ones you provide when you see an opportunity to exceed your customers' expectations. For example, customizing a product/service, baby-sitting a delivery, arranging particularly creative financing, and so on.

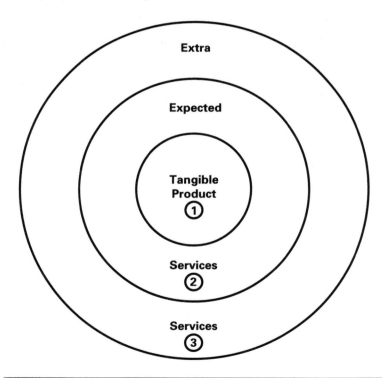

Source: B. Merrifield. THE DYNAMICS OF INDUSTRIAL DISTRIBUTION.

WORKSHEET

INCREASING YOUR CUSTOMER AWARENESS

- Gain insight into the way you think about your customers
- Discover ways to become more market-driven

14.5 The Market-Driven Profile

Which of the following attitudes and practices describe you? If you answer no to any of these practices, think of things that you can change to become less product-oriented and more market-driven.

1. Do you have an organized method for regularly collecting and communicating information to your customers and prospects?

   _____

2. Do you have an organized way of regularly checking in with customers to uncover new needs or problems?

   _____

3. When you uncover problems with your products or services, do you feed back that information to the right people in your company?

   _____

4. Do you engage in joint planning and implementation programs with your customers?

   _____

5. Do you participate in industry and community activities?

   _____

6. Are you committed to giving your customers what they want—even if it means stretching your company's normal operating parameters—or do you try to mold your customers to make things easy for your company?

   _____

7. Do you "go to bat" for your customers? That is, do you sell "internally" to get upper management to bend or throw out the rules to accommodate special requests?

   _____

8. Are you obsessed with professionalism? Do you put a lot of effort into making sure that things are done right the first time? Do you convey this perfectionism to your customers?

   _____

9. Do you keep abreast of industry/political/economic trends and think of ways in which they may impact your customers?

   _____

10. Are you an advocate of change or do you cling to the status quo?

    _____

11. In the final analysis, do you see yourself as working for your company or for your customers?

    _____

WORKSHEET

INCREASING YOUR CUSTOMER AWARENESS

14.6 Creating Realistic Expectations

One important way to make your customers happy is to manage their expectations. You cannot promise a delivery on Tuesday, have it show up on Friday, and expect your customer to be happy. The key is to undersell and overdeliver. Make your promises realistic—perhaps even slightly understated—and then exceed expectations.

Think about how you and your company affect customer expectations and how you can do a better job of it.

1. In your company's advertising, is the primary emphasis placed on product features or service quality?

   _____

2. Does your advertising adequately differentiate your company from the competition?

   _____

3. What expectations are created by the content of your company's advertising?

   _____

4. What image of your company is created by the choice of media used to advertise?

   _____

5. List some better ways to create positive expectations in your company's promotions.

   _____

6. When giving a presentation to a prospect, what expectations do you intentionally create? Do you concentrate only on selling the sizzle and risk misleading people about the steak, or do you present an accurate representation of your product/service?

   _____

7. Are the expectations that you create centered around the features of your product/service, your company, and its reputation, or your qualities as a salesperson and service provider?

   _____

8. What are some ways you can sell yourself better? What can you say or do that will show prospects the benefits of doing business with *you*?

   _____

9. Do you make it clear what customers can expect after the sale in terms of product performance and service quality?

_____

10. Do you and your prospects set up specific success criteria to be monitored after the sale?

_____

11. Do you conceal bad news about your product, service or industry when you become aware of it? Are you straightforward about bad news, or do you let customers find out on their own?

_____

12. Do you or your company have a system for measuring customer expectations, satisfaction, or retention rates?

_____

13. Does anyone seem to care?

_____

? F Y I

INCREASING YOUR CUSTOMER AWARENESS

14.7 The Three Rs of Customer Service

What do customers expect from you and your company? We have distilled service down to its basic elements and found that every interaction with a customer entails three basic components—the Three R's of Service.

Reliability

There are several facets to reliability: fulfilling promises, creating realistic expectations, delivering quality products, and being dependable.

Organizational reliability: Product or service quality; efficient, dependable operational systems; policies and procedures that consistently serve the customer; quality employee training; creating realistic expectations with accurate customer education and communication.

Personal reliability: Timely follow-up on all matters; product knowledge; integrity; and overall professionalism.

Responsiveness

Responsiveness includes the willingness to incorporate flexibility in the decision-making process; giving a higher priority to customers' needs than to company operational guidelines; and timeliness.

Organizational responsiveness: Structuring company policies and operational procedures so that employees can respond to and serve customers in a timely manner. This requires management to empower employees with the authority to give customers what they want, within reasonable parameters. The decision-making process must be moved as close to the customer as possible.

Personal responsiveness: The willingness and ability to work the system on behalf of the customer. Salespeople and other employees must be willing to take the responsibility for customers' problems and, if necessary, sell their solutions upstream.

Relationship

Building positive, loyal, long-term business relationships is important.

Organizational relationship: Focusing on building long-term relationships rather than one-time sales; market research and customer perception research that determine what is important to your target markets; determining and administering guarantees and warranty policies.

Personal relationship: In a nutshell, treating people well. This includes courtesy, recognition, caring, empathy, sincerity, ethical selling, building rapport, establishing trust, and communicating effectively.

WORKSHEET

INCREASING YOUR CUSTOMER AWARENESS

14.8 The Three Rs in *Your* Business

Refer back to the previous FYI on the Three R's of Customer Service. Then give two examples each of specific aspects of reliability, responsiveness, and relationship that are important to your customers.

Reliability

1. _____

2. _____

Responsiveness

1. _____

2. _____

Relationship

1. _____

2. _____

WORKSHEET

INCREASING YOUR CUSTOMER AWARENESS

14.9 How Does Your Company Rate?

On a scale of one to ten, rate your company on the following measures of service quality:

Responsiveness. Do customers get cookie cutter service or does your company treat people as individuals?

1 _____ 2 _____ 3 _____ 4 _____ 5 _____ 6 _____

7 _____ 8 _____ 9 _____ 10 _____

Competence. Does your company have an image of expertise in which customers can place their trust?

1 _____ 2 _____ 3 _____ 4 _____ 5 _____ 6 _____
7 _____ 8 _____ 9 _____ 10 _____

Reliability. How dependable is your product or service? How well does your company follow through on promises?

1 _____ 2 _____ 3 _____ 4 _____ 5 _____ 6 _____
7 _____ 8 _____ 9 _____ 10 _____

Relationship. How well does your company show customers that they care and want long-term relationships?

1 _____ 2 _____ 3 _____ 4 _____ 5 _____ 6 _____ 7 _____ 8 _____ 9 _____ 10 _____

Accuracy. How well does your company avoid mistakes, especially expensive or time-consuming mistakes?

1 _____ 2 _____ 3 _____ 4 _____ 5 _____ 6 _____ 7 _____ 8 _____ 9 _____ 10 _____

Personal Service. How well do service representatives, receptionists, and other front-line people show customers that they are special?

1 _____ 2 _____ 3 _____ 4 _____ 5 _____ 6 _____ 7 _____ 8 _____ 9 _____ 10 _____

Courtesy. Does *everyone* in your company treat customers with this most basic ingredient of human interaction and service?

1 _____ 2 _____ 3 _____ 4 _____ 5 _____ 6 _____ 7 _____ 8 _____ 9 _____ 10 _____

Active Listening. Are people in your company good listeners, especially when it comes to customer problems?

1 _____ 2 _____ 3 _____ 4 _____ 5 _____ 6 _____ 7 _____ 8 _____ 9 _____ 10 _____

Perceived Value. Does your company give customers good value and make them aware of that value before and after the sale?

1 _____ 2 _____ 3 _____ 4 _____ 5 _____ 6 _____ 7 _____ 8 _____ 9 _____ 10 _____

Professional Appearance. Is your company aware of the importance of making a positive impression with a clean, safe, well-maintained place of business?

1 _____ 2 _____ 3 _____ 4 _____ 5 _____ 6 _____ 7 _____ 8 _____ 9 _____ 10 _____

Keeping in Touch. Does your company make an effort to stay close to its customers and solicit their opinions?

1 _____ 2 _____ 3 _____ 4 _____ 5 _____ 6 _____ 7 _____ 8 _____ 9 _____ 10 _____

WHAT'S IN IT FOR YOU

- Take a close look at your company's performance on 11 measures of customer service to determine how you and your company can create greater customer satisfaction
- Identify customer expectations you create and influence (i.e., things you can control)
- Identify problems you can anticipate and respond to (things you can control)
- Identify key customer concerns that you can use to "sell" people internally in your organization in order to give you and your customers better service

INCREASING YOUR CUSTOMER AWARENESS

14.10 How Important Are Customers?

How important are customers? You be the judge. Did you know that . . .

- Five out of six customers who come to you with complaints will continue to do business with your company even if you do not fix the problem, *if they perceive the person who took the complaint as friendly, caring, enthusiastic, and committed to the relationship?*

- Unhappy customers will tell an average of eight to 20 people about their bad experiences? Happy customers tell an average of five friends.

- It costs five to ten times more to acquire a new customer than to maintain a current customer?

- People are willing to pay for better service? A *Wall Street Journal*/NBC News poll asked over 1,500 consumers, "How often do you purchase from a business that has excellent service but higher prices?" Their answers:

All the time	7%
Most of the time	28%
Sometimes	40%
Only rarely	17%
Never	6%
Not sure	2%

WORKSHEET

- Brainstorm ways to increase customer loyalty

INCREASING YOUR CUSTOMER AWARENESS

14.11 Strategies to Protect Current Accounts

You cannot make a decent living or sleep well at night if you are constantly seeking new prospects to replace customers you have lost. Sales and career growth come from maintaining existing customers while simultaneously generating new ones.

In the exercise below, develop three goals that will help you keep your customers happy. Write out specific activities that will help you achieve your goals.

Sample Goal: Keep in close touch with customers after the sale.

Activity: Call or stop by on the 7th, 21st, and 60th days after the sale.

1. Goal: _____

Activities: _____

2. Goal: _____

Activities: _____

3. Goal: _____

Activities: _____

WHAT'S IN IT FOR YOU

- Increase your awareness of people's needs
- As a way to improve your relationships, find ways to meet your customers' personal needs in the course of doing business

INCREASING YOUR CUSTOMER AWARENESS

14.12 Human Needs

We all have needs—some of them basic, others sublime. Think of ways to meet some of the following customer needs:

- The need for recognition

- The need for physical comfort

- The need to be competent

- The need for timely service

- The need to avoid stress

- The need to be understood

- The need for self-esteem

- The need to be remembered

- The need to be respected

- The need to be wanted

- The need to make one's own decisions

- The need for information

- The need for camaraderie

- The need to trust

- The need to be trusted

- The need for emotional support

- The need for laughter

- The need for intellectual stimulation

- The need for meaningful work

- The need for accomplishment

- The need for recreation

- The need for self-disclosure.

INCREASING YOUR CUSTOMER AWARENESS

14.13 How to Make Customers Feel Comfortable

- Use good eye contact

- Smile

- Touch (use only in a professional manner and with appropriate behavioral styles; note it is influential only with Relaters and Socializers)

- Ask questions. (People hear questions better than they hear statements)

- Encourage participation in the sales process

- Listen! Make them feel understood

- Give feedback

- Focus on your customer, and block out all distractions

- Show empathy and be sensitive to customers' needs

- Adopt a sense of urgency about everything you do for customers

- Never try to place blame—it's irrelevant when solving a problem.

INCREASING YOUR CUSTOMER AWARENESS

14.14 Prescriptions for Flexibility

Use the following suggestions to help you adapt to other people's behavioral styles when you are dealing with customers.

	Relater	Thinker	Director	Socializer
NEEDS TO KNOW ABOUT:	How it will affect their personal circumstances	How they can justify it logically/ How it works	What it does/By when/What it costs	How it enhances their status and visibility
DO IT WITH:	Warmth	Accuracy	Conviction	Flair
SAVE THEM:	Conflict	Embarrassment	Time	Effort
TO FACILITATE DECISION MAKING PROVIDE:	Personal service and assurances	Data and documentation	Options with supporting analysis	Testimonials and incentives
LIKES YOU TO BE:	Pleasant	Precise	To the point	Stimulating
SUPPORT THEIR:	Feelings	Procedures	Goals	Ideas
CREATE THIS ENVIRONMENT:	Personal	Serious	Businesslike	Enthusiastic
MAINTAIN THIS PACE:	Slow/relaxed	Slow/systematic	Fast/decisive	Fast/spontaneous
FOCUS ON THIS PRIORITY:	The Relationship/ Communication	The Task/ The Process	The Task/ The Results	The Relationship/ Interaction
AT PLAY BE:	Casual and Cooperative	Structured/play by the rules	Competitive and aggressive	Spontaneous and playful
USE TIME TO:	Develop the relationship	Ensure accuracy	Act efficiently	Enjoy the interaction
WRITE THIS WAY:	Warm and friendly	Detailed and precise	Short and to the point	Informal and dramatic
ON THE TELEPHONE BE:	Warm and pleasant	Business like and precise	Short and to the point	Conversational and playful

WORKSHEET

HANDLING CUSTOMER PROBLEMS

14.15 How You Resolve Customer Problems

Describe two situations in which you dealt successfully with a customer problem. Then describe two situations in which your handling of a problem was unsuccessful.

Successful Resolution 1: _____

What you said or did:_____

Outcome: _____

What you could have said or done better: _____

Successful Resolution 2: _____

What you said or did:_____

Outcome: _____

What you could have said or done better: _____

Unsuccessful Resolution 1: _____

What you said or did:_____

Outcome: _____

What you could have said or done better: _____

Unsuccessful Resolution 2: _____

What you said or did:_____

Outcome: _____

What you could have said or done better: _____

✎ WORKSHEET

HANDLING CUSTOMER PROBLEMS

14.16 How to Evaluate Responses to Problems

Your responses to common customer problems should meet four criteria if they are going to make good business sense. They should:

1. Create customer satisfaction and a sense of loyalty.

2. Have a reasonable chance of success.

3. Be cost-effective.

4. Be within your control to provide.

1. List a typical problem that your customers experience with your products or services.

   _____

2. Think of three or more *creative, new* ways to respond to and solve that problem.
   Those solutions must satisfy all four requirements listed above.

   a. _____

   b. _____

   c. _____

? FYI

HANDLING CUSTOMER PROBLEMS

14.17 Resolving Customer Problems

When one of your customers has a problem with you or your company, follow these seven steps to achieve a mutually satisfactory solution.

1. **Handle the person first, then the problem.** Let angry people vent their frustrations. This alone will go a long way toward resolving the problem. Problems seem less severe after a person has gotten rid of the anger.

2. **Apologize.** This is often left out, but is is a crucial gesture. Offer a sincere, *personal* apology, not one on behalf of the company. Show that you are committed to the relationship.

3. **Show empathy.** Assure your customer that he has every right to be angry and disappointed and that you would feel the same way if it happened to you.

4. **Find a solution.** Resolve the problem *with* your customer, not for her. Ask questions that will get her involved in the process. Some possible questions include:
   How would you like to see this problem resolved?
   What would be an acceptable resolution to this problem?
   If you were in my position, how might you resolve this kind of problem for your customer?
   Would a refund be acceptable to you?

5. *You* **jump through hoops.** Immediately take over and make the recovery process easy for your customer. If there are phone calls to make or forms to fill out, *you* assume responsibility and do the work. If the resolution of the problem is going to be complicated, explain the system to your customer. People feel much better when they are informed than when they are kept in the dark.

6. **Offer compensation.** If the service breakdown was severe enough ("severe enough" is an individual judgment call, but should also be a standard set by your company), you need to say "I'm sorry" with a concrete gesture. Compensation should have these characteristics:

   It should be immediate. Giving a gift long after the fact makes it lose its meaning and appear insincere. Give the gift immediately. For this reason, you must be clear about the parameters for compensating customers.

   Make it meaningful. A meaningful gift is something that has a high *perceived value* to your customer. It should also differentiate you from your competition. Be creative—customize the gift to your customer's personality. Don't send flowers or a box of candy—everyone does that. Know your customer well enough to determine whether a pair of tickets to a baseball game or a hot air balloon ride would be appropriate.

   The gift should be consumable. If you send a calendar or clock to say, "I'm sorry," your customer will be reminded of the incident every time she looks at it. Save those gifts for positive occasions. Your customer should be able to eat or use your recovery gift relatively soon. That way the gift is appreciated, but soon out of sight and mind.

   It should not cost a lot. The combination of high perceived value and low cost to the company is ideal, especially if you are compensating customers regularly. (If you are, correct the situation that is causing these repeated service failures!) Giving away more of your company's products or services may be appropriate (and inexpensive), but only if they won't cause more problems. The worst thing you can do is offer customers more of something that has already caused them grief.

7. **Follow Up** After resolving a problem, with or without a gift, you must follow up. As with any follow-up, you will not only make sure things are OK, you will also look for additional needs that represent selling opportunities. Follow-up is essential because there is nothing worse than a fouled-up recovery. A *recovery* snafu is a guaranteed way to lose a customer forever.

WORKSHEET

HANDLING CUSTOMER PROBLEMS

14.18 Determining Customer Dissatisfaction

Before you do anything to help a disgruntled customer, it is important to determine how upset he or she is. The more upset, the greater and faster your efforts will have to be to correct the situation.

To determine the customer's degree of dissatisfaction, you must do three things:

1. **Listen actively.** Use your communication skills to read your customer accurately. Observe body language. Read between the lines of what is said. Tune in to your customer.

2. **Ask questions.** Avoid misunderstandings. Ask for clarification. Find out how your customer was inconvenienced and how he or she would like the problem resolved.

3. **Trade places.** Put yourself in your customer's place and imagine the frustration *you* would feel.

Your customer's frustration level will fall into one of three levels. After reading the definitions below, write out two examples of typical problems in your company that cause customers to experience these levels of emotion.

Levels Of Customer Dissatisfaction

Bothered. Customers are bothered when service falls below their expectations, disappoints them slightly, or surprises them (negatively), but does *not* cause inconvenience.

Examples from your experience: _____

Irritated. Customers become irritated when they are annoyed by poor service, are mildly inconvenienced, or have lost time but not money.

Examples from your experience: _____

Abused. Customers feel abused by you or your company when they are grossly inconvenienced, have lost a lot of time or even a little money, are personally insulted, unfairly treated, or made angry or upset.

Examples from your experience: _____

HANDLING CUSTOMER PROBLEMS

14.19 Customer Problem/Solution Grid

When Your Customer Is...

You Need To:	Bothered	Irritated	Abused
Express concern and apologize	✓	✓	✓
Immediately make things right	✓	✓	✓
Acknowledge the problem and show empathy		✓	✓
Make a gesture of compensation		Optional	✓
Follow-up			✓

? F Y I

HANDLING CUSTOMER PROBLEMS

14.20 Responding Correctly to Typical Problems

Take one typical customer problem from each level of dissatisfaction in Worksheet 14.18 and write out what you would say and do in those situations.

HANDLING CUSTOMER PROBLEMS

14.21 Courteous Phone Skills

You may or may not answer your own phone. If someone else does, that person should be trained to give customers the best possible impression. If you answer your phone, you need to take the time to do it properly. There are no excuses for rude or unprofessional behavior. Either use common courtesy, or don't answer the phone at all. Rude phone habits can burn leads fast.

The five basic messages that a caller should get from whoever answers the phone are:

1. I will not waste your time

2. I care about you and your business

3. I am competent and well organized

4. I can be trusted to help you get through to your party

5. I am proud of my company and enjoy working here.

There are some *shoulds* that everyone needs to know:

- **Answer calls in no more than four rings.** If your phone traffic is too heavy to allow this, hire an additional receptionist. Remember, a good receptionist is not measured by how quickly she handles calls, but by the positive outcome of each call.

- **Be prepared.** It looks silly when you have to search for a pen and notepad. Similarly, if prices or other information are commonly requested over the phone, that information should be readily available.

- **Identify yourself or your company.** The caller should know immediately who has taken the call. It not only gives information, but adds a personal, friendly, professional touch.

- **Screen calls tactfully.** It is better to make a request or ask a question than sound demanding. "What is this about?" is a rude way to ask, "Will she know what this call is in reference to?" By the same token, "May I tell her who is calling?" is more polite than "Who is calling?" Anything can be said nicely if you try.

- **Don't make customers repeat their stories.** It's happened to you. You call up and tell someone why you're calling. They transfer your call. You tell the next person why you're calling. You get transferred again, and so on. The right way to handle this situation is for the first person to find the proper person to handle the call and tell that person the customer's story. Making customers repeat themselves is making them jump through hoops to get service. That's what happens when front-line people get lazy—they make the customers do *their* jobs. Customers shouldn't have to do the jumping.

- **Maximum hold time is 15 seconds.** If you have to keep someone on hold longer, arrange to call him or her back. Keep closely in touch with people who are on hold.

- **Train, test, coach.** Good telephone skills are common sense, but many entry-level employees lack them. Train them well—tell them exactly what you expect. Don't assume they know how to answer the phone. Test them by shopping yourself; that is, have a friend call to see how she is treated on the phone. Use this insight to coach your people to further improve their skills.

**F Y I**

FOLLOWING UP AND STAYING IN TOUCH AFTER THE SALE

14.22 Assuring Customer Satisfaction

Whether you are a salesperson or a front-line customer service representative, you need to understand some of the things that can go wrong after the sale. Customers become disgruntled for a variety of reasons, most of which turn out to be minor, once they are handled tactfully. Your patience and understanding of human nature will help you remain calm when panic-stricken customers call and demand service.

Selective perception is a common mind-set that customers often adopt after a purchase. They tend to focus on one or two annoying details, despite the overall positive big picture. For example, a new copying machine may work perfectly except for the sound of the motor. The customer might call and complain about the motor and portray it as an intolerable nuisance. He may be stuck in selective perception, focusing only on what is wrong rather than what is right.

People expect their purchases to be perfect and, in general, the more they spend, the greater their expectations of perfection. In fact, the more someone spends, the more they are entitled to perfection. The world is made up, however, of a lot of imperfect but useful products and services.

How should you deal with selective perception? When someone lodges a complaint, check it out to see if it is, in fact, a valid, correctable problem. The motor of the copying machine may be defective. If the customer's complaint is exaggerated, however, you have to do some selling. Put the negative detail in perspective by pointing out the positives, namely the benefits. You can also compare the problem to your competitors' and show your customer that nothing would be gained by switching companies. In addition, you can suggest creative ways of solving the problem. A copy machine can be moved, sound-proofed, or adjusted to.

User error is another common source of frustration for customers. If you have ever bought a computer, you can easily relate to this concept. Computer users usually go through hours of anxiety while they are learning to use the system. This is why a computer installation in an office should be accompanied by a formal training program for everyone who will use it.

Part of a salesperson's job when confirming the sale of a technical product or service is to try to avoid user error. To do so, you must evaluate your customer's technical ability and recommend training if necessary. You must also make your customer aware of the learning period required, during which the full benefits of the product/service may not be realized. This is especially important if your customer will be keeping track of results that prove or disprove your performance claims. The true test of your product/service will come only after everyone is using it correctly.

Buyer's remorse is a catch-all phrase that encompasses all reasons why a customer might regret having made a purchase. It doesn't matter if the reason is selective perception, user error or simply the fear of having made the wrong decision. The bottom line is that the customer has not yet realized the benefits of the purchase. It is your job to assure him or her that you have provided the solution and that the benefits will become apparent soon enough. The more specific you can be, the better. This is the perfect time to remind your customer of your service guarantee, if you have one.

? F Y I

FOLLOWING UP AND STAYING IN TOUCH AFTER THE SALE

14.23 Warning Signs of Dissatisfaction

One of the most difficult things for salespeople to do is juggle the pursuit of new customers with servicing current accounts. This takes some organization, but with the right scheduling, you should be able to find time for each activity.

It costs five to ten times as much to acquire a new customer as it does to maintain a current customer, and that estimate doesn't take your time into consideration. That's why it's important to remain sensitive to your customer's needs after the sale. Pay attention. Look for these warning signs of dissatisfaction.

Decreases In Purchase Volume. Because external factors may be affecting your industry, decreased sales may not be a reflection of dissatisfaction with your product—but you'll never know if you don't check it out. If external factors are not the reason, you may have a situation in which a complaint has gone unresolved. It is not uncommon for customers to fail to express their complaints. Your job is to pull those complaints out so they can be corrected.

An Increase In Complaints. This is obvious. If the number or frequency of complaints increases, you have to quickly and effectively resolve the situation. In addition, you must go one step further. If there is an operational flaw in your company, work to get it corrected. Chances are good that more than one customer is having problems. How many are quietly taking their business elsewhere?

Repeated Comments About The Merits of The Competition. Whether you hear it directly from a customer or through the grapevine, this is a sure sign that someone is ready to defect. If the competition's grass is greener, you have to get out there and resell your company. Increase the perceived value. Build trust again. Bend over backwards if the account is worth it.

A Decline In The Business Relationship. If you find a customer is less cordial during your sales calls or less receptive on the phone, find out the reason. Either you are making a pest of yourself, or he has become less enamored of you or your company's product/service.

New Management. This may not be a sign of dissatisfaction, but when new management is hired, you need to pay close attention. Your task may be as simple as introducing yourself with a phone call or letter and assuring them that their satisfaction is your highest priority, or you may be required to start from scratch—build trust, identify needs and so on to sell them all over again.

Change in Ownership. Whenever your customer's company is sold or absorbed by a larger firm, you need to establish a working relationship with the new people. Sometimes, companies start over by soliciting bids on various products or services. That puts you back at square one. They are now a new prospect, so you'll have to do some homework. One advantage, however, is that your product or service was in place before the change, which is a selling point for you if your track record was good.

If you are lucky, the change in ownership will not affect your relationship with the company. In this case, you simply have to get in touch and assure them that service will continue as smoothly as before the change.

WORKSHEET

FOLLOWING UP AND STAYING IN TOUCH AFTER THE SALE

14.24 Semiannual Account Review Profile

Every six months you should review your accounts. How has the big picture changed? Do some accounts need to be recategorized? What opportunities lie ahead?

Use the following worksheet for this analysis.

- Organization—the ability to compile valuable information to (1) help you evaluate an account's profitability and (2) present an informed overview to your customer during an annual review meeting

Account Profile

Company Name: _____

Street Address: _____

City/State/Zip: _____

Telephone: _____

Background:

Buyers (in order of importance): _____

_____

Products/Services purchased: _____

Growth rate: _____

Buying Characteristics:

When does customer buy? _____

How often? _____ Average order/call: _____

Gross sales volume (yearly): _____

Past sales (last 4 years): _____

_____

Company Goals:

Short-term (as perceived by?): _____

Long-term (as perceived by?): _____

Competitors (for this account): _____

Current competitors: _____

Potential competitors: _____

Your company

Your company/product strengths: _____

_____

_____

Your company/product weaknesses: _____

_____

_____

Your goals for account _____ as of (date) _____

New potential services: _____

Specific account needs:_____

_____Pricing   _____Delivery   _____Service

_____Credit   _____Reliability   _____Other

Profitability Analysis

Profit margin _____ Margin percentage (GMP) _____

Number of calls necessary/year:_____

Average time per call: _____

Travel time per call: _____

Planning time per call: _____

Your cost per hour (CPH):_____   CPH = Direct Cost (DC) ÷ Working Hour (WH)

Your cost per call hour (CPCH): _____   CPCH = DC ÷ CH (Call Hours)

Break-even volume: _____   BEV = DC ÷ GMP

Break-even volume/call: _____   BEV PER CALL = CPCH ÷ GMP

Return of time invested: _____   ROTI = GM ÷ DC

Account classification:_____

WORKSHEET

FOLLOWING UP AND STAYING IN TOUCH AFTER THE SALE

- Gain the ability to act as a marketing consultant by presenting the big picture to your customers on a yearly basis

14.25 Effective Annual Review Meetings

Once or twice a year you will evaluate all your accounts to determine their A, B, C status, among other things. (See Section 2 for other ways to evaluate your accounts.) Once or twice a year, you should also meet with your customers—or at least your best customers—to review where things stand. This is a way to evaluate the account's activities, the industry in general, the economic climate and what to anticipate, competitor's strengths and weaknesses, and so on. This is identical to the research you did when they were still prospects, but now you meet with your customers to get their input.

This annual or semiannual meeting is an opportunity to 1) keep the relationship strong; 2) ask for feedback; 3) introduce new products/services; and 4) shape the direction of future business.

Every review meeting is different, but take the general guidelines below and use as many of them as you can.

1. If possible, arrange a breakfast or lunch meeting. Eating tends to relax people and gives the meeting a more informal tone.

2. Select a place that is conducive to a meeting. It should be well-lit with a large table in a place that won't rush you out after the meal.

3. Invite every significant participant in the account. If there are two buyers, make sure both can attend the meeting.

4. Bring all the spreadsheets necessary to discuss the previous year's business. In addition, bring all the documentation you may need to substantiate your claims regarding industry trends, product reports, etc.

5. Allow an adequate amount of time for the meeting. An hour might be rushing it.

6. Organize your presentation. Use your time logically. Present the past. Ask questions about performance, quality, satisfaction, and so on. Ask about their business and the future. Introduce something new.

7. Give your customers plenty of time to talk. Ask open-ended questions to draw them out and encourage them to say whatever is on their minds. Take notes or record (with permission) the meeting. Send a copy of your notes to your customer as a follow-up.

8. Convey by actions and words your commitment to service and your desire for a long, mutually beneficial relationship.

9. After your review and other discussions, introduce a new product, service, or marketing idea. You can also offer a special discount or promotional package, which are nice ways to thank them for their time and business.

10. Look for opportunities and needs beyond the immediate and obvious. Focus on the big picture as well as the small details.

11. If appropriate, ask for referrals and/or testimonial letters. Your present customer base is one of the best sources of new business.

FOLLOWING UP AND STAYING IN TOUCH AFTER THE SALE

14.26 15 Ways to Stay Close to Your Customers

1. **Show them that you think of them.** Send or fax helpful newspaper clippings, relevant cartoons, Christmas and birthday cards (of course!). Here's a new one—send a card on the anniversary of the day they became your customers!

2. **Drop by to show them what's new.** Always make an appointment or call first—and do it when you're in the neighborhood—but a brief visit to show a new product or leave a brochure is a good way to stay in touch and increase sales or get referrals.

3. **Follow up a sale with a free gift to enhance the purchase.** You should also make an appointment to see how your product/service is being utilized and to suggest other ways to derive more benefits. Customers often do not use their purchases correctly.

4. **Offer "valued customer" discounts.** These can take the form of coupons, letters, or other sales promotions. This not only garners more orders, it also makes your customers happy to be getting such good deals.

5. **Let customers know that they should contact you when they hire employees** so you can train the new people *for free!*

6. **Compensate customers for lost time or money,** if they were caused by problems with your product/service. Have a well thought-out recovery program and stick to it. Better to err on the side of generosity than lose an account out of stinginess.

7. **Be personal.** Keep notes in your customer files on every little detail you know—everything from spouse's name to hobbies and especially their behavioral style.

8. **Always be honest.** Nothing undermines your credibility more severely than dishonesty. Lies have a way of coming back to haunt you. Compare McNeil's handling of the Tylenol incident to Perrier's initial denial of their benzene problem. Why lie?

9. **Accept returns unconditionally.** The few dollars you may lose in the short run is far less than what you gain from acquiring a new customer. For example, ADI, Inc., calculates that it costs them an average of $25 to correct a customer's problem. Their average customer spends $15,000 per year with them. They tell their employees, "Don't quibble."

10. **Honor your customer's privacy.** If you have been a truly consultative salesperson, then you may possess some knowledge that should be kept confidential. Your ethical standards demand that you keep it that way.

11. **Keep your promises.** Never, ever promise something that you cannot deliver. This principle applies to little things such as returning phone calls as well as big things like delivery dates. If you must, baby-sit deliveries and promised service. See that they get done. Your reputation (and your commissions) are on the line.

12. **Give feedback on referrals.** This is the right way to show your appreciation for the referral. Tell your customer the outcome. This is also a good way to get more referrals without asking for them directly.

13. **Make your customers famous . . . for 15 minutes.** If your company has a newsletter, ask customers for permission to write about their success with your product/service. Then send a copy to your customer. The same can be done for industry publications.

14. **Arrange periodic performance reviews.** As a consultant, you should meet annually with your customers to review their competitive posture in their industry, their satisfaction with your company, and any other concerns that may affect business.

15. **Keep lines of communication open.** As in any relationship, assure your customers that you are open to all calls about everything and anything—ideas, grievances, advice, praise, questions, and so on. This is one way you maintain that all-important rapport.

Remember, people do business with people they like!

FOLLOWING UP AND STAYING IN TOUCH AFTER THE SALE

14.27 Referrals: If You Don't Ask, You Don't Get

When prospecting, many salespeople completely forget about present customers. Present customers are an excellent source of new business, but one that is perhaps too obvious. If you have a strong relationship with your customers, you should not feel uncomfortable asking them for favors. Here are some ways to develop new business from current customers.

1. **Ask for referrals within their company.** Sure you've asked for referrals before, but were you specific about it? Probably not. If you direct a customer's thinking internally, you may come up with more prospects. For example, some companies (banks, real estate companies) have more than one branch. Ask if a new branch is opening. Expansions take place all the time and represent new opportunities. People are hired and fired. Fires and floods create changes. People get married and divorced. Births and deaths create opportunities. If you don't ask, you won't get.

2. **Ask for referrals outside their company.** People in business tend to know people in similar businesses. Funny how that works, but if you're specializing in a particular industry, you can take advantage of this small world. When you solve a problem for one customer, he or she may know someone who has a similar need. The key is to not only ask after the sale, but to follow up periodically and ask again . . . and again.

3. **Sell more of the same.** Many companies, especially small- to medium-sized retailers, tend to order conservatively until a product proves its salability. Then they have a hard time breaking out of the habit of small orders. If you see a company that has the capacity to sell more of your product, encourage them to increase their orders and show them how they will benefit. If necessary, offer flexible financing to ease them into the bigger investment. You may also need to consult with them about how they can sell more of your products to current or new target markets.

4. **Cross-sell your customers.** Again, if and only if you see the need or the ability to sell other products, present them to your customers. You have already proven that you are trustworthy, so they will listen when you suggest they carry something else. The same principle applies to services. Once you've solved a problem with one service, perhaps you can tackle another need with another service. Cable television companies do this constantly. Every month they use statement stuffers to try to entice subscribers to sign up for additional services such as HBO.

5. **Upsell your customers.** This is easy to relate to in the computer industry. You've sold a system to a company and they are doing well with it. By keeping in touch and conducting periodic reviews of their business, you will learn how rapidly they are growing. Rapid growth means their computer needs are becoming so much greater. Time for an upgrade to a more powerful, more expensive system. This is natural. The key is to see their increased need before your competitor does, but, of course, that is why you stay in touch.

?FYI

FOLLOWING UP AND STAYING IN TOUCH AFTER THE SALE

14.28 Measuring Customer Retention

How do you know if your customers are satisfied? You can ask, but good surveys are difficult to construct and administer. The most simple and accurate measure of satisfaction is *Customer Retention.*

The Satisfaction Barometer

Customer retention is a valuable measure of a company's product or service quality. Most companies lose, on average, ten to 15 percent of their customers each year. With the cost of acquiring new customers estimated to be six times the cost of maintaining current customers, companies cannot afford to be cavalier about this. Retaining customers must be given as high a priority as acquiring new ones. Consider the fact that in many industries, increasing customer retention by five percent raises the average value of the customer's long-term business by 85 percent. Other reasons to fight to keep current customers:

- Long-term customers generally expand their annual order

- Serving long-term customers is easier because both sides know what to expect; the kinks have been worked out

- Long-term customers are often willing to pay a premium for consistent, valued service.

- Long-term customers are the best source of referrals.

The ideal for internal quality control is virtual zero defects; the ideal for external quality control is zero customer defections.

? **FYI**

FOLLOWING UP AND STAYING IN TOUCH AFTER THE SALE

14.29 Measuring Customer Satisfaction

1. **Define your terms.** To your company, what does retention mean? It may be easier for you to define defection. In either case, you have to devise some measurable way to quantify customer behavior. Magazines and newspapers can use circulation statistics. Insurance agents can use renewal rates. Manufacturers can use data on reorders and annual volume. The shorter your sales cycle and the better you know your customers, the easier your task will be.

2. **Tag your customers.** You have to create a system to keep track of customers. Companies with in-depth customer contact can do this easily, but grocery stores or fast-food restaurants would find this difficult.

3. **Dig in for the long haul.** This is a measure of customer satisfaction that will be analyzed on an annual or semiannual basis.

4. **Find root causes.** If, when comparing this year's retention rate to last year's, you find a decline, seek out the causes. Look for objective reasons. Don't rely on the results of surveys that ask about customer attitudes—these are too subjective. One source of accurate information is defecting customers. Ask them why they don't buy from you anymore. Most will be happy to tell you how you disappointed them. While you're asking, find out what your competitors did *right* to lure them away. Feed this information back to management so things can be changed.

5. **Set retention goals.** No company can keep 100 percent of its customers. Some customers cannot be retained no matter what you do. Perhaps they were shopping price at a time when you were running a sales promotion. Top management needs to analyze the data and decide what defection rate is tolerable, then devise a plan for capitalizing on company strengths, eliminating weaknesses, and attracting the right kind of customers.

6. **Get competitive information on retention rates.** Find out how your company's retention rate compares to the competition. One way to do this is to survey customers who also buy from competitors. to estimate your competitor's retention rates.

7. **Change, measure, monitor, repeat.** After changes are made in your product quality or delivery of service, you need to keep measuring and monitoring your progress and make additional changes as necessary.

8. **What you can do.** As an individual salesperson, you can request information on retention rates or ask that a system be set up to track them if one doesn't already exist. You can devise your own system for your territory. You can also comb through company records and ask former customers why they defected.

FOLLOWING UP AND STAYING IN TOUCH AFTER THE SALE

14.30 Following Up By Style

Relater

The business relationship is important to a relater, so provide consistent, regularly scheduled follow-up. Give lots of assurance that you are just a phone call away. In fact, you will score a lot of points if you give relaters your home phone number. Send Christmas, birthday and other cards. Stop by, if appropriate to make sure all is running smoothly. Take him to lunch, dinner or the ball game once in a while. In general, nurture this customer.

Socializer

In business and love, socializers are the ones who are most apt to buy before they are truly sold. They are also most apt to experience buyer's remorse, so it is your job to keep in touch, make sure everything is okay and assure him that his purchase was wise. Make sure your customer is actually using your product/service. Socializers are easily frustrated by new technology and may shelve rather than learn your solution.

Socializers are usually disorganized. If necessary, you can help him become organized so that your product/service is properly implemented. After all, socializers tend to talk about everything and anything. A purchase that was not implemented property will get as bad a rap as a purchase that was defective.

Thinkers like to quantify their results, so work out a means for measuring the success of your product/service and a timetable for checking those measurements. Make yourself available to answer any questions and assure him that you or someone in your company has the technical expertise to handle any situation.

Make it clear to your customer exactly when you will follow-up and then keep your promise. If you baby-sat a delivery or installation, report to your customer that you did so and that everything is in place as planned.

Throughout your business relationship with a thinker you have to continually prove your credibility, reliability, product/service quality, and value as a supplier.

Follow-up for a director is different than for other behavioral styles. A director isn't concerned about the relationship, she just cares about the performance of your product or service. Assure your customer that you intend to follow-up to make sure everything is okay, but you will not take up much of her time.

Never simply stop by to see a director, they're too busy for that. Call and quickly ask if all is well. If there are complaints, assure her that they will be resolved swiftly and then do so. After the resolution, report back to your customer to inform her that things are back to normal.

Unfortunately, selling to a director does not necessarily give you an advantage for a future sale. You will have to earn the next sale the way you earned the last one—on the merits of your product/service and research.

Thinker

Director

IMPROVING THE INTERNAL CULTURE

14.31 Weekly Improvement Meetings (WIMs)

There are three basic facets to generating business: attracting prospects, turning them into customers, and keeping them as customers. Your specialty is turning prospects into customers. Without your company's help in the first and third endeavors, however, your work will be wasted.

If effective advertising does not attract people to the company, you will have fewer people to sell (or maybe no one). If your company does not provide quality service after the sale, then your customers will be lost out the back door.

For this reason, you have to make sure your company's service is the best it can be. If service is mediocre or poor, then part of your job is to sell upstream. Lobby management to improve service. Do what it takes to raise their customer-consciousness. Give people books and articles and tell them about companies that have positive internal cultures and excellent service.

Go a step further. Take some action to improve the culture and service of your department. The most convincing case study will be the results of implementing the following idea in your department.

The Questions To Ask

Get everyone in your area together for breakfast or lunch weekly, bi-weekly, or monthly. It doesn't matter how often as long as the meetings make a meaningful contribution to the improvement of your department's internal culture. The basic questions to address at the meetings are:

What are we doing right?
What are we doing wrong?
What are our limitations?
What are our high-leverage (high pay-off) activities?
What are our low-leverage activities?
How can we provide better service to our customers?
How can we improve our methods for staying close to our customers?

It's a good idea to periodically include customers in your meetings. Call them Service Improvement Meetings if you want. Invite some of your top customers and feed them well. When they are satiated and happy, ask them for honest answers to some or all of the questions above. You may find the answers that customers give you will differ significantly from the way insiders see things.

Put The Answers To Work

After your group has identified high- and low-leverage activities and ways to improve service, create some goals that will transform the insight into actual changes. Keep track of the measurable results and discuss them at the next meeting.

WORKSHEET

IMPROVING THE INTERNAL CULTURE

- Brainstorm ways to reward and encourage service excellence.

14.32 Reward Excellent Service

Everyone appreciates being recognized for a job well done. There are many ways to recognize people. One way is to create a bulletin board near a high-traffic area such as a cafeteria, lounge, copy room, or coffee machine. The bulletin board would be devoted solely to people who have provided exceptional service. If your sales manager approves, it would be ideal to combine a reward system with the exemplary service board. Rewards could be lunch for two, movie tickets, merchandise, or cash.

Think of at least three other ways to recognize and reward people for delivering exceptional service:

1. _____

2. _____

3. _____

Whom would you approach to implement these ideas?

_____

? **F Y I**

WHAT'S IN IT FOR YOU

- Understand the need for and process of service audits

IMPROVING THE INTERNAL CULTURE

14.33 Use Service Audits to Shop Yourself

Let's say your company intends to improve customer service and has provided training to achieve that goal. What's next? How will you know if the training has paid off in the field? There are two answers—market research and the service audit, also called mystery shopping. Of the two, service audits produce the clearest picture of how customers view your company.

Service audits are simple. People pose as customers and evaluate their shopping experience on criteria that you deem important. They might evaluate sales skills, product displays, return policies, phone courtesy, product knowledge, or innumerable other dimensions. The shoppers can either be people within your company or professional shoppers from a national marketing service firm such as Shop 'n Chek, Inc., of Atlanta, Georgia.

There are two ways to conduct a service audit. One way is to send out mystery shoppers at random to rate your people on various performance criteria. The other way is to establish a baseline of performance by rating people without telling them they are being judged. Then you announce the service audit program and offer incentives. Make it known that mystery shoppers will be coming around during a certain time period. Employees should be told what specific behaviors will be judged so they know what is expected. Cash prizes and other rewards should be awarded to employees who are found to be doing the target behaviors right! Target behaviors can be as complex as giving a good presentation or as simple as a clerk asking, "Would you like fries with your burger?"

The service audit uncovers sales and service strengths and weaknesses. The reports provided by mystery shoppers can be used to improve management practices, operations, services, and the selection and training of employees. The should *not* be used to criticize or punish employees for mistakes.

Shopping yourself provides a way to check the effectiveness of training. It also serves as an accurate means for comparing your company with the competition, *from the customer's point of view.*

[1] The authors would like to thank Carol Cherry, President of Shop 'n Chek, for her contribution to this section. For more information on their mystery shopping and other marketing services, call 800-669-6526.

15 Managing the inner self

WHAT'S IN IT FOR YOU

- Improve your mental attitude and motivation
- Learn to eliminate self-defeating thoughts and visualize success
- Reduce stress and create balance in your life
- Get motivated to exercise and lose weight
- Learn to manage your money and establish some financial goals

"Know thyself" is at least as old as the Bible. Yet it is as contemporary as today. One of the key prerequisites to success in sales (or in any other area of life) is self-knowledge and the use of that self-knowledge to manage your life. A sales career is filled with stress, with rejection, and with intense pressure to perform at increasingly demanding levels—all of which you must be able to manage if you want to have a fulfilling career and a rewarding personal life. This section includes information you can use to take control of your life and reach those personal and professional goals you have set for yourself.

- Identify the excuses you use to get out of working hard or improving yourself

POSITIVE ATTITUDES THAT BREED SUCCESS

15.1 Overcoming Idea and Motivation Killers

"The economy is bad. People just aren't buying."

Whether it's justifying a slow sales period or inventing an excuse for taking the day off, we all occasionally run self-defeating scripts through our minds. But to succeed in sales, we need to replace them with positive, life- and career-affirming scripts that help us work hard and improve ourselves.

Resolve to banish these motivation-killers altogether.

"I'll never make as much money in this field as I want."
"I can't be enthusiastic about this product."
"They don't need my product/service."
"Other salespeople have probably contacted them already about a similar product/service."
"They won't like me."
"I'm not smart enough."
"I need to know my product inside out."
"I can't call on that many accounts per week."
"People don't like salespeople."

Some discouraging scripts pop up when staff are asked to innovate or change an established procedure. Don't let one of these idea-killers keep you from trying out a potentially profitable idea.

"Don't be ridiculous . . . "
"We tried that before . . . "
"It costs too much . . . "
"It can't be done . . . "
"That's beyond our responsibility . . . "
"It's too radical a change . . . "
"That's not our problem . . . "
"We're too small for that . . . "
"Let's get back to reality . . . "
"We've never done that before . . . "
"It would be too hard to sell . . . "
"Let's form a committee . . . "
"Why change things, they're still working . . . "
"You're two years ahead of your time . . . "
"You can't teach an old dog new tricks . . . "
"We've done fine so far without it . . . "
"Has anyone else ever tried it?"
"We're not ready . . . "
"It isn't in the budget . . . "
"If it were a good idea, we'd already have done it . . . "
"We'll be the laughingstock . . . "
"We're doing the best we can . . . "
"It won't work in our industry . . . "
"That doesn't apply to us . . . "

WORKSHEET

POSITIVE ATTITUDES THAT BREED SUCCESS

- Identify the mental potholes that may be tripping you up on the road to success

15.2 Remove Your Barriers to Success

"Mental potholes" may be tripping you up on the road to success. If these barriers apply to you, exorcise them.

Self-doubts. Some people limit their success before they even get out of the starting gate. They do it with negative thoughts that inhibit them from taking risks, forging ahead and being more successful. These negative sentences can be replaced with positive ones through a Daily Thought Diet.

People also create self-doubts by comparing themselves to others. When you compare yourself to someone, you come out either superior or inferior. Neither one is healthy. Avoid comparisons. You are you and that's good enough!

Emotional Baggage. Emotional baggage can be long-term or short-term. Whether you feel a lingering depression from a divorce or aggravation from bumper-to-bumper traffic, you have to leave it all behind you when you walk in the office door. Pretend you're on stage: get into character and put on a happy face. Better still, resolve your emotional baggage so you can truly be yourself.

Inertia. Try not to see your goals as so monumental that you end up paralyzed. Remember that big accomplishments are achieved in small steps. Whenever you think your goals are too far out of reach, break them down into smaller, more easily achieved sub-goals.

Another way to overcome inertia is to periodically review and rewrite your Benefits/Motivation Inventory (See Worksheet 15.7). Remind yourself how important those rewards are. Also, remember that there is no such thing as being lazy. Laziness just means you do not care enough about yourself to put forth effort.

Change Past Programming. Our self-images are formed by innumerable childhood experiences. As a result, we all have "mental tapes" that we say to ourselves, many of which are self-defeating. The key is to become aware of your negative self-talk and stop it in its tracks. When you catch yourself thinking something negative, stop and take the time to defuse the thought. Analyze it and prove to yourself that it is irrational. Then replace the negative thought with a positive one. This is not an easy task, but well worth the effort; and it really works.

POSITIVE ATTITUDES THAT BREED SUCCESS

15.3 The "Building Blocks" of a Happy Life

What are the secrets of a happy life? What are the "building blocks" that all of us should be striving to develop and master? Some of the abilities that follow may seem simplistic, but they truly are the keys to mental wealth.

The Ability to Love. There is no doubt that romance is important. But the ability to love includes more. It means developing the ability to look for and find the similarities—not just the differences—between people. It means genuinely caring and being there to help—a friend or a stranger—when needed, without being asked.

Self-esteem. The ability to love yourself is a cornerstone of mental health. Loving yourself means accepting and appreciating who you are simply because you exist. Too many people make the mistake of basing their self-esteem on their jobs, good looks, big house, attractive spouse, or fancy car. Equating those externals with yourself is ego, not self-esteem. You are not your job, your face, your body, your spouse, your home or your car. Your self-esteem should be based on the fact that you are a unique person with all kinds of abilities and a lot to contribute to society. *That* is enough.

The Ability And Desire To Learn. You should never stop welcoming knowledge from books, television, your experiences, and other people. Learning is a necessity in this age of rapid change. Learning is a mental exercise that keeps your mind sharp and helps prevent diminished mental functioning. An open mind is always more of an asset than a brilliant, closed mind.

A Mission. People thrive when they are engaged in meaningful work, be it volunteer work, odd jobs at home, taking care of a family, a full-time paying job or some other emotionally rewarding activity. We all need things to take pride in, things that give us a sense of accomplishment.

Fun and Laughter. Healthy people can laugh at themselves. The truly gifted can step back and laugh at life when things look bleak.

Having fun is important. You can only maintain your sanity if you take time to participate in activities that are relaxing and truly enjoyable. Sports and hobbies are extremely therapeutic and help you keep life in perspective.

Having fun in life should be a top priority. Imagine being on your deathbed, looking back at your life, knowing you had amassed a fortune but never had any fun. There is no way you would feel successful or content. Fun and laughter are as essential as air, food, and water.

The Ability To Let Go. Life is full of gains and losses. A loss may deserve a grieving period, but at some point you have to move on. Whether it is a job, a pet, a spouse, a car, or a set of keys, you have to accept reality and let go. People who can't let go beat themselves up by obsessing about what could or should have been. It's such a waste of time and energy.

Which "building blocks" have you begun to set in place? Which have yet to be developed? Give some thought to the areas of your life that need improvement, and start building the missing blocks today.

? F Y I

VISUALIZING YOUR GOALS

15.4 The Daily Thought Diet[1]

Affirmations are positive sentences that you say to yourself to replace the self-defeating thoughts that habitually pop into your mind. The daily thought diet is a card or sheet of paper that you create to remind you of who you are, what you believe and what you want to become.

Affirmations for your thought diet should follow three simple rules:

1. They must be stated in the positive. ("I will breathe only clean air" would be used for "I will stop smoking.")

2. They must be stated in the present. ("I am swimming a half-mile a day and loving it.")

3. Like goals, they should be specific, meaningful and measurable. ("I am calling five new prospects every day.")

After you have finished Worksheet 15.5, you will have a daily thought diet. Read it first thing in the morning, once or twice during the day and before going to sleep at night. If your thought diet is the last thing you read before going to sleep, your affirmations will "stick" in your mind far longer than at any other time during the day.

Your thought diet should be broken down into manageable sections. After you have achieved one of the goals on the diet, replace it with a new one.

[1]The authors would like to thank Jim Cathcart for his contribution of this material.

WORKSHEET

VISUALIZING YOUR GOALS

15.5 Your Daily Thought Diet

1. Write out the primary goal that affects you most at this point in time. Be specific.

   _____

2. Write out a half-dozen personal qualities that you are working at developing. State them *positively* in the present. Explain how they relate to your primary goal.

   _____

3. Write out as many minimum daily "to do's" as you can. For example, "I am going to walk for 30 minutes each day." Relate the "to do's" to areas in your life such as work, family, spiritual fulfillment, financial gains, social needs, physical fitness, educational goals and so on.

   _____

4. Now, compile all your affirmations. Be sure they conform to the three basic rules mentioned on the previous page. Copy them onto something that you can keep with you throughout the day. Refer to your thought diet often. The more your affirmations are repeated, the faster they sink into your unconscious mind and become *you*.

? F Y I

VISUALIZING YOUR GOALS

- Understand the value of—
and develop—a storyboard to
help you visualize your goals

15.6 The Storyboard

A good way to reach your goals is to make a storyboard—a visual graphic depiction of your goals whose pictures keep your goals in front of you and your motivation high.

A storyboard can depict the steps along the way to your ultimate goals, or it can be a collage of images showing the end results. To make one, simply get a sheet of poster board, take a pair of scissors and look through magazines. Cut out pictures that literally or symbolically represent your goals. Then paste them on your poster board randomly or in a logical order—whichever best suits the purpose of the storyboard. Put your storyboard where you can see it every day. It will serve as a constant reminder of the goals toward which you are striving.

WORKSHEET

GETTING MOTIVATED

15.7 Benefits/Motivation Inventory

Sometimes you don't realize what you have to gain or lose until you analyze a situation. To get motivated (i.e., committed to personal growth), think about your chosen profession. Ask yourself the following questions and write out everything that comes to mind.

1. If I work through the exercises in this book, how am I likely to improve my performance? (Try to come up with at least six ways.)

   _____

2 How important are those performance improvements? Why?

   _____

3. What are the potential rewards for improving my performance? (Come up with at least three short-term and three long-term rewards.)

   _____

4. Will the rewards be things that I highly value? Will they be worth the effort I expend for them?

? F Y I

GETTING MOTIVATED

15.8 Tips for Sustaining Motivation

Not everyone can remain "up." optimistic and energetic all the time. We all wax and wane in our moods, outlook and energy levels. That's normal. People who are "up" most of the time have many methods to their madness. Adopt some of them to keep your motivation high.

Do What You Love and The Money Will Follow. Hopefully you love sales—the interactions with people, the challenges, the rewards and the unlimited growth potential.

Take Pride in What You Do and It Will Have Meaning. Even if you are starting at the bottom of the corporate ladder, do your job with pride and professionalism. Excellence is its own reward and *will* be recognized. Taking pride and doing the best job you can—no matter what the task—increases your self-esteem, competence and sense of control over your life and work. Not to mention your promotability.

Challenge Yourself With Continuous Self-improvement. Set realistic goals that are attainable in short periods of time. Break larger goals into smaller increments to give yourself frequent opportunities to experience a sense of accomplishment. Success feeds on success.

Reward Yourself for Successes *and* Failures. Salespeople are subject to more than the average amount of rejection in their work, especially if they are cold calling on the phone. Devise ways to reward yourself for your efforts, even when you are not successful. Giving yourself an "E for Effort" will keep you going so that sooner or later you'll be rewarding yourself for a success. Remember, sales can be a numbers game, so every *no* brings you closer to a *yes*.

Think in Terms of a Career Path, Not Just a Job. Commit yourself to doing the best job you can for your present company, but remember that few jobs last forever. Always keep your future destinations in mind while your eye is on the road immediately before you.

Take Absolute Responsibility For Your Life and Career. Realize that you and only you can shape your future. Again, small, positive steps lead to bigger and bigger pay-offs.

HANDLING STRESS

15.9 The Scorch of Burn-Out

People are not unlike machines. You cannot run either one at high speeds for long periods of time without risking burn-out. Burn-out occurs when you are constantly fatigued or stressed by the pursuit of an activity, to the exclusion of virtually everything else. It is manifested in physical and psychological problems that may seem unrelated.

Overachievers are particularly susceptible to burn-out. These Type A personalities thrive on the adrenaline high of being incredibly busy. They cannot say no, but find it difficult to delegate. As a result, they take on more than their share of work.

At the same time, these people often ignore the symptoms of stress. When headaches and back pain occur, they may take aspirin or have a drink to temporarily relieve the pain. People on the fast track to burn-out often know they are harming themselves and tell themselves they must change; but somehow, they never get around to it.

Sometimes people procrastinate in the false hope that things will get better. They blame their stress on external factors such as work load, the business climate, family demands, car problems, traffic, the in-laws and myriad other reasons. Granted, some people do have more sources of stress than others, but that only gives them more reasons to eliminate, manage or reduce it.

You may be approaching burn-out if you have many of the following *persistent* problems:

constant exhaustion

forgetfulness

anxiety attacks

paranoia

depression

boredom and/or lethargy

anger and cynicism

obsession with work/achievement

constant irritability and impatience.

WORKSHEET

- Identify your stress symptoms

HANDLING STRESS

15.10 Symptoms of Stress Checklist

Are you suffering from too much stress?

Use this checklist to determine whether stress is taking its toll on your physical and mental health. For each of the symptoms below, put a check mark in the most appropriate box.

Symptom	Describes 1	Poorly 2	3	Describes 4	Well 5
Constant fatigue	[ ]	[ ]	[ ]	[ ]	[ ]
Low energy level	[ ]	[ ]	[ ]	[ ]	[ ]
Recurring headaches	[ ]	[ ]	[ ]	[ ]	[ ]
Gastrointestinal disorders	[ ]	[ ]	[ ]	[ ]	[ ]
Chronically bad breath	[ ]	[ ]	[ ]	[ ]	[ ]
Sweaty hands or feet	[ ]	[ ]	[ ]	[ ]	[ ]
Dizziness	[ ]	[ ]	[ ]	[ ]	[ ]
High blood pressure	[ ]	[ ]	[ ]	[ ]	[ ]
Pounding heart	[ ]	[ ]	[ ]	[ ]	[ ]
Constant inner tension	[ ]	[ ]	[ ]	[ ]	[ ]
Inability to sleep	[ ]	[ ]	[ ]	[ ]	[ ]
Temper outbursts	[ ]	[ ]	[ ]	[ ]	[ ]
Hyperventilation	[ ]	[ ]	[ ]	[ ]	[ ]
Moodiness	[ ]	[ ]	[ ]	[ ]	[ ]
Irritability and restlessness	[ ]	[ ]	[ ]	[ ]	[ ]
Inability to concentrate	[ ]	[ ]	[ ]	[ ]	[ ]
Increased aggression	[ ]	[ ]	[ ]	[ ]	[ ]
Compulsive eating	[ ]	[ ]	[ ]	[ ]	[ ]
Chronic worrying	[ ]	[ ]	[ ]	[ ]	[ ]
Anxiety or apprehensiveness	[ ]	[ ]	[ ]	[ ]	[ ]
Inability to relax	[ ]	[ ]	[ ]	[ ]	[ ]
Growing feelings of inadequacy	[ ]	[ ]	[ ]	[ ]	[ ]
Increase in defensiveness	[ ]	[ ]	[ ]	[ ]	[ ]
Dependence on tranquilizers	[ ]	[ ]	[ ]	[ ]	[ ]
Excessive use of alcohol	[ ]	[ ]	[ ]	[ ]	[ ]
Excessive smoking	[ ]	[ ]	[ ]	[ ]	[ ]

WORKSHEET

- Identify your sources of stress

HANDLING STRESS

15.11 Personal Stress Inventory

Now that you've identified symptoms, look for the sources of your stress. Don't stop to analyze how stressful the source is; if it comes to mind, write it down.

In each box, list people, situations, or other things that get on your nerves, worry you, upset you, aggravate you, drive you up the wall, or make you fidget—on the job or away from work. Indicate how often they bother you.

	On The Job	Away From Work	Frequency
People			
Situations			
Other			

?F Y I

HANDLING STRESS

15.12 Twelve Ways to Achieve a Balanced Life

Being a Type A personality is not a bad thing, if you learn to control life's stresses. We are all under stress—some more than others—but the key is to *regularly* reduce it and gain a balanced perspective on life. Achievement in one area of your life is not worth killing yourself for, even if you die wealthy.

To avoid or overcome burn-out, heed the advice in the 12 tips that follow. But change yourself slowly. You cannot adopt six or eight new behaviors overnight. Take them one at a time, and before you know it you'll be a new person.

1. **Limit the number of hours you work.** Most workaholics put in 60 to 80 hours every week. Cut back your work load so you're working a normal 40- to 50-hour week.

2. **Set goals and write them down.** Take stock of your activities and determine which offer the highest pay-off. Set goals for these and get rid of as much "busy work" as you can.

3. **Learn to say "No!"** Refusing to take on more work or responsibilities will not lower your worth in the eyes of others. Fend for yourself. Learn to be selfish.

4. **Delegate!** Accept the fact that you cannot do everything yourself and that other people can do good work, especially if they are supervised well. In the long run you are better off spending your time training people than trying to do everything yourself.

5. **Exercise regularly.** This is the best advice we can give you and the one you should act on immediately. *It is the best way to reduce stress.* Exercise makes you stronger in *every* way. Research has shown that people between the ages of 55 and 88 who exercise regularly are mentally sharper. Start now.

6. **Break up your routine.** Salespeople are lucky because their days are so varied. If your routine is very rigid, however, change it around to give yourself some variety. The same principle applies to what you eat. Avoid food ruts, *especially* fast-food ruts.

7. **Take time to relax.** Instead of a coffee break, take some time to kick off your shoes, put your feet up on the desk, close your eyes and daydream, meditate or just snooze.

8. **Eat lunch away from the office.** If you are routinely in the office during lunch, get out. If you can, walk somewhere for lunch and *don't talk about work* with your co-workers. Lunch should be an hour-long mental vacation.

9. **Get out of town.** A change of scenery works wonders, even for a weekend. Plan trips, both short and long. They get you away from it all, and give you something to look forward to.

10. **Spend more time with family and friends.** Workaholics often downplay the importance of people in their lives. People are very important. Keep those connections fun and healthy.

11. **Have fun.** Pursue your hobbies. Take the time to disengage your mind and read, even if you read comic books. Go to sporting events, the theater or whatever you find entertaining.

12. **Lighten up.** This is the most difficult advice to heed, but it may be the most important. Keep things in perspective, the right perspective being that nothing is worth getting sick about. To help you shift your thinking, spend ten minutes in a hospital or nursing home. Suddenly you will see the world differently and will not take life so seriously.

❓FYI

HANDLING STRESS

15.13 Creative Stress Relief

Sales and customer service positions can be stressful. Dealing with the public can be aggravating, especially when customers vent their anger on innocent employees. It takes a positive personality to thrive in sales and customer service, but even the most optimistic person can become stressed out. How can you spell relief? H-U-M-O-R. There are plenty of ways to incorporate humor into the workplace.

The Joke-A-Day Assignment. Each day a different person in your department brings in a joke. At the same time each day, everyone gathers together to listen to it. This five-minute ritual never fails to get laughs, even if the joke is not a knee-slapper.

Cartoon Bulletin Board. Devote a bulletin board to cartoons that people bring in to post for the viewing pleasure of all. At the end of each week, everyone votes on the best cartoon and the winner gets some nominal reward—perhaps just recognition.

As a stress reliever, the bulletin board is more passive and less effective than other methods, but is nonetheless worthwhile, especially when combined with others.

The Decompression Chamber. The next method may sound far-fetched, but it is effective. Set up a small room devoted exclusively to humorous stress relief. Equip it with a television and VCR, humorous videos, comic books, audiotapes and other toys. Encourage people to escape there during lunch hours or coffee breaks. Once it's established, you'll probably find the CEO holding meetings there.

The Great Wall of China. A company in San Diego roped off a small area against a brick wall outside its building. Employees bring in cheap dishes, cups, saucers, glasses, and serving plates that they buy at garage sales, flea markets, and discount stores. When they need to blow off some steam, they gather up some china, go out to the wall and have a ball smashing china against it. What an incredible idea!

Massages. Massage can be a delightful treat. Many massage therapists specialize in office mini-massages. They visit stressed-out employees at their desks and spend ten minutes or so loosening them up. Imagine how great people would feel if your department sponsored massage breaks on a weekly basis.

Can you think of other ways to reduce stress at work? Brainstorm some ideas and then suggest them to someone who will listen.

GETTING IN SHAPE

15.14 Changes are always M.A.D.E.

Losing weight and getting in shape is not something that happens to you—it is something you do to yourself. Granted, it is not easy for most people; but that can be said of any type of change. Change is a fact of life, something we all must learn to welcome and implement more readily. The key is to control change, rather than waiting for change to control you. By staying in control, you make change an ally rather than an adversary. Changes that are M.A.D.E. by you enhance your self-esteem. Changes that are forced upon you can undermine it. Work on the former and keep the latter in perspective.

M = Mental Pictures. First, create a new mental picture of yourself. Visualize how you will look and feel when you have accomplished your physical goals. You will be more trim and lean. You will be strong and limber, with good cardiovascular fitness. Picture yourself as the new you as often as you can. Add the image to your storyboard.

A = Affirmations. Add your new self-image to your daily thought diet. When you talk about yourself to others, do so in a positive way. Don't hesitate to discuss the changes you are working on. By making your goals public, you increase your commitment to them.

D = Daily Successes. Success is earned in small increments. Build confidence everyday by setting up ways to experience success. That means practicing "slender behaviors" daily—eating well, exercising and thinking the right thoughts about your new healthy life-style. Be sure to reward yourself as often as possible for your successes. Don't reward yourself by cheating on your diet or skipping your exercise. Instead, treat yourself to a pleasurable experience.

E = Environmental Influences. Make your environment work for you by surrounding yourself with positive influences. Avoid people and situations that make you uncomfortable; that is, lead you to temptation. Find a support person or group. People who have support groups are far more likely to succeed than those who go it alone.

You are what you think. To change any habit, you must first change your thoughts, feelings, attitudes, values and behaviors. The process that M.A.D.E. you what you are today can work for you to make you what you want to be tomorrow.

✎ WORKSHEET

- Analyze your present eating and exercise habits
- Set and achieve goals for improving your physical fitness and diet

GETTING IN SHAPE

15.15 Your Weight Loss and Exercise Program

This is an exercise that incorporates self-observation and goal setting. You may need more paper and several sessions to complete this worksheet. As you reach your goals, take yourself through this process again and create new goals.

1. Study your current eating habits. List all the bad habits that prevent you from reaching your target weight.

   _____

2. List the ways you can change your poor eating habits.

   _____

3. List all the excuses you use for not exercising for 20 minutes three to four times per week.

   _____

4. List all the things you can change so you *will* exercise more.

   _____

5. Decide to change NOW. Write three specific weight-loss (if appropriate), nutrition and exercise goals. Assign a completion date for each.

   _____

6. Write as many *affirmations* as possible that will motivate you to eat well and exercise regularly. Include these in your daily thought diet.

7. Write three affirmations that will change your body image and self-esteem. (These are different from the goals and affirmations above.) Add them to your thought diet.

   _____

8. List three people who can help you with your goals, through emotional support or by participating in sports with you. Specify when you will talk to them about this.

   _____

Start NOW with a commitment to eat right, lose weight and exercise regularly.

❓FYI

GETTING YOUR FINANCES IN SHAPE

15.16 Money Management

Errol Flynn once said, "My problem lies in reconciling my gross habits with my net income." There is no doubt that a great deal of satisfaction in life comes from your ability to spend money. But far too many people overspend to sustain a life-style that they really cannot afford. Instead of building a portfolio of assets, they build a portfolio of debts.

Financial maturity (aka self-control) means living without some things now so you can have more later. Focusing on the long-term is the only way to get ahead.

Most people live in the present and are financially immature. Their attitudes are "I work hard. I'm not going to deny myself what I want" or "I may not be around tomorrow. Why should I worry about it?" More often than not you are around tomorrow . . . and tomorrow arrives much sooner than you expected.

There are three basic things you must do to get ahead financially: live within your means, pay down your debt, and save money.

Living within your means may require some adjustments. Many people create budgets for themselves, but adhere to them as poorly as most people adhere to diets. The past is the best predictor of the future. If you have little self-discipline now, that's probably how much you'll have tomorrow. Maybe not.

The best way to live within your means is not to necessarily go without, but to spend less on your essentials and indulgences. Do you have to live in a $1,000 apartment? Would an $800 apartment serve you just as well? Do you have to eat in restaurants so often? Eating at home is much less expensive. When you do eat out, why not settle for less expensive food? Do you have to buy Georgio Armani ties or would Pierre Cardins at half the price suffice? And must you drive a car that serves your transportation *and* ego needs? You get the idea.

Paying down your debt is a step you must take before you can hope to save money. Most people have become accustomed to paying outrageous interest rates on credit card balances. The key is to pay these off and learn to pay cash.

Compile a list of your debts—every one of them. Include on this list the interest rate and the minimum monthly payments of each card. Then pay off the balances, starting with the card that charges the highest interest.

Save money, but do it with a plan. Simply saying you will save X percent of your income is too vague. You have to set specific savings goals that will provide you with an incentive. For example, you should save for next year's taxes, a new car that you will eventually need, clothes and so on. Determine when you will incur these expenses and figure out how much per month you should save to meet the goals.

Be realistic. Avoid the myth that winning the lottery or earning X amount of money will solve your problems. If you haven't gotten the hang of managing money yet, a windfall will go the way of your past income. Learn to manage your money so that, when the lottery does make you rich, you will be set for life.

 WORKSHEET

GETTING YOUR FINANCES IN SHAPE

- Set specific long- and short-term financial goals

15.17 Financial Goals Worksheet

SHORT-TERM GOALS
(One Year)

	A, B, C Priority*	Goal	Target Date	Time to Complete	Approximate Cost	Cost per Month
SAMPLE:		Develop a Cash reserve	July 1	10 months	$2,000.00	$200.00
1.						
2.						
3.						
4.						
5.						
6.						
7.						
				TOTAL	$ _____	$ _____

LONG-TERM GOALS
(Two Years or More)

	A, B, C Priority*	Goal	Target Date	Time to Complete	Approximate Cost	Cost per Month
1.						
2.						
3.						
4.						
5.						
				TOTAL	$ _____	$ _____

Add cost per month from Short-Term Goals $ _____

Total per month needed to reach all goals $ _____

*A = Must Do
*B = Ought to Do
*C = Nice to Do

SECTION

Appendix

Self-Diagnostic Test

Someone once said, "The ability to move fast is less important than first knowing your starting point. Otherwise, the faster you go, the more lost you'll get." That statement is certainly true for your career development. While you want to move quickly and steadily up the ladder of success, you first need to know where you are today, right now. First you need to ask yourself two questions:

1. Am I cut out for a career in sales?

2. At what stage am I in my career development?

   The following Self-Diagnostic Test should help you find out.
   First, take the test yourself as a self-rating device and evaluate your answers. Next, ask a customer to fill out the questionnaire and share the answers with you. Third, ask your manager or supervisor to do the same thing. Then compare the three sets of responses. The result will be three perspectives that will help you use this book to chart your future success in sales.

Rate Your Performance

As you rate yourself, focus on what you actually do in your day-to-day practice as a sales professional rather than what you think you should be doing.

1-5 Rating System

1 = poor or never
2 = Fair or rarely
3 = average or sometimes
4 = good or usually
5 = outstanding or always

	My Rating	Sales Manager	Typical Customer
Knowledge about your company			
Knowledge of products and service			
Study your prospect's situation/company			
Control the selling situation			
Demonstrate empathy			
Demonstrate concern for customer			
Manage time			
Set goals			
Set profit objectives for territory			
Follow a prospecting system			
Use call schedules			
Consistently classify prospect by potential			
Set sales objectives for accounts			
Use a call report system			
Use a prepared sales presentation			
Develop rapport			
Follow up/follow through			
Listen			
Ask for the sale			
Recover (turn negative situations around)			
Ask for referrals			

After rating yourself, try the exercise again through the eyes of your typical customers. How would they rate you?

Ask your Sales Manager to rate you and then compare all three perspectives. Determine your developmental needs after reviewing your scores.

INDEX

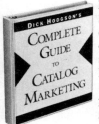